Passport to Wine Knowledge

Jean-Pierre Adam

"PASSPORT TO WINE KNOWLEDGE" is a concise book of the science and technique of wine, which offers a collection of information's and suggestions targeting the reader whose work or personal interest touches on a relating topic.

Based in part on my view that wine is not just a product for plain consumption, but a part of modern civilization, the volume spans a range of regional and time periods. draw upon an understanding of certain geographical and political conditions as possible factors, using general straight forward language in an effort to create a thorough yet accessible resource.

The author concludes with some thoughts about "the fragility of wine", which he sees as a "living property, typically requiring the collaboration of art and patience, of time and care".

Overall this writing is designed to pay a kind of tribute to such processes as well as to enlighten and provoke thoughts.

Mary-Beth Pappas
Media Publishing LLC
Alexandria, Virginia

"If you enjoy history and geography, this is a fine example of a book, for you to read. It will not only give you insight and understanding with the wonderful scenes of the world, but provide you with a thoroughly comprehensible vocabulary how wine found its place in the civilized world".

Edouardo Beringer
History Professor
University of Miami
Florida

"Passport to wine knowledge, overdue for a long time, is a tremendous writing about the science and technique of wine.

Some specific information's give the reader an excellent description in a clear presentation. My compliments to the author, a long time friend of mine".

Dr. David Skinner
Washington D.C.

PASSPORT TO WINE KNOWLEDGE

PRESENTATION OF A BOTTLE OF BORDEAUX
BY JEAN-PIERRE ADAM, CHEF-SOMMELIER
AT A THREE STARS RESTAURANT IN MIAMI-BEACH, FLORIDA

PASSPORT TO WINE KNOWLEDGE

)
_ _
(

A CONCISE BOOK OF THE SCIENCE
AND TECHNIQUE OF WINE

AND

THE HISTORY OF CALIFORNIA
AND FRENCH VINEYARDS

BY JEAN-PIERRE ADAM

Contents

Disclaimer 9

Acknowledgments 10

Foreword 11

CHAPTER ONE   Wine Approach 13

CHAPTER TWO   Origin of the Vine 17

CHAPTER THREE   The Degustation 23

CHAPTER FOUR   Chemistry and Medicinal Effects on Wine 37

CHAPTER FIVE   How to Become A Wine Connoisseur --- Choosing and Storing Wines --- The Laws of the "Appelation d' Origine Controlée" in France 47

CHAPTER SIX   Varieties of Vines GrownAround the World 53

CHAPTER SEVEN   The Wine History of California 59

CHAPTER EIGHT   The Wines Districts of France 81

    SECTION A   Alsace 85

    SECTION B   Bordeaux 101

    SECTION C   Burgundy 139

    SECTION D   Champagne 167

    SECTION E   Côtes Du Rhône 183

    SECTION F   Languedoc, Roussillon, Provence ....

    SECTION G   Loire Valley 191

    SECTION H   The Cognac and Armagnac Wine Districts 199

CHAPTER NINE   The Fortified Wines and their Areas of Production in Europe 209

CHAPTER TEN   Conclusion 223

CHAPTER ELEVEN   Reference List 227

Disclaimer

THE AUTHOR AND THE PUBLISHER ARE DISCLAIMING
ANY INFORMATION CONTAINED IN THIS BOOK,
FOR MISLEADING OR FALSE INTERPRETATION ON
ANY CHAPTERS PRESENTED HEREWITH.

THIS BOOK IS FOR INFORMATIONAL PURPOSES ONLY
AND THE AUTHOR DOES NOT ASSUME REPONSIBILITY
FOR ANY INACCURRACIES OR OMISSIONS.

IN THE OPINION OF THE AUTHOR, THESE WRITTINGS
ARE TRUE AND ARE NOT ATTEMPTED TO GEAR
THE READER TO INCONCLUSIVE THOUGHTS.

Acknowledgments

The author wishes to express his appreciation to:

Mr. Louis Orizet, Engineer in Agronomy and author of the book, *Les Vines de France*, for his remarkable assessment of the recovering of the French Vineyards since World War II.

Mr. Alexis Bespaloff, for his comprehensive introduction and up-to-date guide of the wines of the world in his book, *The Signet Book of Wine*.

Mr. Robert G. Mondavi and his family for the latest documentation on the Robert Mondavi Winery in Oakland, Napa Valley, California.

The Conseil Interprofessionel des Vins d'Alsace (C.I.V.A.) for the latest information on the vine-growing industry in Alsace.

The House of Clicquot-Ponsardin Champagne, Reims, France, for the biography of Madame Clicquot, *Her Peaceful Conquest of Russia*, written by the Count Bertrand de Vogue, President of the National Academy in Reims.

Sopexa, Paris for the illustrations and colored maps of the wine districts of France.

I also wish to express my gratitude to the winegrowers from all over the world, especially the ones in California who practice the most modern techniques to insure quality and consistency, and those winegrowers from tiny areas in France whom I did not mention but who deserve to be complimented for their continuing efforts to promote their wines, namely those of the Côte Basque, the Jura, the Jurançon, the Minervois, and the Savoy.

Foreword

Passport to Wine Knowledge has been in the making since early this century for the edification of all students. It also is written to be a reference book for sommeliers, restaurateurs, wine-store clerks, and hotel managers. Finally, it is directed also to all wine novices who are interested in learning and studying the history of wine, the evolution of the wine industry in the old and new worlds, acquiring knowledge on how to taste wine and how to talk about wine through the imaginative evocation of the idioms of the wine expression.

Therefore, it is a real opportunity to discover the enjoyments of wine from an old pioneer country like France and those of a new geographic location such as California with all their past and eloquent history and wonderful geography.

In this foreword, I would like also to summarize the knowledge for which the retail-merchant needs to do justice to his job and his wares; it is for him to pass on the benefit of his knowledge to his customers: by selling the wine which meets the customers' requirements (good ordinary wines for everyday use, and more imposing wines for special occasions); by offering the right wines to go along with particular dishes; by drawing up a suggested list of wines for a meal, without too many different varieties; and by advising on the order of serving wines and their proper temperature at consumption.

In giving the inexperienced customer a foundation in this aspect of civilized living, you will often find that you have made not only a convert, but a friend. Wine is not just for plain consumption, it is a part of modern civilization.

It has been a privilege for me to be exposed to the industry of wine during my forty years spent in the United States and to have been responsible for the promotion of fine wines from all the countries of origin in the most grand hotels, the best restaurants, and all the good wine stores in the states of Florida and New York. In writing *Passport to Wine Knowledge*, I have included remarkable essays in the chapters of Degustation and Medicinal Dietetics of Wine.

This manuscript has not been elaborated as a wine-label book; on the contrary, it is a serious instrument on how wine is produced including the history and science of such production, while at the same time giving to the consumer the most information about the various wines to increase one's enjoyment of each and every wine of quality.

Jean-Pierre Adam
Maître, Commanderie d'Amérique de la Confrérie des
Chevaliers du Taste-vin, Certified Wine Educator

CHAPTER ONE

Wine Approach

THE VINE PLANT: ITS GROWING FACTORS

THE VINE ORIGINATED FROM THE "VITIS" SPECIES AND GROWS MOSTLY IN WARM TEMPERATED AREAS OF THE GLOBE. ACTUALLY, THE METEOROLOGY DICTATES HOW AND WHERE THE VINE IS ABLE TO GROW. MANY CENTURIES AGO, IT HAS BEEN RECORDED THAT THE VINE WAS GROWING IN ENGLAND, IN ICELAND, IN RUSSIA AND IN THE FAR-EAST, BUT NOT ANYMORE.

THESE COUNTRIES HAVE NOW ESSENTIALLY TWO SEASONS: COLD AND WARM. ALSO THE SOIL IS ANOTHER BIG FACTOR TO THE VINE. THE VINE IS MORE AT EASE WHEN GROWN IN SANDY OR MIXED STONE-GROUNDS. WHEN GROWN IN A SILICA SOIL, THE VINE PRODUCES LIGHT SUPPLE WINES. WHEN GROWN IN A CLAY SOIL, IT PRODUCES WELL-COLORED AND FULL-BODIED WINES. IN CHALKY SOIL, THE WINE HAS A TENDENCY TO BECOME ROBUST, BUT WITH AN EXCELLENT SCENT.

New vine shrub at an early stage
of blooming

INTRODUCTION

The grapevine has the appearance of a never changing creation of God. During its lifetime of 25 to 30 years, it shows sometimes the winegrower a deceptive feeling of stability.

Despite this thought, the grapevine has a tendency, like every plant to gain in this area of evolution and therefore implies a partial change in the science of agronomy.

In less than thirty years for example, the French vineyards have build up a new face like never before in the past, due to the frenzy of transformations which bowl over the planet. Everything has contributed; the rage of mechanization, the decrease of the labor force, the better knowledge of the wine maker also played a large part in that role, the technical assistance, the reforms of structures and a guardianship much more understandable of the government agencies.

Nowadays, the vine better nourished and better taken care of, the components with the whole new science of oenology assures us of a very important volume of food wines.

The average consumer hides his ignorance behind common areas on a very discouraging bad faith. So confident to make an error of judgment, but so confident to never be cheated, he suspects ahead of time any bottle which is presented to him and for bravery, attests that no one can assure him, and is glad to close his eyes over the sincerity of such label.

It is scarcely known the effort followed by the entire profession. It is bad judgment not to know the control vigilante of the government agencies which are present to guarantee the harmlessness of the wine and the sincerity of its presentation.

THE VINE STOCK

Thevine is a plant issued from the *Vitis vinifera* species which used to grow all over Europe and adapted to the different climates and soils of each region; however, the vine grows at its best in temperate areas and consists therefore of a great number of varieties.

The vine stock is considered a climbing shrub or a small tree with the following components:

1. The climbing plant which bears the shoots on canes.

2. The leaves whose functions are to absorb nutrients and carbon dioxide. The leaves, assisted by sunlight, transform the sap into elements, especially sugar, necessary for the grapes. It is therefore one of the most important elements of the vine stock.

3. The roots with respiratory and nutritive functions.

4. The nodes staggered on the canes on which the leaves, the buds (future canes), tendrils (supporting elements), and bunches of grapes are located.

5. The fruit in the shape of marbles or berries are joined together into bunches. The fruit develops after the pollination of the flowers.

The life of the vine starts at the end of winter and with the first sunshine of the year. On top of the canes pruned by shears, small shoots appear in the form of sap which is called tears of the vine from the old stock, awakened by the thrust of new saps. The buds are the next to emerge under the influence of warmer temperature. Little, tender leaves then grow, in the middle of which can be seen tiny bunches of future grapes. The flowering stage comes as early as June. The berries start to take shape until they reach their volume and weight.

CHAPTER TWO

Origin of the Vine

WINE - THE DELIGHTFUL BEVERAGE

The origin of wine dates back long before the Antiquity area and we could agree that beside the mastering of the horse, the wine really has been the genius discovery of man, with the help of the climate and the soil composition.

Cited in the Bible are hundred fold references on wine. For example, during the wedding at Cana, Christ changed water into wine so the festivities would not be overshadowed by its lack of it. Later the wine had been identified as the blood of Jesus Christ and in due course was consecrated as such by the by Church. Wine had become an indispensable element in Church activities as well as in the duties of hospitality. The records of ancient monasteries show us clearly that monks had always been allowed to drink wine on high feast days with their meals.

Nowadays, we live in a modern world and wines are negotiated all over the world. It has however sometimes become ludicrous to condemn wine in the name of a false conception of hygiene and dietetics. Wine is not the alcoholic beverage responsible for a variety of sickness when over indulged. Alcoholism, due to hard liquors is increasing crimes and automobile accidents and they are a few of these perpetual problems.

We have never consumed in the history of humanity so much sodas and spring water of all kind, also a huge variety of fruit juices and other types of cola beverages.

Recently, a distributor was barred from promoting one of its products on a foreign market, for the reason that the bottled water involved with had excessive amount of arsenic content. It has been mentioned in an article and written in the Wall-Street Journal and inquiries, now, are closed. Thousand of these bottled water were sent back to the United States to the distributor. Nobody knows, however, where these bottled water were shipped again to a different market.

On a physiologic point of view, wine like nearly all the food products supplied to the market for daily consumption are subjected to artificial chemical adulteration.
In America, we call it "PRODUCTIVITY".

Wine has been regarded for centuries as a basic ingredient of human food. It was described by a clergyman of the seventeenth century as follows: "After bread comes wine which is the second health food given by the Creator." Before those times, it had been known that wine was a necessary part of the diet as essential as bread. The popular saying was: "Go eat with joy your bread and drink your wine to one's heart content."

Wine is, first of all, an antiseptic and used to be given to the Greek and Roman armies sent abroad. At that time dysentery was rampant. Typhoid and cholera were common sicknesses and hard to cure. Hence, the Greek and the Romans were responsible for the planting of the vine across Europe in pursuit of new lands. At the height of the Roman Empire, the occupation stretched from the deserts of Africa to Scotland.

During the Napoleonic era and during the Battle of Austerlitz, it was mentioned in a general's journal that wine handed out on a daily base to the troops gave them mental and physical stamina. It helped to fight weariness and maintained the strength and morale of the soldiers.

Also of interest, in rural areas of France, it was well known that housewives added wine to soups as it was known to add healthful benefits to the meals. Wine carries with it all the vitamins found in grapes: vitamin A which has beta carotene to help ward off cancer, vitamin B which contributes to mental alertness and provides energy, and vitamin C to combat fatigue.

ANTIQUITY

The use of the winepress goes back to the very high Antiquity as evidenced by the sacred books of the Hebrews and at the funeral engravings of the Egyptians. The winepress with the large wood screw has been in existence since the year 23 A.D.

Wine was preserved in "dolia", big-bellied jars smeared with cobbler's wax, resin, sulfur and plaster. The 'seriae' were small amphorae and pointed in order to be planted in sand. The wood barrels unknown at that time in Italy, were made in Gaul (former name of France). For the transport, lamb's skins were used and is still seen in Spain.

It would be too long to study the detail on how the wine was cared for at, but let us say that many practices of the present days were in place at the time of the Romans and Greeks, including many adulterations that were practiced throughout the world.

Among the practices in use at that time were concentration the use of heat and the plat rage. Also additives were incorporated such as honey, salt, clay, lees, water and other flavorings. Filtering through linen sleeves also affected the integrity of the wine product.

The amphorae were stored in an upper level room called apothecia often designed to be in the passage where kitchen smoke would exit probably to hasten the aging. These amphorae's were shut with a cork plug, smeared with wax, had on their collars a label with the name of the vine-growth and the name of the Consul in function at that time.

PREHISTORY

The vine dwells today all along the Mediterranean Coast, but it is not because it occupies this geographical area of election that one must attribute the merit to be at the origin of the wine.

Geology tells us by its fossil remains that the Cusses is in the same family as Vitis and was a forerunner of Vitis. It haunted already immense forests during the secondary era.

Favoring an equal climate and warm weather, these Cusses vines spread very far towards from its birth in Asia to all the Occident countries from Thrace to Greece, to Egypt and then to Italy.

It is only during the Tertiary period that the specific form of the "Vitis" type started to be recognized. The uniform temperature and the Luke warm weather of Miocene area endorsed the dispersion of the vine all the way to the farthest regions of the globe from the Polar Circle until Japan.

During the Quaternary period, the vine was seen in Greenland in North America, in Japan and in the entire Europe from Iceland to Greece.

Therefore, it is to be concluded that the vine is clearly a native plant about whom the Paleontology development grew mainly in Europe, which exclude the legend of the Orient, which actually is the cradle of vine.

When mankind became sedentary, the wine-grape started to be regularly seen with the debris of the first ages.

It also was noticed that in the Prehistoric meridian station the stalks and peeps of the grapes were accumulated in compact masses. Therefore, one can conclude that man probably used them to prepare beverages. From then on, the fermented juice acquired new virtue by the instant transformation of sugar into alcohol.

MYTHOLOGY

Mythology is not the subject of this book. Nevertheless, I would like to establish the etymology of the word "wine" in the different languages of the period of Antiquity

The word wine derives from the root "vena" which means love.

Vena is therefore the radical root for all those Europeans of Caucasian ancestry:

The Swen named the wine "gvinal"

The Georgian "gvino"

The Mingrelian "gwini"

The Celtic "gwinien'

The Latins "vinum"

The Germans "wein"

The Italians "vino"

The English "wine" and the French "vin"

HARVEST AND VINIFICATION

The vine occupied such a large place in the lives of our ancestors that at the time of the harvest, all normal life was suspended. Popular celebrations took place during those times. They were strictly in obedience to formal rites.

The wine grapes were picked-up, pressed, and trampled in the field, then later in the cellars (torculariumvinarium). All people living at the time of Antiquity (Greeks, Hebrews, Egyptians, Latin's and Gauls) practiced the crushing or stamping by foot. It was done with naked feet but with a strict cleanliness, the grape juice flowed out and was put in amphorae's for fermentation.

Wine is one of the most fascinating and mysterious art; by its complexity and the secret of its behavior, wine experiences the shrewdness of man.

The testimonies which is given to us since the early ages, prove to mankind on which high level it is up-held.

It was always a focus of dedication therefore to cultivate the vine. One is really surprised to find out that among the routine, the superstition and empiricism, and the perfections of methods of culture of our far away ancestors remain to-day. This perfection has been explained by our modern science, but has not been modified.

The leave of the vinestock has been as a matter of fact the insignia of the Centurion's commandment.

It has been described through all civilization that the prestige of the wine-grape is associated with the chaff of the wheat and symbolizes fertility under the brush of the painter or the chisel of the sculptor. Its shows that wine has always been beneficial, like a practical mystic prestige. The precariousness literature on wine has however not survived the times of war and the influx of the weather.

The two most important Greek literary subjects still in existence are the one from Magon, a Carthaginian, who was called the father of the rural economy "Rusticationis parens"and from the Hellenic literature

"The Geoponic Greeks" an important collection, dated from the tenth century. The essential has been written by Caton, Varron, Columelle, Palladius, Virgiles (The Georgics") and Pline (natural history).

From all the links of the agricultural science, the vine forms without any doubt, with the association of wheat, one of the oldest crops.

Let's take an example from the Egyptian wine culture. It was well known that during the Greek and Roman occupation, the wines produced in Egypt were very much praised and in demand. Cleopatra was said to have served Ceasar with wine from Meroe, which was produced near the fourth cataract of the Upper-Nile River.

In the 1900s', an Egyptian scientist named Gianaclis started to set-out and search the type of soil on which selected vine-stock could be grown. At the same time he tried to find out how good the wine of his ancestors tasted as evidenced in the writings of Virgiles, Horace and Pline. Perhaps in the last 3000 thousand years the tastes changed a lot? He came to the conclusion that the tastes of the ancient Egyptians were not fundamentally different than the ones in the modern World.

Gianaclis and his team eventually found a soil very different from the alluvial soils which came down the river and were deposited in the delta and the Valley of the Nile. These soils were buried under the sand close to the border of the desert. Over the years, in order to match the right technique and the right vinestock to the climate and the soil, seventy known grape varieties were tried. By now and after a half of a century of effort the wine of the Pharaohs have been resurrected and Egypt is exporting again, especially to Russia.

CHAPTER THREE

The Degustation

THE SEQUENCES,
WHEN TASTING A GLASS OF WINE

I- Give a gentle swirl to the glass

II- Then take a long breath
   and let your sense of smell work

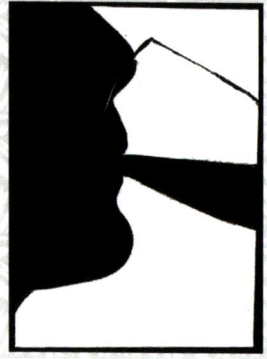

III- Taste the wine slowly, by simultaneous strokes

The art of degustation is conditioned by the following:

1. Intuition
2. Reflection
3. Perception
4. Technical skills
5. Silence

Actual degustation

1. Visual Examination

The wine analysis starts with the eye. The following cliché is retained when:

1. We look at it
2. We breathe it
3. We taste it
4. We talk about it

The pleasure of analyzing the wine comes first with the sight of the wine. At that point, you will like the wine or dislike it.

Suppose your first impression of a wine is dubious. The dark weight with lead scent leads you to not seek further examination.

Instinctively, the taster is looking ahead for other deceptions. The taster becomes more severe and is ready to criticize more.

THE DEGUSTATION

The degustation will never have the assertion to the results in arithmetic numbers having a hard time to help the hierarchic classification of the products within themselves to put in relief their virtues to disclose their defects.

Aside of the growths, the degustation informs on the origin, the type and the vintage year. In short, it is a way of precious information for the judgment of a wine.

To understand well, its indispensable character, it is good to remember that between an ordinary and a great vintage wine, there is chemically small differences that the analysis is not able to reveal.

It is nevertheless true to say that the wine is like a physical embodiment and an essential vital part, despite these unverified differences.

HOW TO COMPARE AND DRINK WINE

The degustation is more than a technique because it appeals to all the senses. It is an art whose object it is to judge and appreciate the sapidity and scented properties of the wine. It is the only art, by the way, having recourse to all the senses except for the sense of hearing. The art of wine-tasting is to judge the characteristics of a fermented grape juice which has come to maturity. Three senses are involved: sight, smell, and taste.

SIGHT

The taster looks at the wine poured in a glass with a stem. He holds the glass by the stem to eliminate any body odors and to keep the upper part of the glass free of any finger touching that could warm the glass and the wine. We like to recommend a ten-ounce all-purpose wineglass. One exception, however, is when tasting Cognac. Cognac is served in brandy glasses, also called snifters. Very small and very big glasses are not recommended, they are less comfortable than those with a bowl whose size is somewhere between an orange and a large apple, so that the applied warmth releases the Cognac's bouquet when you hold the bowl in your palms.

Coming back to our examination of our wine, the sight recognizes the color and brilliance: pale or dark yellow, with golden or greenish tints for white wine; light or dark red shades of color going from ruby to garnet for red wines; pale red for rose wines, sometimes with a coppery tone.

The wine will be seen at its best if it is held to the light in a very clear uncolored glass. Cut glass enhances the color and the brilliance. Remember that judging a wine takes less time than reading about it.

For the taster, ability to concentrate mental activity is necessary in having a productive degustation. Therefore the degustation is an excellent lesson for the mind.

SMELL

The second sense for the degustation is the sense of smell which is one of the basic senses. This sense seems to be exercised less and less, probably due to our type of civilization. The sense of smell collects the *bouquet* of the wine which may be strong, delicate, or fresh. It will be full in full-bodied rich wines. It sometimes recalls certain fruits or flowers. The best way to smell the bouquet is to fill the glass halfway and roll the wine around the sides of the glass to release the scent. The bouquet of the wine gives you a strong first impression of the wine itself. If the wine has any serious faults, they can be discerned by smell. You can then avoid the unpleasant experience of tasting a bad wine. Occasionally, a wine may be corky (revealed by a pronounced smell of cork). This happens much less frequently than many people think. Inexpensive white wines, for example, often cause an unpleasant prickly sensation in the nose, a sign of an excess of sulfur dioxide, used to stabilize wines.

From time to time you may come across a red wine or a white wine that has a suspicious brown color and a bouquet reminiscent of a sherry without any of the fruit of a good wine. Such a wine is described as maderized, the result of having been oxidized. This may have been caused by overlong aging in wood, a faulty cork that let air into the bottle, or it may be the natural evolution on a wine that is just too old. Another warning signal is a sour, vinegary smell, which indicates that the wine contains an excess of acetic acid. If you have ever left out a glass of wine overnight, what you will smell and taste the next day is an excess of acetic acid.

When tasting better wines, especially those made from one of the classic grape varieties, you should look for a bouquet that is typical of the origins of the wine. In general, younger wines have more fruit in their bouquet (more of the smell of the grape), while older wines show a more refined and subtle character. The perfume manufacturers discovered long ago that the sense of smell is probably the most evocative of all senses.

OLFACTIVE ANALYSIS

This can perhaps reduce our gourmet vocabulary. The novice, for example, may give up on the olfactive analysis, in general, due to laziness, ignorance, or by inaptitude. Incapable of discerning the scents that a wine can offer, the novice backs up behind this excuse: "What is so good about giving us so much aggravation when it is so simple to drink it down?" Be careful about awful complaisance, it will soon lead you straight to gulping it down, instead of drinking it.

In reality the sense of smell is of great nobility. The thought organizes itself with it. The repeated olfaction suggests remembrances and comparisons, and prepares the joys of the palate. It proposes reflective thoughts and introduces us fully to the spiritual emotion.

THE AROMA

The first of the phenomena perceptible to the nose, the aroma comes essentially from the grape. Hence, it is called *bouquet primaire* or *bouquet original*. The aroma is specific for each vine variety. It is constant, but the tonality is variable according to the vintage year and the nature of the soil. An example of the most typical aroma is the one provided by the Muscat grapes. Most of the great wines have specific aromas that are very special like the cabernet grape, the syrah, or the gewürztraminer. As a general rule, the aroma softens during the period of fermentation.

It is for this reason that the wine makers of Muscat have limited the action of the fermentation by blending some alcohol in order to give to the finished product its full aroma.

THE BOUQUET

The meaning of bouquet is simply a flower-bunch scent.

Note and memorize:
When someone asks you to define aroma and bouquet, what is your answer?
The bouquet is the effervescence of blooms.
As mentioned before, the scent of the aroma is mostly given by the grape itself. Therefore the aroma is also called *primary bouquet*. The secondary bouquet appears during the fermentation. It is the result of the yeast.

The same secondary bouquet gains its maximum intensity at the end of the fermentation. It becomes smooth with the passage of time and shades off after a few years to become the *bouquet tertiaire*.

THE GUSTATIVE EXAMINATION

Human beings have a lesser gustative sensibility than olfactive sensibility. On the other hand, the gustative sensibility is quicker.

There are a few hundred odors which have their proper area of sensory excitations on the tongue. Among them are the sweet, the bitter, the acids, and the salty.

THE SWEET

The impression of sweet is not in relation to a determined chemical structure. Among the sweet substances, there is a group of sweet called oses, holosides and polyols.

THE BITTER

The bitter is above all the characteristics of alkaloids (brucin and quinine).

THE ACIDS

The hydrogen ion (H+) is responsible for the acid impression. As a general rule, all the acids have a salty flavor except for the salicylic acid which is slightly sweet and picric acid which is bitter. The acid impression is in relation to the ionization of the environment.

THE SUGARS

Among the sweet substances found in wine which are essentially left over from non-fermented sugars (reduction sugars), there is also the glycerin with a powerfully sweet taste but without odor. Glycerin gives to wine its mellowness, and it is a normal residue from the alcoholic fermentation. Glycerin is variable and is dosed between four to ten grams per liter; however, sweet wines like Sauternes hold as much as twenty grams per liter.

Eighteen grams of sugar is needed to provide one degree of alcohol.

$$S = sugar$$

$$S/18 = X \text{ of alcohol}$$

The bouquet tertiaire develops during the aging in barrels first, then in bottles.

In the first stage, it is the result of an oxidization treated gently with the component of the wine. In the second stage, it is the reverse phenomenon, it is called reduction. The final bouquet is above all the task of nature. It is the bouquet indeed which gives to the wine its distinction, its harmony, and its nobility.

The most common types of odors found in the great wines are as follows:

Ethereal, acetone, ethylic ether, acetate of ethyl

Aromatic odors: menthol, geraniol

Ambrosiac odors: vanilla, jasmine, linden flowers

Metallic odors: mercaptan

Balsamic odors: camphor, carnation

Empyreumatic odors: coffee, resin, grilled almond, tobacco

Caprylic odors: animal odors

To close this section, note that only the nose is able to reveal the accidental odors which cannot be traced by the analysis, for example: the taste of cork, fuel oil, tar, or molds.

SENSE OF TASTE

Do not smoke while tasting wine, but sponge your palate with a piece of bread. The sense of taste analyses the sapidity and the touch in order to register the thermal and pressure sensation.

The flavor of the wine will inform the experienced taster about its origin, the nature of the soil it comes from, the vine that produced it, its age, and the methods of wine-making employed. The tongue and the palate will catch the aftertaste: some wines are fruity, others are flat or lacking in aftertaste, or they are harsh or full-bodied.

At which temperatures should wines be served?

White and rose wines should be served cool but never iced (between 44° F and 54° F for dry wines). Sweet wines should be served even cooler.

Champagne and sparkling wines should be served slightly chilled. The bottle should be placed in an ice-bucket two hours before consumption. In general, it is not recommended to put ice cubes in the wine.

Red wines should be served at room temperature, or *chambre* (between 58° F and 64° F).

In order to achieve this, depending on the temperature of your cellar or the exact location of storage of your bottle, it is recommended to keep the bottle standing upright in the room where it is consumed, for two days. If your bottle was kept in a too cold area, do not heat the bottle of wine, but let it come to the room temperature in a natural way.

ALCOHOL

Alcohol is known to be the structure of the wine (its frame), or it is this structure which supports all other elements. At the same time, it is a fundamental ingredient to conserve wine. When the wines are powerful or strong in alcoholic degree, over certain years they become known as quality wines. Some people unfortunately buy wines based on their alcohol content.

Alcohol is definitely a necessity for quality, but it is not the essential element. It is important to say that alcohol should not be the main concern at a tasting, despite the fact that the palate is flattered by alcohol.

However, we should never confuse a naturally produced wine with distilled alcohol. Wine comes from the natural chemical and biological transformation of sugars and wine. It does not have the degree of toxicity of distilled alcohol which is a carbonaceous chain ethanol capable of oxidizing.

One should also consider the manner in which a person drinks. On an empty stomach, alcohol travels very rapidly into the duodenum and in less than half an hour is absorbed by the blood; however, if the stomach is full, the alcoholic absorption will take place much more slowly. The combination of alcohol and oxygen allowing for an oxygenating process at the normal rate of 100 mg (0.35 ounce) per kilo of body weight per hour can be virtually complete when we drink wine in a reasonable dose without other heat sources.

To quote once more the research of Dr. deBruigne, "The freed energy can be fully absorbed in the progress of cellular respiration, thus providing a true source of calories."

To conclude this short chapter, here is some advice to follow when you plan to go to a party or a dinner: Half an hour before starting to drink, take a tablespoon of olive oil or the edible oil you have at hand. This will coat your stomach, and the wine will have a longer time to penetrate the duodenum, or eat a slice of bread before any drinking. The bread will act as a sponge in your stomach. When partaking of a wine degustation, imbibing too much alcohol can dull your senses which must be intact to fully appreciate the use of all your senses, so be sure to make use of the spittoon on hand, and spit out the wine after having tasted it to your satisfaction.

ACIDITY

The acidity is healthy and has a youthful longevity. A wine can be guaranteed for several years if it has an optimum acidity content of four grams expressed in sulfuric acid or sulfates. This acidity is formed by the amount of different acids: tartaric, malic, lactic, citric, succinic, and acetic. The tartaric and malic acids exist in normal doses in the grape itself. The tartaric acid is more or less stable; however, part of it becomes insoluble during the first cold months of winter and becomes bitartrate of potassium. The malic acid regresses in the wine as lactic acid. It is then called malolactic fermentation. The succinic acid is the one which gives wine its vinous flavor. All these acids exist in the wine either as a free condition or as a salted condition.

COLORING MATTERS

Coloring matters also play an important role and contribute to the formation of the fruit in wine consumed young. They also contribute to the bouquet in wine submissive to aging.

The coloring matter is also a polyphenol and is located in the skin of the raisin except in the case of the vine growth called tinting growth where it exists in the pulp and is located in the juice of the grape.

The coloring matter derives from pyrocatechin also called oenolic acid and is specific to each vine stock, evidenced by the chromatography.

It is usually insoluble in water. It dissolves in alcohol little by little in proportion to the processes of formation of the fermentation. These properties are used by wine makers in order to obtain wines more or less colored at will and in a natural way.

However, some countries are using full artificial tinting which is more easily controlled, but be careful. If you drink some wine and spill a drop on your white shirt, you cannot erase the spill with water. Or if you bought an inexpensive bottle of wine for cooking chicken, after cooking a while, you will have a blue sauce.

Later, the coloring matter becomes resin and, under the presence of oxygen, stays insoluble. It becomes at that stage brownish and drops to the bottom of the bottle.

As a result of an error in manipulation, the white wines contain a little bit of red coloring matters, these coloring matters are called stained (tâchés). The discoloring may be obtained by the use of *noir animal*, a powder coming from burned animal bones. The use of it is strictly enforced by the law and by the I.N.A.

The coloring substance does exist in the white wine, but it not visible. As a result of this prejudice, the white wine turns yellow and later maderized. Moreover, the addition of an alkaline substance in a white wine will turn it greenish by the reaction of the invisible coloring substance. This explains why it is so difficult to perfectly stabilize wines, and the amateur must understand that these deposits are less a flaw than a guarantee obtained by natural channels.

The secondary bouquet is usually floral or fruity. Sometimes it even becomes a fruity-floral complex which shows a certain steadiness, able to characterize the wine's growth. For example, in the Beaujolais *grands crus* or great growths which are consumed mostly when they are young, one can observe the following constancies:

> Brouilly: prune, peony
> Chénas: almond, violet, amber
> Chiroubles: red currant, prune
> Fleurie: iris, violet, amber, musk, réséda
> Juliénas: peach, raspberry
> Morgon: apricot, red currant, kirsch
> Moulin-à-Vent: prune, violet, musk
> Saint-Amour: peach, reseda
> Régnié: blackcurrant, cherry, peony

This later wine village has been elevated to the great growths *Grands Crus* appellation in the early 1980s.

Do not be confused with the Beaujolais de l'année, that is, the Beaujolais of the year, the grapes where harvested. It is also called Beaujolais Nouveau or Beaujolais Primeur.

It has been a trend since the 1970s for the Beaujolais winemakers to sell their wine ahead of time in order to cash in for their new equipment needed for their harvest. It is estimated that thirty percent of all Beaujolais is sold early. Of course, the end of the year's holiday celebrations prove to be a good incentive to enjoy a light-bodied wine which complements any meal and will not make too much of a dent on your wallet. The sales have been so successful even in the United States that by November 15, the Beaujolais is shipped by air to be provided for the Thanksgiving holidays.

THE TANNIN

To close this chapter, here is a last word about tannin. When you taste a great wine, an astringent substance comes into the composition. Tannin gives a certain body to wine, but it is also known for its therapeutic virtues. It gives a determined role in the feasibility of *pasting* (or collage). Therefore you can better appreciate a limpid or clear wine. Chemically, the tannins of wine are polyphenols derived from the catechin acid. Their importance varies according to the wine growths. For one, the tannin of the Gironde/Bordeaux is rich in tannin. Red wines contain around three to four grams, but can reach up to nine grams in certain years. White wines however are limited to a half gram.

Above all, tannin gives to wines its wellness or flashy taste. When there is too much tannin, the wines are biting, harsh, astringent. Too little tannin causes the wines to be thin or meager. If the white wines are not in that wellness of state, it is because of their weak tenure in tannin. The natural sources of tannin are the stalk and seeds. In certain years, however, the winemaker can add tannin derived from the gallic acid. New oak barrels can provide a lot of tannin, at first a little excessive but lessening with time to later render a very gentle bouquet.

THE BOARD OF LOCUTIONS

Nothing could better finish this section than a board of locutions. Here are the terms used by qualified wine tasters in order to express their gustative emotions. In speaking of overall qualities, tasters will use the following words: distinguished, elegant, grand, charming, graceful, stylish, fine character, noble, fine, and skillfully made. The following selection is divided into six classifications: palate, gown, constitution of the body, vinosity, nose, and freshness, smoothness, bitterness. Each classification has locutions for qualities and for flaws.

BOARD OF LOCUTIONS I

Selection	Qualities	Flaws
Palate	Lively, fruity, sharp, tasty, evocative, sensual, mature, luscious, robust, complex, consistent	Deceptive, vulgar, heavy, mediocre, rancid, untidy, at a turning point
Gown or Robe	Clarity, rubis, shining, ambered, pure, of gold-green crystalline, well-dressed, transparent	Bad-dressed, fishy, tern, broken, too much gown, crumpled
Body Constitution	Rich, fleshy, muscle, full, well fed, robust, powerful, meat, copious, fine, subtle, delicate, elegant, refined	Lean, made too narrow, thin, badly-built, skinny, unbalanced, coarse, vulgar, common, unrefined, hollow, gaunt
Vinosity	Generous, warm, with a lot of pep, nervous, heady	Poor, flat, vulgar, flabby, weak, soft
Nose	Scented like a flower-bunch, appealing, enticing, appropriate for age, enticing, good nose, bristling with truffles, subtle, rich, raspberries, perfumed	Vulgar, faded, muted, worn out, without charm, faded, wilted, stale, ungrateful
Freshness, Smoothness, Bitterness	Tender, firm, supple, slippery, plump, mellow, smooth, virile, caressing, voluptuous, lined, creamy, velvety, mouthful, oily, ardent, melted	Sharp, biting, acidic, green sour, harsh, astringent, raw, tart, barren, clinched, aggressive, rough

BOARD OF LOCUTIONS II

Here is some vocabulary to use when you talk about wine. The terms and definitions are not as technical as the Board of Locutions I. These are the most used expressions to clearly spell your impressions of a wine in the correct term.

	Favorable	Unfavorable
General Character of a Wine	Clean, elegant, full, velvety, soft, tasty, vigorous, rich, robust, warm	Harsh, unbalanced, heavy, light, poor, thin, weak, insipid, thick, sharp
General Character of the Color	Brilliant, clear, gleaming, ruby, crimson, amber, sumptuous	Cloudy, dull, pale, faded
General Character of the Alcohol Content	Lively, generous, powerful, heady, strong	Cold, flat, light, weak, lifeless
General Character of the Sugar Content	Mellow, sweet, dry, smooth, unctuous, silky	Insipid, sugary, harsh
General Character of the Bouquet or Aroma	Fine, fruity, rich in bouquet, spicy perfumed	Burned, flat, corky

HOW TO DRINK AND COMPARE WINE

You will soon realize that one of the great pleasures of drinking wine is to talk about them and to compare impressions. Trying to describe the color, the bouquet, and taste of a wine is much less difficult when you are talking to someone who has the same wine in his own glass. The vocabulary of wine tasting may seem vague or difficult at first, but you will discover that its terms are fairly specific and easily understood by anyone who has tasted several wines.

Although professional wine tasters may use technical terms to pinpoint certain characters, a tasting locution form does not need to be extremely technical. The only way to learn about wines is to try different bottles and to be aware of what you are tasting. A good way to define your impressions more accurately is to compare several bottles at a time.

The appellation contrôlée laws were based on earlier attempts to control the authenticity and quality of French wines which were in turn made necessary by the confusion resulting from the complete replanting of the French vineyards after their destruction by phylloxera toward the end of the nineteenth century. Phylloxera is a plant louse that was unwittingly brought over from the United States on American rootstocks and which began to infest the European vineyards about one hundred years ago.

Various methods were proposed to eliminate the phylloxera epidemic devastating the vineyards of one country after another, but the technique that finally worked was to graft European *Vitis vinifera* vines to native American rootstocks from the eastern United States that were resistant to this insect. Eventually, every single vine in Europe (and most of those in California) was grafted onto an American rootstock.

In conclusion to this chapter on the degustation, it is very important to understand—and can't be repeated enough—that wine behaves like a living element. Wine has the inconstancy, the weaknesses, and is faint-hearted. As a famous doctor said years ago, the wine is a physiological serum. Therefore, it has that complexity, that instability, and also the vulnerability.

CHAPTER FOUR

Chemistry and Medicinal Effects on Wine

Wine is not a simple alcoholic liquid but a complex substance created by the mysterious processes of nature. It is a living product containing yeast, enzymes, and vitamins. It makes no claim to be a complete food, but it is a food which is easily digestible and in balanced proportions provides the body with: Mineral salts, sugar, glycerol, organic acids, aldehydes, ketones, tannins, proteins, trace elements, and so on. The latest research shows that wine contains important enzymes (polyphenol). Its bacterial qualities give it an indispensable value in preserving health. Where infections originating in water or food are concerned, it can play an important preventive role, and it can be very valuable during epidemics. It is also useful for its synergic enhancement of anti-infectious therapy. "Thus, wine seems to answer a real human need, both of the mind and the body. It is very rare for there to be any medical objection to a natural, simple wine, drunk in moderation with meals. For a healthy person, it is safe to say that its benefits far outweigh its defects. Everything depends on the amount and the quality." (Ribereau, 1961)

In 1802, Chaptal discovered six constituents in wine. In 1968, scientists have identified more than two hundred. Drink wine in good measure. This is my main concern about consuming wine. Consumption of wine is overall very harshly criticized by most diet advocates.

Here is the range of the chemical components of the wine as identified by Professor Forgrand. (University of Bordeaux)

Indicated in weight by liter.

Alcohol......................	56 to 120 grams
Dry extract	17 to 32 grams
Total acidity	1.5 to 8 grams
Volatile acidity	0.5 gram
Glycerin...................... ...	3.5 to 15 grams
Bitartrate of potassium	1 to 5 grams
Free tartaric acid	less than 1 gram
Malic acid	1 gram
Sugar	1.5 to 4 grams
Sulfate of potassium	0.15 to 4 grams
Succinic acid	0.7 to 1.4 grams
Tannin	1 to 3 grams
Gum	1 to 4 grams
Sulfuric acid	0.1 to 0.3 grams
Ashes	1 to 3.5 grams
Coloring matters	a few centigrams
Density	0.995 to 0.997 gram

Researchers know that wine contains a very small quantity of chlorine, fluorine, borine, iodine, silicium, copper, zinc, and iron. Mrs. Randoin also revealed that wine contains the vitamins C and B. The aromatic substances, the organic acids, the pectic products, and albuminoid are found in the dry extract, so was oenidol recently discovered. With all these useful elements, how can we contest the value of wine as an alimentary product?

Thus a liter of red wine provides around eight hundred calories, enough to form a supply of food by itself. However it cannot be a sole alimentary base, but just a saving element of substitution or a comparison.

(32oz = 800 calories

(24 oz = 600 calories

6 oz glass of wine= 150 calories)

In their obsession, health technicians persist in comparing the alcohol found in wines to the distilled type of alcohol. They have both the same calorific power, but their harmfulness cannot be compared.

Wine has beneficent biochemical effects on the organism and very serious studies have been done about it. For instance, glycerin exists normally in our intestinal tract divided into fat bodies. There it combines with phosphates which are becoming glycerophosphates utilized by the organism. Sugar is dependent on the glycogenic function of the liver and registers itself as a saving element. The many acids of wine reinforce the acidity of the chime and raise the bile and pancreatic secretions.

As per Dr. Dougnac, wine is among the only beverages in which the pH (2.7 to 3.2) is the closest pH of gastric juice (2 to 2.5).

The tannin excites the smooth fibers of the digestive tract, as per Doctor Weissenbach. The phosphate under the organic element is a powerful accelerator for the nutrition and for the azotes exchanges.

For a long time, Professor Charvin had revealed the mechanism of the action over the mineral salts. Their ionization by the humoral phenomenon contributes through catalysts to wake up supple affinities. Thus, all the dastases are dependent on a metal.

When one knows the importance of these substances in the metabolism of the human body, one understands better that when bringing these metals under the assimilable forms, wine assists the complicated mechanism of the human being. Wine acts over the great organic elements of the human being. Introduced in the mouth, it provokes reflexes on the nervous centers, the salivary glands, and gastric glands. Professor Pachon describes this process, "Agreeable sensations are born when wine is scrutinized, smelled, and tasted. They favorably modify the psychic tonus of the individual and provoke automatically the start by the direction of the psychic reflexes from the secretion of the craving juice."

When arriving in the stomach, wine accelerates the secretions, it even provokes the afflux in the stomach of white cells which are of the sources of the oxidant ferments.

During the fourth Convention of Doctors, friends of wine from France, the effect of wine over the digestive tube has been described as follows: "Wine is a seasoning, it promotes the action of the amylas, accelerates the gastric circulation, and thanks to its vitamins B in particular, releases and stimulates the gastric secretion." The stimulating effect of wine operates normally on the function of the hepatic cell of the subject when wine is utilized at normal doses. All the phenomena brought to mind above, are an important condition which can only be conceived in the perspective of a "reasonable consumption of good wines."

The most important part of the health technician's quarrels deals with the cirrhosis of the liver at first, then on the effect of wine over the nervous system.

It is known that since the early ages, man has given way to stimulants. In China, the stimulant is poppy. In the Orient, it's opium and hashish, in the East it's coffee and tea; however, the Occident has been lucky to produce wine.

If man is banned from these stimulants and is an addict of strong substances, he will be tempted sooner or later to use alcohol, cocaine, or morphine. Professor Letourneau explains this mechanism: The use of various substances has for its main motive the desire of aiding human beings to emancipate themselves from the ordinary conditions of life: misery and the worries of his daily life. Those things give him a forgetful moment and the appearance of a refuge for a short while."

All the citations of these serious practitioners conclude that the moderate use of wine produces a light excitation, a sensation of well-being, and a decrease of fatigue. Professor Pousson puts it well: "Wine restores the joviality of man, improves his judgment, inclines to attachment, pleasing the senses, warming up the heart, and stimulating the brain."

In order to complete this chapter, there is one more last point we should consider, it is the one connected with the bacterium power of the wine.

This matter could not be denied without doubt by the thinkers. Even before the discoveries of Doctor Pasteur, our ancestors, for ages, utilized, by instinct, the bacterium power of the wine, even in surgical matters, to sterilize the wounds.

Why, since centuries ago, was white wine recommended to be consumed, with oysters? It was the same measure of precaution. Very soon people began to use vinegar in salads. Without doubt, our ancestors had observed these precautions to sterilize these uncooked foods.

Abuse of wine as well as abstinence lead us to the formula of Professor Fiessinger, a member of the Academy of Medicine, "An adult man and in good health can drink without danger with his meals one gram of alcohol-wine per kilogram per weight of his body and per day." For example, a 170-pound man can drink 85 grams of wine per day with his two meals.

EXPLANATION OF TECHNICAL WORDS USED BY WINE GROWERS

It is not unusual to find wine terms while reading wine magazines or books that are not explained by the writer. In order to clarify these terms, they will be listed alphabetically.

Acids: In the composition of wine, there are a certain amount of acids. If too little, the wine is flat or tasteless, if too much, the wine becomes spoiled or sour tasting of vinegar. By the way, the French words *vin aigre*, meaning sour wine, then became *vinaigre*, vinegar.

Acidity:　There are two types of acidity, the volatile acidity and the fixed acidity. The volatile acidity is the combination of all the fatty acids produced mainly by the acetic acids. An acetic acid has a threefold origin in wines: the oxidation of the acetal itself produced by the oxidation of ethylic alcohol, during the alcoholic fermentation and during the aging of the wine; the action of the acetic bacterias and from some definite yeasts; and the action of the anaerobic bacterias. Please look for the words: acetal, ethylic, anaerobic. The grape juice practically does not hold any acetic acid. When diluted with liquids, it develops into vinegar. The vinegar itself has been known since the age of Antiquities and has been used as a condiment. If the volatile acid exceeds 0.9 gram when the wine is ready to be bottled, it means that the wine is sick. It is called by the French words *vin pique* (turned sour, spoiled, or pickled). Such wines are improper for consumption and are legally forbidden to be sold to the public. They are usually taken to vinegar factories or are distilled. The volatile acidity is mostly issued from the acetic, butyric, formic, and propionic acids. They assist in giving to wine its bouquet and its stability. The acetic fermentation takes place only in the presence of air and is produced by a microorganism called the acetobacter, the chemical formula is as follows:

$$\text{Alcohol} + \text{Oxygen} \qquad \text{Acetobacter}$$
$$CH_3CH_2OH + O_2 \qquad \text{Acetic Acid} + \text{Water}$$
$$CH_3COOH + H_2O$$

Total acidity means the fixed acidity plus the volatile acidity.
The fixed acidity: This acidity comes from the tartaric, malic, and citric acids.
They are present in the grape and during the fermentation. They are desirable, natural vegetal acidities which give the wine an agreeable tartness.

Aeration of the musts: A good aeration (ventilation), also called oxygenation, is obtained by removing the grape from the stem; this is called *égrappage*. This method activates the fermentation by letting the oxygen of the air pass freely through the grapes in order to activate or bud the young yeasts, present in the grape.

Collage:　The method which consist of adding to the wine after the fermentation is over, a proportion of a broth of fish or caseine or gelatin, or fresh blood from animals or beaten egg whites to clarify the impurities of the wine (floating solid elements). It is a very important and mandatory operation once the wine has been fermented.

Cuvage or cuvaison: This is the practice of letting the grapes ferment during a certain period of time from one day to ten days. The coloring elements for obtaining a red wine is the aim of this operation. If a white is desired from colored skin grapes, the grape is not macerated with the grape's juice. If the winegrower is looking to make a rose or pink wine, the grapes are left to slightly color the grape's juice, for example: White Zinfandel or Rose from Provence.

Chaptalization: When the grapes are harvested, they sometimes do not contain enough sugar in order to raise the alcohol content that the winegrower is seeking. As a finished product, the wine being chaptalized is less vulnerable to excessive acidities. Chaptalization is done by adding honey and water or beet sugars into the must during the fermentation. The word chaptalization comes from the inventor's name, M. Chaptal, who was Napoléon's minister of agriculture.

Débourbage: This operation consists of separating the main impurities present in the must. They are mostly coming from remains of soil and organic substances. It is done with anhydride-sulfureous acids and is especially used in the vinification of white wines.

Débourrage: Operation consisting of carrying out a first draw-off in order to separate the wine from its dregs (or in French *bourres*).

Slow fermentation: The slow fermentation is the transformation of the lactic acid of the must into malic acid with the aid of malolactic bacterias, which are natural ingredients of the grape juice. This a very important factor which conditions the wine to bring down the total acidity of the wine and therefore promoting a harmonious effect in the wine.

Tumultuous fermentation: This is the transformation of the grape sugar into alcohol with the aid of the yeasts naturally present in the grapes or yeasts prepared in laboratories.

Dregs (or *Lies* in French): Dregs are formed by the thick substances settling at the bottom of the barrels during the fermentation. A wine which is on its *lies* or on its *bourre* is called a wine *sur lies* when the wine has not been drawn off, for example: Muscadet sur lies, Sauvignon Blanc sur lies. This is applied mostly to white wines to give them an enhanced vegetal flavor.

Marc (pronounced *mahr*): Once the grapes have been pressed, the leftover substances like the stalks, seeds, and skins of the grapes are called marc. The marc is still usable for distillation or sometimes it is blended with sugared water in order to get a type of wine called *vin de piquette*, mostly kept for the help to consume.

Plastering: The addition of calcium sulfate (or gypsum) to lower acid musts to induce the necessary degree of acidity level. This process is not allowed in France, but accepted, for example, in Spain for making sherry. It is also used in warm weather climates for the same reason.

MANIPULATION OF WINE

AUTHORIZED MANIPULATIONS

Manipulations which do not constitute fraudulent practices, according to the wine laws of France and dated August 1, 1905, are:

- The treatment of white wines and rosés by the ferrocyanure of pure potassium. This chemical term means a voluminous salt, yellow in color, odorless and soluble in water. Do not be confused with ferrocyanure ferrique which is not authorized. It is insoluble. It has been proposed as an exchanger of ions, especially, in order to eliminate copper and lead.

Let me point out that in the United States, ferrocyanure ferrique mixed with ferrocyanure of potassium is used to a certain degree.

- The blending of wines together.

- The adulteration of white wines, either by addition of concentrated musts or with a blending of sweet wine.

- The freezing of wines.

- The pasteurization of wines.

- The collage or pasting of wines using *kieselguhr*, a German word, used to clarify silicious deposits.

Professor Deflanche, once described this soil as a microscopic type of seaweed, constituted with one cell only.

- The coloration of wines obtained only by addition of grape caramel.

- The clarification of white wines slightly stained, using purified charcoal.

- The treatment with pure sulfurous anhydride.

- The addition of citric acid crystallized pure.

- The addition of tanin.

NON-AUTHORIZED AND FORBIDDEN MANIPULATIONS

Article 3 of the legislation on wines, dated August 1, 1905, decreed that all forbidden and non-authorized manipulations of wine are considered an infringement and are punishable by a large fine and jail term. The legislation against the fraud (or swindle) relies on the laws of 1905, modified in 1912, in 1929, and by the last decree of 1938.

The best wording one can apply when talking about fraud is "an adulterated wine", translated as *un vin frelaté*. This means a wine which has been denatured with some type of blending in order to give it the appearance of qualities it does not possess. There are three main elements to disclose that fraud: Inhibitor of the alcoholic fermentation; artificial coloration; and plastering (platrage)

It is also strictly forbidden to sell wines obtained by blending or to sell wines unsuitable for consumption. The manipulations are considered fraudulent when the winemaker or a wine broker has, as his objective, the modification of the natural state of such wine.

Other forbidden manipulations include:

- Mouillage: The addition of water to wine, even if it is known by the buyer.

- Addition of foreign products such as sugar or marc that is not authorized. The same applies to the addition of coloring matters, of products like sulfurous acid, nitric acid, hydrochloric acid, salycilic, and boric acids or similar products.

- Sodium chlorure above one gram per liter.

- Forbidden also is the use of figs, caroubs, mowra flowers, clochettes, rice, barley flour, and other sugar products.

- Glucose: The use of glucose in the vinification for the purpose of the preparation of a second press wine.

- The manufacturing of wines by diffusion.

A wine of diffusion uses the process of diffusing water in the vats containing marc, where the alcohol remaining produces piquette, or wines obtained by the action of water and the marc (pressed grapes). Piquette is known in France as an alternative to producing wine, and it is mostly for the help, but there are always shrewd people willing to take a risk by cheating. Any manufacturing of wine by diffusion is required to be declared three days in advance at the nearest state collection office.

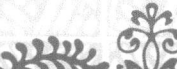

WINE AND HEALTH

Wine has been regarded for centuries as a basic ingredient of human food. It was described by a clergyman of the seventeenth century as follows: "After bread comes wine which is the second health food given by the Creator." Before those times, it had been known that wine was a necessary part of the diet as essential as bread. The popular saying was: "Go eat with joy your bread and drink your wine to one's heart content."

Wine is, first of all, an antiseptic and used to be given to the Greek and Roman armies sent abroad. At that time dysentery was rampant. Typhoid and cholera were common sicknesses and hard to cure. Hence, the Greek and the Romans were responsible for the planting of the vine across Europe in pursuit of new lands. At the height of the Roman Empire, the occupation stretched from the deserts of Africa to Scotland.

During the Napoleonic era and during the Battle of Austerlitz, it was mentioned in a general's journal that wine handed out on a daily base to the troops gave them mental and physical stamina. It helped to fight weariness and maintained the strength and morale of the soldiers.

Also of interest, in rural areas of France, it was well known that housewives added wine to soups as it was known to add healthful benefits to the meals. Wine carries with it all the vitamins found in grapes: vitamin A which has beta carotene to help ward off cancer, vitamin B which contributes to mental alertness and provides energy, and vitamin C to combat fatigue.

MEDICINAL EFFECTS OF THE WINE

In order to complete this chapter, there is one more last point we like to touch, it is the one connected with the bacterium power of the wine.

This matter could not be denied without doubt by the thinkers. Even before the discoveries of Doctor Pasteur, our ancestors, for ages, utilized by instinct the bacterium power of the wine and this also in surgical matters, to sterilize the wounds.

Why, since centuries ago, was white wine recommended to be consumed with oysters? It was the same measure of precaution. Very soon came in usage the vinegar with salads. With no doubts our ancestors had observed these precautions to sterilize these uncooked foods and for that matter the possibility of carrying germs.

Abuse of wine as well as abstinence lead us to the formula of Professor Fiessinger, a member of the Academy of Medicine.

"An adult man and in good health can drink without danger with his meals one gram of alcohol-wine per kilogramme per weight of his body and per day."

Example: A 170 lb man can drink 85 grammes of wine per day with his two meals. (approx. 2 pounds= One kilogramme)

CHAPTER FIVE

How to Become A Wine Connoisseur

-o-

Choosing and Storing Wines

-o-

The Laws of the "Appellation d'Origine Controlée" in France

How to become a connoisseur of wine

Many stories have been written over the years on how wine was produced and consumed and for different reasons. In our modern society, wine became an accessory to our dining pleasures, as well as a way of toasting friend that you would like to treat well. It is also a tradition to baptize new ships by bouncing a bottle of Champagne against the front hull. Any prestigious sporting event will also command a toast with wine.

There is no snobbish bearing when you believe that you are a connoisseur as long as you don't brag about it. You become a connoisseur like you become a good cook, taking notes, experiencing, and finally you know it.

In this world, not everybody likes to consume wine. A lot of people are content to drink iced tea, fruit juices, cola beverages, or milk with their meals. Some prefer whisky. Some others will tell you that wine gives them a headache, yet others drink beer and some other will tell you that wine is expensive. Nevertheless, the consumption of wine is growing and there are countries that you never would have imagined which are now growing and exporting wine to markets. Here are some steps to follow.

To become a connoisseur in wine requires a full knowledge of understanding, distinguishing, and evaluating a certain wine. Note that tasting wine and consuming wine is strictly limited to any exaggeration. You will not become a connoisseur overnight. As a novice, you will be looking for a certain wine which flatters your palate. Every palate is different, but your taste will become narrower when you will come upon your choice. It can be a robust red wine (strong in alcohol content), a white wine (light and acidic), a sweet wine or fortified wine, or a semi-dry pink wine. Once you have discovered your choice, you will stay with it for a while until your palate is absolutely certain that your mind has set on it. Later on, you will be exposed to a different wine which you also enjoy to taste and more than once. This is due to a change in your taste buds. You were not completely satisfied with your first choice, also your way of living might have changed or evolved, even your own body has perhaps matured, as you reach the peak of your age.

At that time you know what you would like to taste the most:

A Burgundy type (more masculine)

A lighter red wine such as Beaujolais

A Rhône wine (more meaty and robust)

A Bordeaux type of wine (with a lot of softness, more feminine)

Your stage of maturity has now reached its peak. From now on, it's just a matter of what you can afford in the vast category you choose. On an informal basis, it's like a teenager finding his or her first girlfriend or boyfriend. You might find him or her after two or three encounters, then you finally settle for your real choice, the final choice: the marriage of a couple. You will have good years and bad years!

A last word when choosing your wine, be aware that all so-called wine expert-reporters will write about the quality of a wine, not so much on a negative side but more appropriately, the positive qualities. They are all wrong. They are told to promote a wine so it will sell. On the contrary, a wine expert does not necessarily give you information on the constitution of the wine. They keep their own remarks and don't publish them.

Various wine publications are jumping on the wagon to publicize that the harvest of top-ranking Bordeaux wines for example will be "good, not so good, or passable." The same applies for any regions producing wines. They are paid by importers and distributors to tell their readers of the up-coming distributions of wine which are not yet even bottled. Wine is like a delicate baby. First, it has to age in the barrel, then in the bottle in order to mature properly.

THE SHIPPING OF WINE

Here is an example of how wine is shipped after production. A wine-shipper gives an order to a wine producer for a container of 750 cases of wine of a specific vintage year, let's take, for example, a Merlot wine.

After the contract is signed by both parties and after the usual custom papers are ready, the wine is loaded on a container truck (usually not refrigerated) and brought to the nearest harbor of exportation. There it stays a couple of days before being loaded on a ship which has the right of passage to a foreign country. Suppose the wine is to be shipped from Europe to Baltimore, Maryland. The sailing is not always smooth, and the ship may encounter stormy weather. Anyway, the voyage will take ten days. Eventually, the container will be unloaded within the next forty-eight hours and shipped by truck to the importer's warehouse. The temperature on July 25, 2005 was 101° F in Baltimore.

The importer has a demand from three wine-distributors: an order from Washington, D.C. for 250 cases, another for 200 cases in Chicago, and 300 cases in Cincinnati. Within the next eight days, the wine is delivered to the respective parties. From then on, it is distributed by regular truck in the next fifteen days. For example in Washington, it may go to thirty-five wine retailers where the wine stays approximately between three and six months until sold. These handlings take around six weeks from the producer to the retailer.

There is, however, a faster but more expensive way to send wine: by air-cargo with a charge of between fifteen and twenty dollars per case. Your wine can then be obtained in four days, which is the case for Beaujolais wine (or Beaujolais Nouveau) which was harvested in early September and was ready for consumption in New York or San Francisco for the Thanksgiving holidays at the end of November.

CHOOSING AND BUYING WINE

The range of wine available in stores varies greatly from country to country. If you live in France, Italy, or Spain, the local supermarket will only stock wine from each of these countries. In the United States, is it better to buy wine from a grocery store or a national wine merchant chain? To answer this question, one must consider the wine being purchased.

The competition between national chains and supermarkets is very severe. It wouldn't be surprising for a wine distributor to remove all the stocked wine in a store and place its own line coming from a different grower or shipper. If you would like advice about special bottles of origin such as Barolo, Mosel Wines, Loire wines, even Vintage Ports, or imported Cognacs, then the best place to go is the independent wine merchant or the national chain. These people employ at least one wine clerk who has good knowledge of their stock and origin. They are, generally, also invited to regular wine tastings each year. They are therefore able to help you select what you have in mind.

SERVING WINES

Historically, room temperature referred to dining-rooms without central heating, so red wines don't taste their best if served too warm. On the other hand, a complex red wine should not be chilled, nor should any red wine be warmed near a heating device. The wine becomes numb and will lose its bouquet. A temperature of 65° F would be an ideal temperature. White wines and rosés should be iced in buckets to come to a chill of no colder than 40° F. The refreshing quality of any chilled white or rosé wine will enhance its virtue.

In general, all light red wines which grew on the most northern part of their countries must be served rather on the cool side, such is the case for Beaujolais wines, Bardolino wines, or California red Burgundy types.

Last, but not least, make sure you lock your cellar. Be certain of the location of your key, and should you find the need to delegate, give the key to a person of integrity.

APPELLATION D'ORIGINE CONTRÔLÉE IN FRANCE

The meaning of this term is to give a name to a specific area and control it. These laws provide and constitute a guarantee from the legislator of the place named on the label and where the wine has been bottled and by whom. The French legislators, under the pressure of wine growers, decided to create in 1935 the Appellation d'Origine Contrôlée.

An independent organization, Institut Nationale de l'Appellation d'Origine (I.N.A.O.), was founded. It had to first set up a chart of the great wines and alcohols (Cognac and Armagnac). The Institute, above all, received the mission to look after the observance during the stage of production, to respect the rules of control for each entitled vineyard locality, to create a wine label spelling the contenance of its origin and give strict conditions of what the bottle of wine contains, the proof of alcohol and the variety of grape utilized.

The character of a wine is bound up with the place where it is produced: the soil and the subsoil, climate, situation, and local vegetation all play a part in giving the wine its own quality. If any one of these changes, then the wine changes too, but these natural factors, although they are essential, are not the only ones involved. Man, in the person of the wine grower, also plays a decisive role in choosing the varieties of vines, the methods of cultivation, wine making, and in deciding how to keep the wine.

The combination of these natural and human factors gives the wine its own original quality and is expressed by the Appellation d'Origine. This is why it is necessary to describe fine wines, wines which have this original quality, by the name of the place they come from. The Appellation d'Origine may only be used for wines made according to the local practice in the place named on the label. The category Appellation d'Origine Contrôlée (A.O.C.) offers a double guarantee: origin and quality.

STORING WINES

The ideal place for storing wines is a cool cellar where the temperature is a constant 50 to 55 degrees year round. The area is to be dark and free of vibrations. Light is the number one enemy for wines because it spoils them after a while. Never store bottles in your kitchen or dining room. Always store the bottles lying down in a horizontal position, never upright.

More and more, builders and architects are planning special wine cellars for custom homes at the behest of the buyer; however, they are still a rarity, even in new restaurants. By the way, next time you go to a restaurant, carefully find out where the wine bottles are stored. They might be stored in an improvised corner in the kitchen, and the house wine bottles might be sitting behind the bar counter. Ninety-eight percent of bottles stored in areas mentioned above will show no aroma or will smell like the cork, finally they will be shady, and the color will fade.

This lack of foresight will prove that people not familiar with storing wine bottles will have problems sooner or later, they will suffer a loss.

If there is no shortage of funds, and if you have a space available, you could always look for and purchase an insulated wine cellar with humidity control and temperature control. There is now a large selection offered in sizes and prices.

If you intend to have your own cellar, it is important that you keep track of your stock and use a notebook in order to show what you have purchased and the date of purchase. If you keep good records, your experience will count to your advantage. Also, your knowledge of vineyards and their vintages will assure you of becoming a fine connoisseur of wines.

CHAPTER SIX

Varieties of Vines Grown Around the World

WHITE GRAPE VARIETY

Aligoté: Grape used in Burgundy, France, that plays a second role to Chardonnay. Produces quiet acidic wine. It is the perfect wine to use as an apéritif in adding black currant syrup or wild blackberry syrup, (crème de mûres). This well known apéritif is called Kir, named after the Bishop Kirr of Dijon, the capital of Burgundy. History tells us that Bishop Kirr launched the drink after being confronted with all the small winegrowers of the northern part of Dijon who hardly sold their product at that time due to the poor quality of the Aligote.

Chardonnay: This variety's correct name is actually Pinot-Chardonnay. It is at its best grown in Burgundy and in the Pays d'Oc in southern France. Pinot-Chardonnay produces the Cadillac of the white wine in France. It is unmatched anywhere. A lot of cuttings were shipped around the world, but due to the climate and soil of different countries, it produced rather semi-dry wine or even sweet wines. It is unthinkable to taste a Pinot-Chardonnay full of scents, heavy and artificially flavored with wood. The most famous villages in Burgundy producing top Pinot-Chardonnay are: Montrachet, Puligny-Montrachet, Meursault, Chassagne-Montrachet, Aloxe-Corton (Grand Cru Corton-Charlemagn), Chablis, Pouilly-Fuissé.

Chenin Blanc: Chenin Blanc is mostly planted in the Loire Valley. The soil and climate, however, fits the variety to be planted in New Zealand and also in South Africa where the growers called it Steen. The Loire Valley, especially around the city of Tours, produces the pearl of Touraine called the Vouvray issued from the Chenin Blanc. California also produces very drinkable wines, labeled as Chenin Blanc.

Colombard: Originally used for making Armagnac and Cognac, it is used more and more in Southwestern France. It is a white-skinned grape. It produces a crisp, lightly floral, easy to drink wine. It was tried in California for a while to make inexpensive jug wine, it is now in retreat. South Africa is also planting that variety and it is used mostly for blending.

Folle Blanche/Gros Plant: Mostly planted around the estuary of the Loire River and around the area of the city of Nantes. It is also known as Gros Plant. It produces wine on a slight bitter side, excellent when consumed with fresh raw oysters or shellfish.

Gewurztraminer: The first large producer is Alsace, France, where it produces a dry, perfumed; and pungent wine. Gewurztraminer can be served as an apéritif. It compliments the goose liver terrine or pâté and desserts.

Here are a few grand crus Gewurztraminer found in the States:
Jean-Marie Haag: Gewurztraminer Alsace, Grand Cru "Zinnkoepfle", L'Esprit Sélection de Grains Nobles.
Léon Beyer: Gewurztraminer Alsace Quintessense Sélection de Grains Nobles
Robert Faller & Fils: Gewurztraminer Alsace

Gewürz means spicy flavor. Gewurztraminer is issued from the Traminer grape. Like all wines from Alsace, it goes through a cold fermentation not colder than 48° F. As for the German wines, they are processed through a hot fermentation. In other words, the juice fermenting is heated to 65° F. Therefore all German white wines are light in taste, the aroma is less pronounced, and overall made on the sweet side, while Alsacian wines are dry.

Grenache Blanc: Planted mostly in the Languedoc and Rousillion in southwest France and all the way to the Pyrénées Mountains and there on in Spain, the North Lyanza region. This variety is vastly used for blending purposes of Ri as it is recognized as a "VDN Appellation".

Marsanne: A leading white variety planted in the Northern Rhône Valley producing a wonderful white Hermitage. This full-bodied wine can age up to ten years. Well known variety in Australia.

Müller-Thürgau: Müller-Thürgau is a cross-breed between the Riesling growth and the Sylvaner growth. It is used only in Germany to make high-volume wines such as Liebfraumilch, a commercial brand well known in the States. Its light sweet side is to the liking of all palates.

Muscadet: A variety planted along the Loire Valley, producing the famous Muscadet wine. Muscadet grapes ripen early and produce a fairly dry wine where scents of spices are emphasized. No better wine could be served with shellfish than Muscadet.

Muscat: Muscat is above all a sweet table grape that you can find during the season in most fruit stores or supermarkets. It is grown in Alsace, the Midi, and in Italy. The Muscat wine, a strong-scented and delicate wine complements desserts and, in Italy, is mostly used in elaborating sparkling wine. The best varieties of Muscat are: The Muscat de Petits Grains and the Muscat of Alexandria.

Pinot Gris: Produces spicy, full-bodied wines known as Pinot Grigio in Italy, Belli Grigio in Slovenia, and Grauburger and Rulander in Germany. The name Tokay was also used for that growth but has been deleted by the European Union because of the conflict arisen with the wine growth, Tokaji, produced in Hungary. Grown in Alsace, Austria, and Germany.

Riesling: One of the better species of grapes, planted mostly in Germany and in Alsace, France. In France, it is vinified as a bone dry wine with a lot of aroma. The finished product of Riesling in Germany is on the semi-dry side due to a different type of vinification. The area where the Riesling grows the best is along the Nahe and the Moselle rivers, also on the sharp hills of Rheinpfalz on the right side of the Rhine River.

Roussanne: Grown in the Rhône Valley. It produces the famous Hermitage. It is also planted in the Languedoc and Rousillon area near the town of Perpignan.

Sauvignon Blanc: A glorious vinestock planted in many parts of the world with a temperate climate and hot sunny days. In the Bordeaux area of the Graves and the Sauternes, it found its niche. The soil (gravel) gives to the wine its very special aroma which characterizes the bouquet of all the great white Bordeaux. When combined with Semillon, it is semi-dry or sweet. Between Pouilly sur Loire and Orléans, in the province of the Loire, the Sauvignon Blanc is called Pouilly Fumé. Other areas where it is cultivated are California, Washington State, South Africa, Australia, and New Zealand. Sauvignon Blanc is vinified on the dry side, while in other countries it is on the semi-dry to sweet side and usually with a strong cedar scent.

Semillon is the grape that gives us the famous Sauternes. Its distinguished character is created when attacked by the noble rot, or *pourriture noble* in French, producing wines with outstanding fineness which define its legendary breed and elegance; however, the dry climate of California prevents this beneficial fungus from forming naturally on grapes, and consequently, Semillon is often marketed as a dry wine. The scientific name of the noble rot is *Botrytis cinerea*.

Sylvaner: Sylvaner is not classified as a noble grape like the Riesling but produces agreeable refreshing table wines. It is mostly grown in Germany and in Alsace, France.

Traminer: This vinestock was introduced by the Romans in the early A.D. 800. Traminer comes from the village of Tramin or Termeno in the Italian province of Tyrol. There are many types of Traminer: red, blue, and white. Also many names have been used including Traminer Aromatico, Traminer Musque, and Gewurztraminer. Gewurztraminer is the legal name required by law in Alsace, France, since 1970. It is now associated with Alsace and has an appellation contrôlée d'origine. It is today the most planted variety as is the Riesling in Alsace. California and Washington State also grow a type of Gewurztraminer in a sweet style due to their warm summers.

RED VARIETY OF GRAPE

Barbera: Native of Italy. Produces mellow, semi-dry wines, deep in color. The region of Piedmont is the location of Barbaresco Barolo, the villages where the Barbera grape is grown.

Cabernet Franc: Mostly planted in the Bordeaux area of France. Produces softer wines than Cabernet Sauvignon. It ripens before the Cabernet and helps for the blending of the most important wines produced in Bordeaux such as Pauillac, Margaux, St. Julien, and St. Emilion.

Cabernet Sauvignon: The traditional variety of Bordeaux planted in many countries. It ripens later than the Cabernet Franc in France. The Cabernet Sauvignon brings finesse and depth of flavor to the wine and needs three to five years to develop graciously.

Carignan: Largely planted in Southern France in the area called the Midi, also in Spain and California. Produces full bodies wines.

Chianti: The region of Tuscany with Florence as its capital is where the famous Chianti wine grows. Chianti is the best-known wine produced in Italy, sometimes mediocre, sometimes excellent. As a result, an inner zone of Chianti Classico was formed by a *consorzio* (united producers of the inner zone of Tuscany). The production is around twenty percent of the total wines made in Chianti. Such wines bear neck labels depicting the Gallo Negro, a black cockerel on a gold background.

Cinsault: Variety mostly used for making rosé wines. Largely planted in the Rhône Valley of France and in the Midi area.

Gamay: Gamay produces the famous Beaujolais wine, located just above the Rhône Valley, seven miles from Macon along the Saône River and the slopes of the mountain chain, facing east and south. Its production is over 1,000,000 hectoliters: The top growths are named after the ten villages, located each on top of the hills: Moulin à Vent, Chiroubles, Brouilly, Juliénas, Morgon, Chenas, St. Amour, Fleurie, Côte de Brouilly, and Régnié. What makes Beaujolais so special is the granitic soil, a rather distinctive *gout du terroir*, or taste of the soil. The wine of Beaujolais is at its best when consumed young. One more note about Beaujolais wine, it tastes better slightly chilled or at cellar temperature between 50° and 60°. The wine really tastes all the fresher and seems even more delightful.

Grenache: This variety produces red and rosé all along the Mediterranean Coast. These wines are very pleasant and fruity. They tend to age quickly. One of its top lines is the mellow wine from Banyuls.

Malbec: A growth with good tannin content, best known in Bordeaux for blending. Used also in Argentina's better wines.

Merlot: A well-known species in Bordeaux and all the Midi area. It produces a soft wine with a lot of fruit aroma. It is used more and more in California and in Australia, also Chili, Argentina, Italy.

Mourdevre: This is a quality wine growth used mostly as a table wine in the South of France.

Nebbiolo: This wine grape is a better species in Italy and grows a lot in the Piedmont area where it produces the famous Barolo and Barbaresco. Requires some years of aging before consumption.

Pinotage: A crossbreed of Cinsault and Pinot Noir, produced mainly in South Africa. At its best, the wine has a rich plum fruit aroma.

Pinot Meunier: Best known as the third variety used in the creation of Champagne.

Pinot noir: The number one grape used in Burgundy and in Champagne. In other parts of the world, the variety is more difficult to grow and not easy to vinify because of the lack of color in the skins.

CHAPTER SEVEN

The Wine History of California

1. The Legend

2. The Napa Valley

3. The Sonoma Valley

4. The Mondavi Domain

THE ESTATE WINERY OF ROBERT MONDAVI IN OAKLAND
NAPA VALLEY, CALIFORNIA

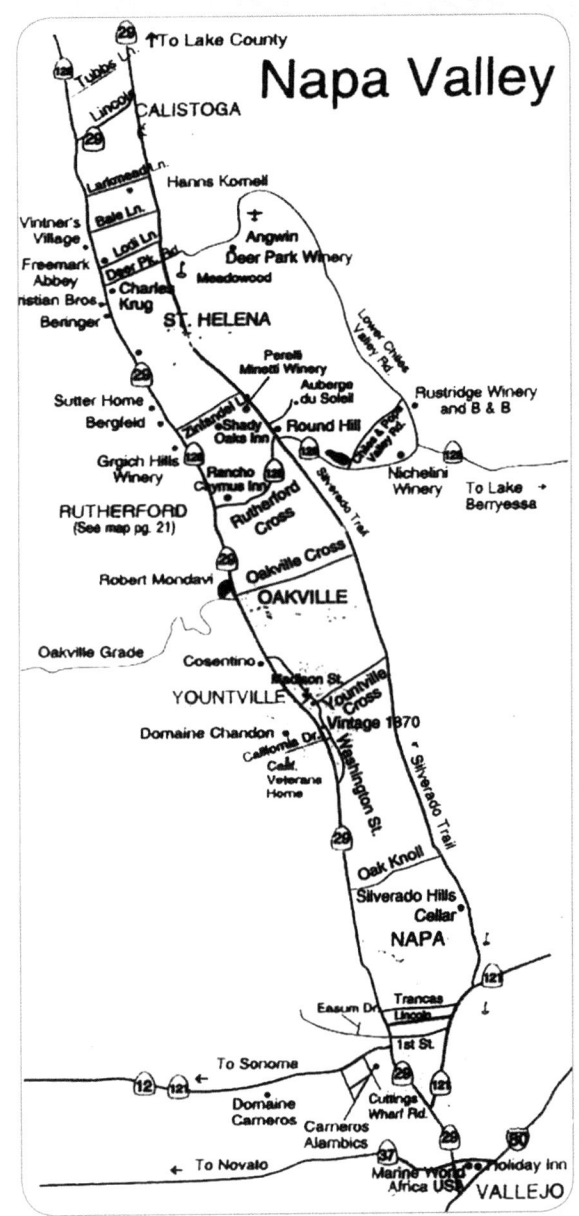

THE MAP OF NAPA VALLEY, CALIFORNIA

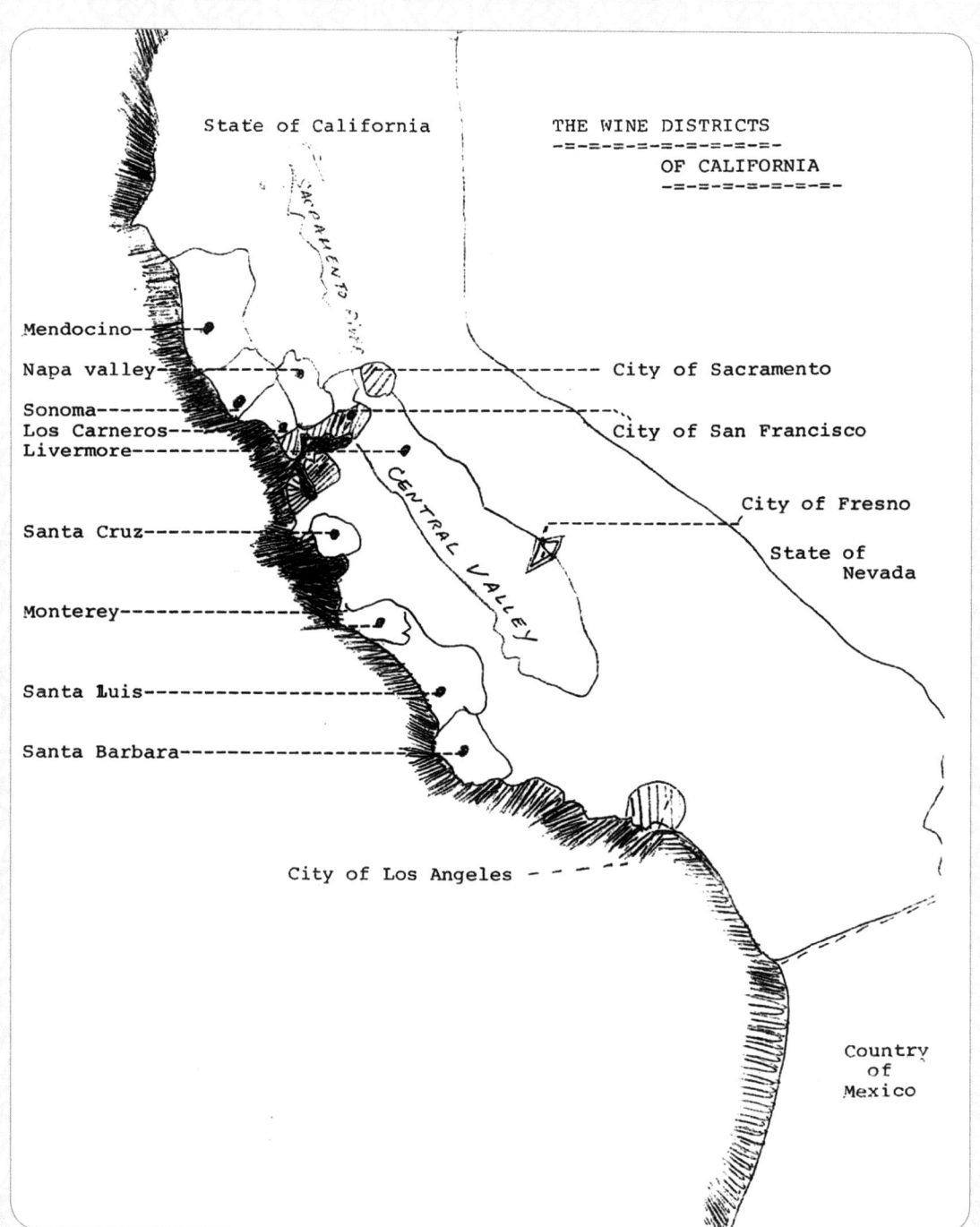

State of California

THE WINE DISTRICTS
-=-=-=-=-=-=-=-=-
OF CALIFORNIA
-=-=-=-=-=-=-=-

Mendocino--------

Napa valley---------------

Sonoma--------- ---------------------- City of Sacramento

Los Carneros---

Livermore---------------- ------------------ City of San Francisco

Santa Cruz------------

-------------- City of Fresno

Monterey-------------------

State of
Nevada

Santa Luis-------------------

Santa Barbara-------------------

CENTRAL VALLEY

City of Los Angeles - - - -

Country
of
Mexico

The early wine stages

The vinestock variety, *vitis vinifera*, came to North America in 1524, when Cortes, the Spanish Conqueror of Mexico, directed the land owners to grow vine, thus it became one of the industries of the New World.

He ordained that for five years, the holders of land grants must plant one thousand vines per year, for each one hundred Indians living on their land. As it was the case of the best wine districts in Europe, the vineyards in California had their beginnings through the help of the Church which needed wine for sacramental purposes.

In 1769, Father Junipero Serra planted vines at the New Franciscan Mission in San Diego, all the way south. It was called the Vineyard of the Mission. It has been said that the wine was harsh, coarse, and without character. It was, however, a good start and the feasibility of viticulture was then established in California.

The first commercial plantation of vines was made in 1824 by one of the early settlers at Little Pueblo of Los Angeles. Six years later, a Frenchman from Bordeaux, Jean-Louis Vignes, started a vineyard about where Los Angeles Union Station now stands. By the middle of the nineteenth century, his wines and brandies were known throughout the State of California. Within a generation, wine making became the principal industry of the Los Angeles area. The total production still remained small, nevertheless, four million gallons of wine were produced in 1875. The gold rush of 1849 had been highly beneficent also for California and brought a demand for all good things, including wine.

Four thousand years ago, the Greeks and the Phoenicians sailed into the estuary of the Gironde, not far from Bordeaux and were impressed by the favorable conditions for growing wine in this area.

The same must had happened to this vast open land of California, where all these new fortune hunters came, but the smart and skilled new emigrated wine makers recognized the hills and valley around the San Francisco Bay, the Sonoma area, and the Napa Valley. They, also after tremendous hard work, found their own liquid gold.

Nowadays, with only one or two exceptions, the wineries which dominate the wine production in California had been founded by immigrants who came from other important wine-growing areas in Europe.

In 1875, California produced four million gallons of wine, a small amount for these times. The winegrowers exported mostly to South America, but did not develop a serious domestic American market.

The average American also was a whisky drinker. In short, he was a transplant from the austere Protestant cultures of northern Europe where the wine culture did not flourish, and where wine consequently was not a habit of daily life, at least among the common folk.

Two generations later, the Act of Prohibition was declared from 1919 to 1933 and had a decisive influence on the shape of the wine industry of California. It was also a misguided triumph of legislated morality. The clause of the Prohibition law allowed wine making for home use only and for the immediate family. Sacramental wine growing was tolerated, but all commercial wineries had to close down.

The vineyards themselves had to be uprooted and replaced by varieties of vine like the Thompson seedless. The thick skins of that variety could withstand the rigors of transportation across the United States. The Thompson seedless was also a high-yielding variety of table grape.

It takes seven years to harvest table grapes, but the development finally came after the 1940s. California winegrowers received a real boost, first they joined together to create a self-help society called the California Wine Institute whose purpose was to educate Americans in the pleasures of drinking wine and especially California wine first. Secondly, a vast generation of young wine writers schooled in Europe tried to impress the readers, but with the patient efforts of the California Wine Institute, the change in American drinking habits finally arrived. The task was to teach the Americans how to drink it, when to drink it, and how much of it to drink.

By 1970, the annual production of California wines was 425 million gallons, the area of cultivated vineyards was 695,000 acres. The annual consumption in 1970 was 1.60 gallons per person over twenty-one years of age; in 1995 it was 1.70 gallons.

History

In the sixteenth century, the Pilgrims emigrated to the northeastern region of North America, a new land where they could freely practice their religion. They were followed by millions of other emigrants from all over Europe over the next centuries. A lot of these emigrants did not drink hard liquors like whisky, vodka, or rum. They mostly drank tea, coffee, milk, and later on fruit juice or lemonade. It is undeniable to say that the history of the California wine industry is also part of a collision between two cultures in a new country.

The white Americans of Saxon Protestant descent (W.A.S.P.), were a large group among these newcomers who were industrious, organized, but somewhat naive and provincial people. Wine was not produced in their former countries of origin, but they were able to ferment grains to make whisky.

To the contrary, the emigrations of Catholics at that time were from southern and central Europe where wine was produced. They were family loving, wine loving, and perhaps backward but urbane.

In the 1940s, on the eve of WWII, two young brothers raised in the northeast of the United States had the ingenuity for marketing wine.

Ernest and Julio Gallo, whose parents emigrated to the United States in the nineteenth century from the Piedmont wine district in Italy (Chianti and Barolo district), settled in Modesto, California. They became the leaders at that time in the wine industry. They moved with vigorous innovations in their campaign. They started with the big state of Texas, where their marketing research team questioned all wine drinkers about their tastes, their preferences in selecting full-bodied wine or light wine, their preferences of sweet wines or dry wines, or if they preferred red, rosé, or white wines.

It became a triumph of the great American free enterprise.

The single event in the post-prohibition history in particular was, however, the element of war in Europe in the 1940. At that time, millions of American soldiers were sent to England in preparation of the invasion in France and further to Berlin. When they got the go signal, they drove through hundreds of wine villages, from the Loire Valley to the Chablis area, then Burgundy then Alsace, across the Champagne area, the Rhine River, and the Moselle.

The winegrowers from France, Germany and Italy welcomed the Allied Forces with more than a glass of wine. All soldiers, young or old were exposed to the family life of the old country. When welcomed into someone's home, you were treated with a glass of wine first. When it comes to food, wine, and entertaining friends, the Europeans possess a tremendous amount of *savoir faire*. Eating and drinking are authentic rituals in Europe, and every home always has several bottles of wine set aside for these highly-regarded ceremonies.

After WWII, a large number of U.S, Foreign Service officers traveled through Europe, they too became acquainted with wines from France, Germany, Italy, and Spain. California wine production in 1875 was four million gallons. In 1975, it was 425 million gallons. In one hundred years, the production has increased a hundredfold.

There is still a gap between consumption in Europe and consumption in the United States, nevertheless, it has almost doubled in the short time of thirty-five years in the States.

THE MODERN WINE INDUSTRY OF CALIFORNIA

The state of California produces a tremendous variety of wines at different prices and of different styles. After the prohibition, the wine industry started at zero, that was in 1933. All table grapes grown at that time were not fit for making wine. For example, the Thompson seedless grape with a thick skin and a fleshy pulp could not be used. The one variety at that time and good for all climates was the Zinfandel.

It is still today the most widely-planted red vine. Zinfandel conjures an image of a sweet pink wine, but being from a red grape it produces deeply colored wines. With the ingenuity of the cellar master, Zinfandel can easily be handled by adding richly-flavored blackberry scent, spices, or cedar flavors.

By 1960, the Federal Regulation tried to change the industry and a lot of cuttings of different varieties were imported from Europe and planted on any adaptable climates around California. Those who enjoyed Zinfandel and wanted to know about its origin were surrounded by the variety's mysterious lineage.

It is said that in 1880, Count Haraszthy, a new wine grower, had introduced Zinfandel to California; however, the facts contradicted his claim because after many years of research, a breakthrough was made in 1967 when a U.S. pathologist made his discovery.

The State of California offers practically the entire range of climatic conditions to be found anywhere in the wine zone. Most of the Europeans vinestocks are cultivated in California. Despite their diversity, the wine lands can be divided into two large categories:

I. The Central Valley, from the Sacramento valley to the San Joachim Valley, the Coast Range, and the Sierra Nevada, along with the San Bernardino area of Southern California. These areas are often flat, hot, fertile, and mostly irrigated vineyards. In this Wine Zone are grown not only grapes for the production of brandies, Sherries, or Ports, but what is called the standard wines of California (a lot of inexpensive, ordinary wines) often marketed under the traditional generic names, like Chablis, Rhine wine, Burgundy or Claret; however, in the last twenty years, these generic names have been reclassified as Chardonnay, Pinot noir, Merlot, or Cabernet Sauvignon.

II. The North Coast Counties near the San Francisco Bay is the other principal vine-growing area. It includes the areas of Mendocino, Sonoma, Livermore, Los Carneros, Napa, and Santa Cruz. The finest grape varieties transplanted to California are produced here.

THE ZINFANDEL MYSTERY

In the 1960s, a pathologist noticed a plant named Primitive in Southern Italy that looked identical to Zinfandel. The pathologist then sent cuttings to the University of California at Davis where it was later proven through isozyme fingerprinting and DNA tests to be the same as Zinfandel. It was a scientific proof of its origin, but some still believe that Zinfandel came from the East, pointing to Croatia and the Balkans countries. In California, the Zinfandel vine is the most widely planted of all the vines. While I do not hear of any planted in Eastern Europe where it once had been traced, Zinfandel is perhaps suitable to the California climate and soil but produces a light-bodied red wine, common to the *vin de table* or *vin ordinaire*. With all the chemistry applied today, it is easy to drink a well-blended oaked Zinfandel or a well-blended perfumed flavor one, using plums, or raspberry extracts. In general, it is quite difficult to train all these American wine novices and make them switch for example to a Cabernet Sauvignon which is producing a fuller and more aggressive wine in California. I would say more refined is a better description.

In the twentieth century, a common red wine grape was developed in California during the prohibition years as a juice grape for home winemakers. It was a varietal named Bouchet which produced a red juice. It was a cross between *teinturier du Cher* and grenache. It was a hybrid varietal with a deep color producing a high sugar content. It was usually a good blending for cheap bulk wine. It still ranks fourth in acreage among California wine grapes. At that time, the California wines were linked with Zinfandel. Zinfandel became a top varietal name brand in California. Zinfandel is a tough varietal, but produces a huge quantity of grapes. It is, however, blended with the Bouchet varietal.

Zinfandel, easily pronounced or shortened as Zin became the highlight of American wine. Unfortunately, it cannot be compared to a higher quality wine. The Bouchet species is called in France "JUS TEINTURIER"(a dyeing grape-juice). This varietal is therefore used in blending and is the most natural way in adding color to juices having not enough color. It is grown in the area of south of France, adjacent to Spain, where it has been known for a long time.

NAPA VALLEY HISTORY

The Napa Valley is a relative latecomer to the wine business. Until 1823, the Napa Valley was inhabited only by the Wappo Indians. Around that time Father Jose Altimira went through the valley and was looking for a site to build a mission with vineyards next to it. He later settled on a location in adjacent Sonoma.

Like Sonoma County, the land was abundant and the many streams and rivers provided the necessities of life for the Indians. Among the few explorers who came for an eventual settlement was George Yount. He was given a land grant in Napa by General Mariano Vallejo and built one of the first wineries in 1836. Yount planted the coarse mission variety, and the rest is history.

The geographic and meteorological factors have created a series of weather patterns or a special microclimate in the Napa Valley.

The temperature can vary as much as ten to twelve degrees from one end of the valley to the other. During spring, summer, and fall, you can always count on sunny days and cool evenings.

The valley can be traveled by the two main roads that run its length from Napa to Calistoga up north, a tiny village known for its mineral springs. The area at that time was populated with deer and bears. Most of the productive land was included in Mexican land grants and not available to the pioneers who ventured through the valley.

The confrontations that led to the Bear Flag revolt in Sonoma and to the declaration of freedom from Mexico and statehood for California finally opened the door for the settlement of the Napa Valley. Before the end of the nineteenth century a few Germans planted vineyards, mostly with the white variety of Germany. They were: Charles Krug, Jacob and Frederick Beringer, and Jacob Schram. Their successors are still firmly implanted in the wine business.

Another strong influence in the development of the Napa Valley was mining which had its heyday at the end of the nineteenth century.

In 1860, cinnabar (quick silver) was discovered a few miles northwest of Calistoga. At that time, quicksilver was much in demand; it was used to recover gold and silver from ores by almagamation, in the manufacture of explosives, drugs, and paints. Napa County became the leading producer of quicksilver in the 1900s.

The Napa wines continued to grow in reputation and the area attracted more and more winegrowers until it almost came virtually to a halt during the prohibition time from 1925 to 1933.

THE SONOMA VALLEY HISTORY

The history of Sonoma County is the history of the California wine industry. Legends and personalities both rolled into one. The flags of seven countries have flown over the county: Spain, England, Imperial Russia, Mexico, the Bear Flag, and the United States. The rolling hills, the green meadows, the rugged coastline, the streams and rivers, the mild climate, and the rich soil served the early inhabitants well.

The county's 1600 square miles have seen the peaceful Miwok, Wappo, and Porno Indians flourish at that time. The early 1800s saw a change for the Indians and Sonoma County that was never to allow such an easy existence again. The Spanish had made general claim to California in 1521 with the conquest of Mexico, but Sir Francis Drake claimed the area for the Queen of England, Elizabeth I, when he reached Drake's Bay in Marin county in 1579; however, no long permanent term settlements were made until the early nineteenth century for this area.

The Russians who were looking for a way to provide for their settlement in Sitka, Alaska, explored down the Pacific Coast and finally established a settlement at Ross, an archaic name for Russia. They built a fort, a chapel, and a stockade on the site and set about with great determination to produce what they needed for themselves and the Sitka settlement. They bartered with the Indians, the Californios (Mexicans living in the area), and Yankee traders and explored the Russian River, Mt. St. Helena, and named the California poppy, *Eschscholtzia californica*.

The Russians' grape-growing and wine-making activities indicated the potential of developing the grape culture in the northern part of the state. Both the Yankees and the Mexicans were alarmed by the Russian venture and were greatly relieved when the Russians sold out to John Sutter of later Gold Rush fame in 1841.

Meanwhile, the Mexicans had also been busy making their mark on the area. General Marino Vallejo accompanied Father Jose Altimira as he established the last of the California missions, Mission San Francisco Solano de Sonoma in 1823. Vineyards were planted, the Indians were baptized, and the mission grew until orders for secularization arrived in 1834 from Mexico.

Few people realize that there is such a range of climatic conditions in California, even the best individual districts are not familiar to most consumers because their wines are marketed by brand names rather than California place-names. There are several important grape-growing areas in California, but most of them do not produce the premium table wines with which we are presently concerned.

The great Central Valley stretches for three hundred miles from Sacramento down through Lodi, Escalon, Modesto, and the length of the San Joaquin Valley beyond Bakersfield. This vast region, along with the smaller district between Los Angeles and San Diego, produces about ninety percent of the grapes used to make California wines, mostly from table and raisin varieties. The best land for varietal wines, however, lies near San Francisco and includes the counties of Napa, Alameda, Contra Costa, Santa Clara, Santa Cruz, Monterey, and San Benito.

Sonoma, which is located north of San Francisco, has been the first large area planted with vines by the same Franciscan missionaries who introduced viticulture to Southern California in 1769.

Agoston Haraszthy, a native of Hungaria and of noble background emigrated with his family at that time and established an extensive vineyard in Sonoma in! the 1850s called Buena Vista, which is still producing wines today.

Other wineries in this region are Sebastiani and Korbel (known primarily for its California sparkling wine) ..Italian Swiss Colony one of the two biggest commercial wineries is located further north in Asti. The largest California winery E.& J. Gallo is in Modesto, in the San Joaquim Valley; it is said that Gallo produces one out every four bottles of wine sold in this country.

The Napa Valley is generally considered to have the finest soil in California for the premium grape varieties like Cabernet Sauvignon Pinot Chardonnay or Pinot Noir

A number of well-known wineries are located there like Beaulieu Vineyard, one of the top producer of Cabernet, also Christian Brothers, Inglenook Charles Krug and Louis Martini. Hans Kornell is also there with Heitz Cellars and Souverain. The new winery of Robert Mondavi is the most modern in Napa and the new generation of Robert Mondavi are concentrating on the productions of top varietal wines only.

CLASSIFICATION OF THE WINE DISTRICTS

THE NAPA VALLEY VINEYARDS

Wappo Hill Vineyards

Robert Mondavi and his wife, Margrit, chose the name Wappo Hill for their property in the late 1970s to honor the Native Americans of Napa Valley. The Wappo are a distinct group of three tribes who spoke similar languages and lived in the foothills and valleys of the Mayacamas Mountain. Because of their staunch resistance to the Spanish, the early explorers called the members of these groups *guapo* or brave. Eventually, as English-speaking pioneers settled into the area, the Spanish term became Wappo, the name by which they are known today.

Huichica Hills Vineyard, Carneros District

Huichica (pronounced wee-cheek-ka) was the local Native American tribe's name for the small, burrowing owls that live in the windswept hills of this region. These owls were believed to have supernatural powers. The name Carneros means ram or sheep in Spanish. The Carneros District was designated a viticultural area in 1983.

The Robert Mondavi family purchased the initial property of 485 acres in 1988. Three hundred and sixty acres of vines were planted over the next three years. An additional ninety-four acres were acquired in 1995 and planted in 1998.

To Kalon Vineyard, Oakville District

To Kalon is a Greek word meaning the beautiful. The vineyard of To Kalon is located in the Napa Valley, Oakville District. It was originally planted by a winegrower pioneer in 1868. Robert Mondavi and his family purchased acreage of this vineyard which is adjoining the Robert Mondavi Winery in 1966. This is a micro-climate region of the number two classification. The To Kalon Vineyard, located on the famed Oakville bench has well-drained alluvial, loam, and clay soils on the Valley floor and gravelly loam on its slopes. The Cabernet Sauvignon is one of the main varieties planted in To Kalon.

CLASSIFICATION OF THE WINE DISTRICTS

During the late 1980s and under the leadership of the University of California in Davis, a classification of the wine districts was created.

First, an appellation status designated as the American Viticultural Area (AVA) was given, similar to the French Appellation Contrôlée law.

For example, the Oakville district, which is the center of Napa Valley, is differentiated from the other Napa Valley areas primarily because of its mid-valley location. It is southerly enough to be cooled by morning fog from the San Pablo Bay to its south but northerly enough to enjoy warm afternoon sunshine. There is also a tremendous variation in the soil types within the Oakville area, but they are all quite distinct from other districts within the Napa Valley.

Secondly, a classification has been given to five wine regions by the accumulation of Heat Summation Units, in other words, the "degree days" above 50° F, during the growing season from April 1 to October 31.

Region I: 2500 degree days or less
Region II: 2501 to 3000 degree days
Region III: 3001 to 3500 degree days

The Stags Leap District, Napa

The Stags Leap District is named for the hundred-year-old legend of a stag that eluded hunters with a dramatic leap across the jagged outcropping of palisades on the eastern flank of the Napa Valley. The Stags Leap District begins seven miles north of the town of Napa, on the Silverado Trail. One mile wide and three miles long, the district is bounded by rocky hillsides to the east (distinguished by the 2000-foot palisade, Stags Leap Ridge) and the Napa River to the west. In 1989, Stags Leap District became the first viticultural area in the United States to be specified an appellation based on the distinctiveness of its soil. The steep eastern hills retain and reflect the afternoon temperatures to rise, while breezes from the San Pablo Bay maintain cool morning and evening temperatures.

The soils of Stags Leap District are unlike any other in the Napa Valley, retaining less water than most other soils, resulting in intensely-flavored fruit.

A GREAT WINE BENEFACTOR OF THE LATE TWENTIETH CENTURY: MR. ROBERT G. MONDAVI

At ninety years old, Mr. Robert G. Mondavi remains the world emissary of American food and wine. His vision was to create California wines that belong in the company of the great wines of the world. Having successfully achieved this goal, his wisdom as founder and Chairman Emeritus of Robert Mondavi now guides his sons and daughter in their leadership of the Robert Mondavi family of wines.

Born in Virginia, Minnesota to parents who emigrated from the Marche Area of Italy, Mr. Mondavi was greatly influenced by old world traditions. "My passion for bringing wine into the American culture was motivated by a desire to plant deep into the soil of our young country the same values, traditions, and daily pleasures that my mother and father had brought with them from Central Italy: good food, good wine, and love of family," said Mr. Mondavi. This passion sparked a revolution in the American food and wine experience.

A graduate of Stanford University in 1937 with a degree in economics and business administration, Mr. Mondavi understood that marketing was as critical as winemaking expertise in achieving success in the wine industry.

Upon graduation, he joined his father at Sunnyhill Winery in St. Helena and later, after convincing his father to purchase the historic Winery of Charles Krug, he upgraded the technology of the family enterprise, determined to raise quality.

Robert was guided by an inherent spirit of discovery. In 1966 at age fifty-three, he established the first major winery built in the Napa Valley following the repeal of Prohibition in 1933. His goal was to combine European craft and tradition with the latest in American technology, management, and marketing expertise.

To celebrate the pleasure of wine, food, and the arts, the Robert Mondavi Winery was built as an enduring landmark with a sense of California history as reflected in its mission-style architecture. In fostering a wine culture in America, tours and wine tastings were initiated to educate the American palate. Throughout more than three decades, the Robert Mondavi winery has provided the creative setting for jazz and classical concerts, art exhibits, and culinary programs.

At the Robert Mondavi Winery, in the late 1960s, Robert pioneered many fine winemaking techniques in California, including cold fermentation, stainless steel tanks, and the use of French oak barrels. A sales and marketing leader, he was responsible for popularizing dry-fermented oak-aged Sauvignon Blanc as Fumé Blanc—a move now acknowledged as the catalyst for the recognition of this grape variety in America. Robert also initiated blind tastings in the Napa Valley, allowing consumers and the trade to evaluate wine quality.

The comprehensive wine and food program founded in the late 1960s has greatly evolved over the years. The Great Chefs program was established in 1967 as the first winery culinary program in the U.S. This program has featured such luminaries as Julia Child, Paul Bocuse, Alice Waters, Thomas Keller, Jean and Pierre Troisgros, and Joel Robuchon.

During the latter half of the 1980s, Robert Mondavi launched the Mission Program to counteract the anti-alcohol campaign that was gathering force in America. "At Robert Mondavi Winery, we view wine as an integral part of our culture, heritage, and the gracious way of life," said Robert. The Mission Program educated media, trade, and consumers about the health benefits of moderate wine consumption.

Robert has long believed that great wines should be recognized internationally. In 1970, Robert Mondavi Winery was among the first to export premium California wine. This international outlook also led to partnerships with prominent wine families of the world embracing the belief that great wines result from the quality of the climate and the people who create them. The framework for these partnerships was initiated in 1979 with the House of Baron Philippe de Rothschild in Pauillac, Bordeaux, France. "The idea was to take our different cultures and traditions along with the best materials and know-how from Bordeaux and California, to create a wine with its own style, character, and breeding," said Robert.

Opus One was the result of this partnership. More recently, this international outlook has led to alliances with the Frescobaldi family of Italy (Marchesi de Frescobaldi), the Eduardo Chadwick family of Chile (Vina Errazuriz) and the Oatley Family from Australia (Southcorp/Rosemount Estate).

With sons Michael and Tim, now in command of the Robert Mondavi Company, Robert is immersed in his great adventure as a major benefactor of cultural and educational institutions. COPIA: the American Center for Wine, Food, and the Arts, a world-class cultural center celebrating the bounty of the American table, opened in November 2001.

Enhancing an already extraordinary contribution to the California wine industry, Robert and his wife, Margrit, made a substantial personal gift in late 2001 to the University of California in Davis, to establish the Robert Mondavi Institute

for Wine and Food Science and to name the campus's new center for performing arts. The Robert and Margrit Mondavi Center for the Performing Arts opened in October 2002.

An uncompromising perfectionist, Robert has been guided by the following belief, "If you wish to succeed, you must listen to yourself, to your heart, and have the courage to go your own way." The Robert Mondavi Company continues to reflect this core philosophy of its founder. These and other lessons of his life are the subject of his autobiography, *Harvests of Joy: My Passion for Excellence*, published in 1998 by Harcourt Brace & Company.

THE WINES OF CALIFORNIA

The gradual development of the California wine growing started at the end of the nineteenth century. It is mostly due to the flow of immigrants to California from Europe, some with money and some without. They were mostly skilled in wine making.

Some Spanish monks established themselves in the early sixteenth century, living in monasteries as a community. They produced sacramental wines and sold their extra production to the neighborhood communities. The most prominent vintners at the time were as follows:

From France:
Georges de Latour: Established the famous wineries of Beaulieu Vineyards, recognized today as BV.
Paul Masson: Paul Masson Vineyards.
Jean-Louis Vignes from Bordeaux.
Etienne Thee: Founder of Almaden Vineyards.

From Italy:
Ernest and Julio Gallo (Napa Valley): Very successful winemakers who, in Texas, were the first to use the new marketing technique to penetrate all markets. At that time, wine was mostly sold in bulk and in gallons for the upcoming supermarkets. They had to go in a completely new direction, and having the courage to do so, became nationally well known.

Other winemakers of Italian descent: Pedroncelli, Seghesio, Louis Foppiano, Sebastiani, Louis Martini, Robert Mondavi.

From Czechoslovakia:
Korbel: The house of Korbel Champagne.

From Hungary:
Agoston Haraszthy: Founder of Buena Vista Vineyards.

From Germany:
Wente, Charles Krug, Beringer, Schram. Wente Bros. Wineries.

From Finland:
Gustave Niebaum: Founder of Inglenook Vineyards.

From Ireland:
Concannon: Concannon Wineries.

The better-known wine producers in California are:

Almaden

Beaulieu Vineyard

Beringer

C.K. Mondavi (Charles Krug)

Ernest and Julio Gallo Wineries

Franzia

Korbel

Robert Mondavi

Louis Martini

Meridian

Mirassou Vineyards, Santa Clara

Pappio Vineyards

Sutter Home

Weibel

Wente Bros.

Next are the best known among smaller vineyards, specializing in fine wines:

SMALLER VINEYARDS, SPECIALIZING IN FINE WINES

Acacia
Alexander Valley Vineyards
Arrow Creek
Beaulieu Vineyard
Benzinger
Brogle
Buena Vista
Cakebread
Caymus
Chalone
Château St. Jean
Clos du Bois
Clos du Val
Crest Hawk
David Bynum
Estancia
Far Niente
Fetzer
Firestone
Freemark Abbey
Geyser Peak
Grgrich Hills

Groth
Gundlach-Bunschu
Haans Kornell
Heitz Wine Cellars
Hess Collection
Iron Horse
Kendall-Jackson
Charles Krug
De Loach
Lohr
Markham
Matanzas Creek Winery
Merryvale
Robert Mondavi
Morgan
Mount Veeder
Sebastiani
Simi
Stags Leap
Stemmler
Sterling Vineyard
Rodney Strong

1999

CHARDONNAY
RESERVE

ROBERT MONDAVI WINERY

1990

CABERNET SAUVIGNON

RESERVE

ROBERT MONDAVI WINERY

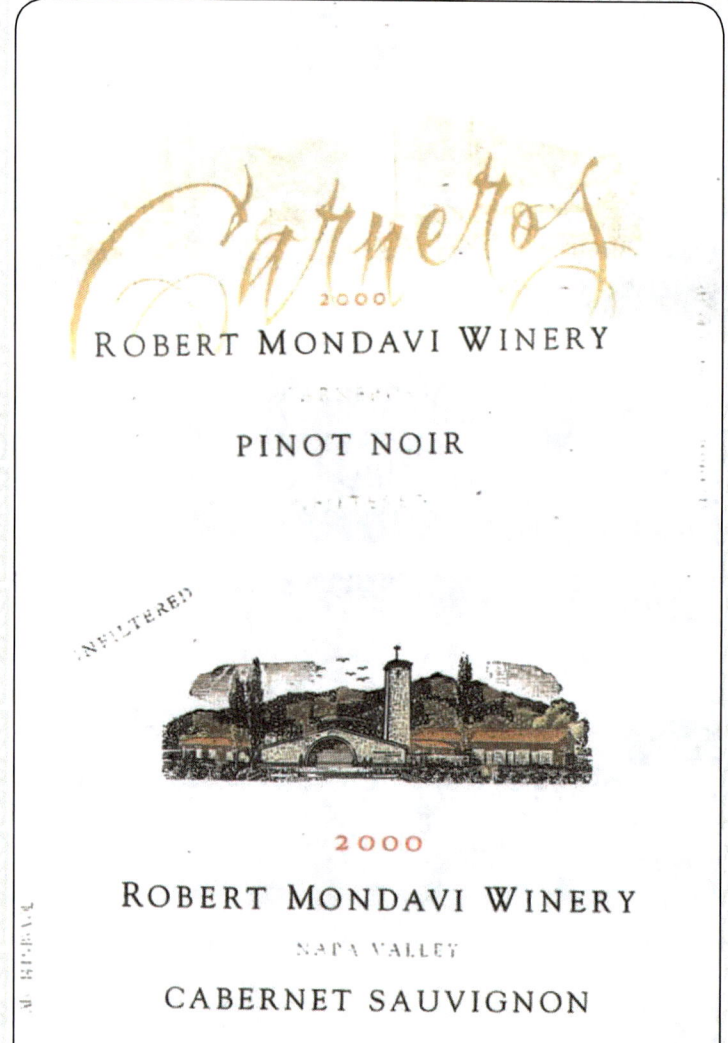

Robert Mondavi's Lifetime Achievements

1962   Chairman of Wine Institute

1981   Co-founded the American Institute of Wine and Food with Julia Child and Richard Graff

1982   "Winemaker of the Year" - American Wine Society

1983   "Commandeur de Bordeaux" - Grand Conseil du Vin de Bordeaux

1986   "Man of the Year" - Wines and Vines magazine

1988   "Man of the Year" - Decanter magazine; "Hall of Fame" Award - California Restaurant Association Educational Foundation

1990   "Merit Award" - American Society of Enology and Viticulture

1990   "Wine & Spirits Professional of the Year" - James Beard Foundation

1991   Beverage Industry's "Man of the Year" - Christermon Foundation; "Ambassador" and "Master of Aesthetics of Gastronomy" Award - Culinary Institute of America

1991   National Business Hall of Fame - Junior Achievement, Inc.

1992   Honorary Chairperson for Life and "Winemaker of the Year" - American Institute of Wine & Food, California State Polytechnic University at Pomona

1993   Honorary Master of Wine - Institute of Masters of Wine

1995   Bay Area Business Hall of Fame - Bay Area Council; Honorary Degree "Associate Member of Cornell Society of Hotelmen" - Cornell University

1996   Torch Bearer - International Olympic Committee

1997   First ever "California State Fair Lifetime Achievement Award," Wine Spectator's "Reader's Choice Award"; "International Achievement Award" - World Trade Club; "Business Leader of the Year" - Harvard Business School Association of Northern California

1998   European Wine Council's "Lifetime Achievement Award"

1999   "Patron of the Arts Award" - The Songwriter's Hall of Fame, NYC

2000   "The F. Norman Clark Entrepreneur of the Year Award," California Travel Industry Association; International Food & Beverage Hall of Fame, Doctor of Oenology, Honoris Causa, by Board of Trustees of Johnson & Wales University, Hall of Fame - Di Rona (Distinguished Restaurants of North America)

2001   Recipient of the "Wine Industry Integrity Award"

2002   Lifetime Achievement recognition from: the California State Assembly, the American Food and Entertaining Awards by Bon Appetit magazine and TV Food Network and Wine Enthusiast Magazine Wine Awards; Presidential Citation, University of California at Davis; Degree of Fine Arts, Honoris Causa, California College of Arts & Crafts; Order of Merit of the Republic of Italy, Government of Italy

2003   US House of Representatives, "Distinguished Honorary Member of the Agricultural Leadership Alumni": Award of Merit - Winemaker of the Century," Confrerie de la

ROBERT G. MONDAVI

Robert has long believed that great wines should be recognized internationally. In 1970, Robert Mondavi Winery was among the first to export premium California wine.

This international outlook also led to partnerships with prominent wine families of the world embracing the belief that great wines result from the quality of the climate and the people who create them. The framework for these partnerships was initiated in 1979 with the House of Baron Philippe de Rothschild in Pauillac, Bordeaux, France.

"The idea was to take our different cultures and traditions along with the best materials and know-how from Bordeaux and California, to create a wine with its own style, character and breeding," said Robert.

Opus One was the result of this partnership. More recently, this international outlook has led to alliances with the Frescobaldi family of Italy (Marchesi de Frescobaldi), the Eduardo Chadwick family of Chile (Vina Errazuriz) and the Oatley Family from Australia (Southcorp/Rosemount Estate).

With sons Michael and Tim, now in command of the Robert Mondavi compagny, Robert is immersed in his great adventure as a major benefactor of cultural and educational institutions.

COPIA: the American Center for Wine, Food and the Arts, a world-class cultural center celebrating the bounty of the American table, opened in November 2001.

Enhancing an already extraordinary contribution to the California wine industry, Robert and his wife, Margrit, made a substancial personal gift in late 2001 to the University of California in Davis, to establish the Robert Mondavi Institute for Wine and Food Science and to name the campus' new Center for Performing Arts. The Robert and Margrit Mondavi Center for the Performing Arts opened in October 2002.

An uncompromising perfectionist, Robert has been guided by the belief that, "If you wish to succeed, you must listen to yourself, to your heart, and have the courage to go your own way". The Robert Mondavi compagny continues to reflect this core philosophy of its founder.

These and other lessons of his life are the subject of his autobiography, "Harvests of Joy: My Passion for Excellence," published in 1998 by Harcourt Brace & Compagny.

THE LATEST FAD IN MARKETING

In the last thirty years, a large number of new wineries have sprung up in California, as well as in Australia, New Zealand, and South Africa. Some have converted their operation from making mostly sweet wines and Sherry wines to now producing semi-dry wines, red and white, issued from a variety of vinestocks imported from Europe. All these winegrowers are in a learning stage and are presently flooding the market with mediocre and inexpensive wines

The way they label their wine bottles is also quite an interesting fact. These new growers are searching for a catching marketing tool in order to attract the young generation of our time to buy their products without even putting the origin of these wines. A weird design fashion is used to label these wine bottles. Amazing but true, and when you look for the wine-department aisles, be ready for a good laugh. You will see kangaroo tails, wild boar, giraffes, roosters, goats, monkeys, lizards, fish, and toads on these clever labels.

European producers, influenced and compensated by the American wine industry, are now showing funny designs on their labels like "Fat Bastard, Old Fart Wine, Red Bicycle!" Labels with such designs are not permitted to be sold in Europe. They would be an insult to all vinegrowers.

What has wine to do with this type of labeling? To a connoisseur, it is ludicrous, with no class and not serious at all. It is more like sensationalism at its worst. Due to the ignorance of the public and the lack of regulated wine laws, everything, is permissible and will endanger the hard work of prominent winegrowers.

FUSÉE (PRONOUNCE "FEW-ZÁY) IS THE FRENCH
TRANSLATION FOR ROCKET, AN IGNITED
CYLINDRICAL PROJECTILE.

ABOUT A GLASS OF "FUSÉE WINE"?
THIS IS THE TRUE LABELING AND PACKAGING
OF A CALIFORNIAN VINTNER.

CHAPTER EIGHT

The Wines Districts of France

The Wine Districts of France

SECTION

    A ALSACE

    B BORDEAUX

    C BURGUNDY

    D CHAMPAGNE

    E CÔTES DU RHÔNE

    F LANGUEDOC
       ROUSILLON
       PROVENCE

    G LOIRE

    H THE COGNAC AND ARMAGNAC DISTRICTS

WINE·GROWING AREAS IN FRANCE

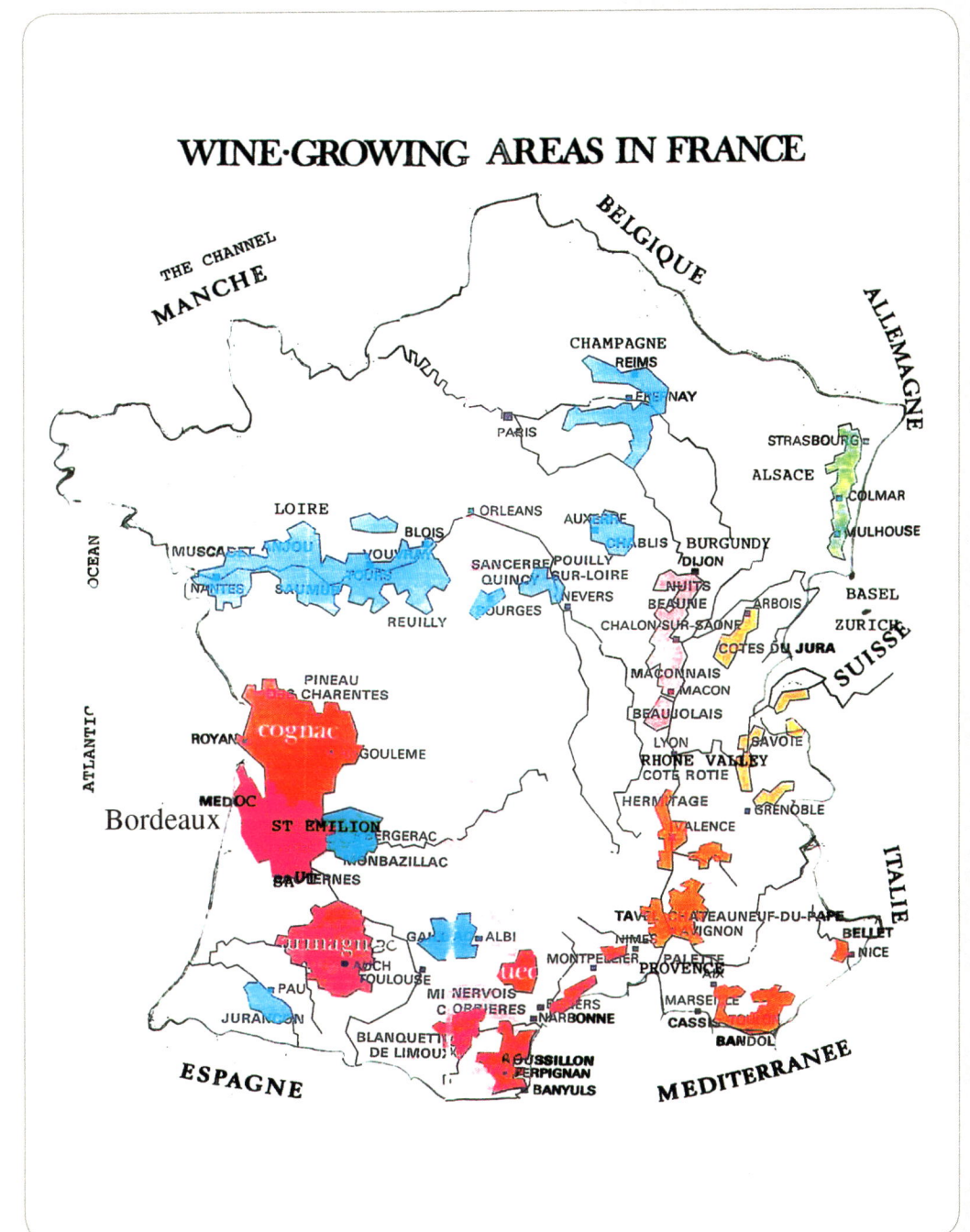

THE CHANNEL
MANCHE

BELGIQUE

ALLEMAGNE

CHAMPAGNE
REIMS
EPERNAY

PARIS

STRASBOURG
ALSACE
COLMAR
MULHOUSE

LOIRE
BLOIS
ORLEANS
AUXERRE
MUSCADET ANJOU VOUVRAY TOURS
NANTES SAUMUR
REUILLY
SANCERRE
QUINCY
BOURGES
POUILLY
SUR-LOIRE
NEVERS
CHABLIS BURGUNDY
DIJON
NUITS
BEAUNE ARBOIS
CHALON-SUR-SAONE
COTES DU JURA

BASEL
ZURICH
SUISSE

OCEAN

PINEAU
DES CHARENTES
cognac
ROYAN
ANGOULEME
MEDOC
Bordeaux
ST EMILION
BERGERAC
MONBAZILLAC
SAUTERNES

MACONNAIS
MACON
BEAUJOLAIS
LYON
RHONE VALLEY
COTE ROTIE
HERMITAGE
VALENCE
SAVOIE
GRENOBLE

ITALIE

ATLANTIC

armagnac
GERS ALBI
AUCH
TOULOUSE
PAU
JURANCON
MINERVOIS
CORBIERES
NARBONNE
BLANQUETTE
DE LIMOUX
ROUSSILLON
PERPIGNAN
BANYULS

TAVEL CHATEAUNEUF-DU-PAPE
AVIGNON
NIMES
MONTPELLIER
PROVENCE
PALETTE
AIX
MARSEILLE
CASSIS
BANDOL
BELLET
NICE

ESPAGNE

MEDITERRANEE

THE WINES FROM FRANCE

VINEYARDS IN FRANCE ARE GROWING SOUTH OF THE LINE WHICH EXTENDS FROM THE LOIRE VALLEY THROUGH THE CHAMPAGNE AREA, TO ALSACE.

NINETY PER CENT OF FRENCH VITICULTURAL SOILS ARE CALCERREOUS, MEANING HIGH IN LIMESTONE CONTENT. SOME AREAS LIKE CHAMPAGNE AND THE COGNAC REGIONS HAVE AN EXCEPTIONAL HIGH PROPORTION OF LIMESTONE THIS MEANS THAT THE VINE PLANT MUST BE PLANTED WITH GRAFTING STOCK, CAPABLE OF RESISTING LIME CARBONATE. A VINE PLANT NOT RESISTANT TO LIME CARBONATE WILL FALL VICTIM TO CHLOROSIS (AN ABNORMAL CONDITION OF THE PLANT IN WHICH THE GREEN PART LOSES ITS COLOR AND TURNS YELLOW AS A RESULT OF A LACK OF CHLOROPHYL PRODUCTION).

CHEMICAL ANALYSIS HAVE SHOWN THAT THE ROOT SYSTEM HAS TAKEN ABOUT 250 CHEMICAL SUBSTANCES FROM THE SOIL.

DRINKING WINE IS A WELL TOLERATED MEDICINE WHICH CARRIES AMONG OTHER THINGS, ASSIMILABLE MINERAL ELEMENTS.

WHEN YOU DRINK WINE, YOU DO NOT ONLY CONSUME A SIMPLE LIQUID, BUT A NATURAL BEVERAGE, WHOSE COLOR AND TASTE VARIES ACCORDING TO REGIONS, THE VINTAGE YEARS AND THE TYPE OF VINEYARDS.

IT TOOK MANY CENTURIES OF OBSERVATION, FAILURES, SET-BACKS AND SCIENTIFIC RESEARCH TO ASSIGN TO EVERY VINE PLANT, ITS POSITION TO PROVIDE US TODAY WITH BETTER WINES.

NOWADAYS, THERE IS A BETTER STABILITY OF PRODUCTION, ESPECIALLY IN FRANCE, SINCE THE REVISION OF THE WINE LAWS OF 1953.

THESE LAWS ALSO BETTER PROTECT THE BUYER AGAINST ADULTERATION OF WINES, FRAUDS AND MISDEMEANORS.

THE ANNUAL PRODUCTION OF WINES AMOUNTED IN 1970 WAS 60 MILLION HECTOLITERS IN FRANCE.

THE APPELLATION CONTROLÉES WINES AMOUNTED ONLY 15% OF THAT AMOUNT GIVING US A TOTAL OF 8 MILLION HECTOLITERS OF "A.C." WINES WHICH REPRESENT AROUND 310 MILLION BOTTLES OF 0.75 CL (THE UNIVERSAL TYPE OF BOTTLE).

SECTION A

The Wines of Alsace

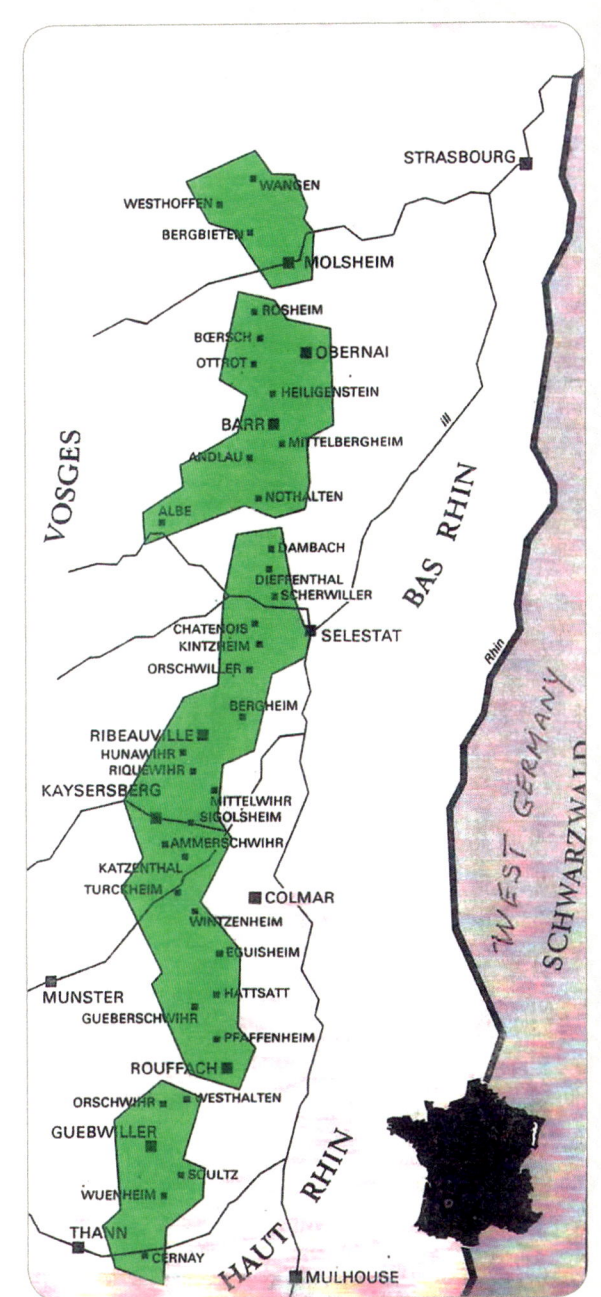

MAP OF THE WINES FROM ALSACE

BOTTLE OF ALSACIAN WINE

All wines in Alsace are bottled in a green slender tapering bottle, while the German Rhine district has a brown glass bottle, the Moselle district uses a pale green color bottle.

In 2002
The wine district of Alsace produces 160 million bottles of A.O.C. wines, making it the second wine region for white wines after Bordeaux.

PASSPORT TO WINE KNOWLEDGE

THE WINES OF ALSACE. FRANCE

ALSACIAN HEADDRESS WORN IN ALL VILLAGES'S LOCAL CEREMONIES.
NOTICE THE FRENCH BADGE ON THE LEFT SIDE OF THE HEAD-DRESS.

HISTORY

In the seventeenth century, when Louis XIV, the King of France, traveled to Alsace, his coach stopped for a while near the top of the Vosges Mountains. The king, then, looked down and was told that the elongated plain that he saw was the plain of Alsace with the vineyards in foothills all along. He was said to have remarked, "What a beautiful garden!" This part of Eastern France shares borders with Germany as delineated by the Rhine River almost naturally.

If you heard or read about the Maginot Defense Line, built just before WWII, that is where it started in Huningue, a town two miles away from the Swiss border and the city of Basel.

Alsace is a gentle, verdant landscape of trees covered slopes, orchards, and vineyards. Medieval villages fit snugly into the hillsides covered with vineyards. Cobblestone streets are particularly ravishing made with pink granite stones and half-timbered houses. They remain a remarkable heritage of another time in life. Slender steeples tower over these villages. Each spring, the storks come back to their precariously perched nests.

This is France even though most of the villages have Germanic sounding names such as Ammerschwihr, Beblenheim, Bergheim, Sigolsheim, and Rouggach. This is the legacy of this area's bitter history. After being wrenched back and forth between France and Germany for the past three centuries, Alsace considers itself resoundingly French.

Yet people there speak their own hard-won Germanic dialect and have a way of life distinctly different from the rest of France. As for the culinary art, Alsace is known to boast some of the best eating places to be found in France.

The grapevine, though only distantly related to present-day varieties, existed in the geographical region that was to become the Rhine Valley long before the appearance of man. Fossilized leaves of *Vitis*, found in the region of Constance, provide formal proof of this.

Later periods of glacial activity destroyed many species of vegetation, but those *lambrusques*, or wild vines, still commonly found in forests along the Rhine even a century ago are descended from isolated patches of *Vitis* vines that survived the climatic rigors of the time.

The fruit of the vine was appreciated by the prehistoric population, as can be seen from the heaps of grape pips discovered during the excavation of lake settlements; however, although the fruit of the vine has been used in the region since time immemorial, the evolution from simply gathering the wild grapes to the actual cultivation of the vine only took place after the Roman conquest.

From the earliest days of the present area, vestiges indicate the growing importance of viticulture: heaps of grape pips, fragments of wooden casks, then gradually vine motifs beginning to be used to decorate pottery or in bas-relief carvings. As early as A.D. the second century, records mention the transports of wine along the Moselle and Rhine Rivers and prove how soon the commerce of wine began.

Germanic invasion in the fifth century brought viticulture into temporary decline, but surviving documents show how quickly the vineyards regained even greater importance under the rule of the Merovingians and Carolingians, thanks to the foundation of numerous abbeys and convents at that time.

Canon Earth reveals, in his survey of the history of viticulture in Alsace, that documents dating from before A.D. 900, mention more than 160 winegrowing localities.

The great importance of the Rhine vineyards can be judged from one of the articles in the Treaty of Verdun in A.D. 843 which divided up the empire that had been created by Charlemagne. This expansion continued without interruption until it reached its zenith during the sixteenth century. The numerous houses in the Renaissance style that can still be admired and visited throughout many wine villages bear witness to the prosperity of that period when large quantities of Alsace wines were exported throughout Europe.

At that same time, many different regulations came into force concerning the grape varieties (amongst which mention is already made of Traminer, Muscat, Riesling, and others), their cultivation and their vinification, as well as extremely lucrative taxation to the benefit of the municipalities, the monasteries, and the nobility.

GEOGRAPHY

Although wines were not invented in Alsace, there is no doubt that they have been enjoyed here during the last twenty centuries. The Alsacian vineyards and villages had suffered from destruction and battles during WWII. The vineyards are now admirably replanted since 1945 and the villages now show an image of prosperity.

The province of Alsace is situated three hundred miles east of Paris. The area starts at the first hills of the Jura Mountains, flanked by the Swiss border to the city of Basel, Switzerland. There, the Rhine River takes a twist, turns to the right, and flows to its estuary in Holland. The Rhine River is like a natural boundary between France and Germany until it flows further down through Germany well north of Strasbourg. The area of Alsace is no wider than forty miles and its length no more than two hundred miles. On the left side of the Rhine, the tall mountains of the Vosges are visible and act like an immense windbreaker for the lower vineyard hills.

The vineyards of Alsace stretch over one hundred miles north to south and their locations face east and southeast. The wine villages are connected with the famous secondary road named the Wine Road (*La Route du Vin*). All of these villages were built during Medieval times and remain the same to this day. Some are walled and have two or three huge fortified entrance doors like Riquewihr and Turckheim. In Turckheim, as a tourist attraction, you still can see and hear on summer nights the famous night watch guard in his fifteenth century uniform strolling along the narrow side streets, shouting: "All is well, you can sleep in peace now."

The capital of Alsace is Strasbourg, a well-known large city, with its gorgeous pink sandstone cathedral. Strasbourg is the seat of the Council of Europe. Further south, fifty miles from Strasbourg is the city of Colmar, a small capital of its own. It seats the prefecture of the Haut-Rhin district. Colmar is a very picturesque city. The modern town is built around the old city which is bustling with tourists year round. It is the site also of the most visited museum in France, the Museum of Underlinden, famous for the painting of Mathias Gruhewald, one of their most and unique artistic creations from the Middle Ages of the entire area of the Rhine. The painting is entitled "The Retable of Issenheim" and was painted between 1512 and 1516.

At first sight, *la Route du Vin* is simply as pretty as a picture postcard. Compact ranks of vines, historic walled villages, ancient half-timbered houses, Romanesque and gothic churches, renaissance wells, the proud ruins of medieval castles, attractive traditional inns, and cool inviting wine cellars all combine to make a charming and unforgettable itinerary; however, its real secrets are revealed only to those inquisitive visitors who take the time to go off the beaten track.

It takes time to discover the soul of the wine road, to meet the winegrowers, to taste their wines, to stroll through these medieval villages until far from the crowds, high above, amidst the vines that line the vineyard trails, the visitor can admire the views that are reserved only for the happy wanderer.

At every stop, the culinary genius of Alsace becomes more apparent and makes it easy to understand why with the complicity of its wines, this is one of the most gourmet regions of France. Every one of its hundred miles gives the visitor an opportunity to enter into the spirit of this wonderful region. From spring to October, festivals of wine and wine fairs are taking place which all keep the traditions alive and celebrate the wine of Alsace.

At the heart of the wine region, and only a few miles from Colmar, the famous Château de Kientzheim seats the Confrerie St. Etienne, a wine brotherhood. This castle used to be the home of the Baron Lazare de Schwendi and now, houses the museum of the wines of Alsace. From a fascinating recreation of a winegrower's cellar down the centuries, the magnificent surroundings serve to highlight the beauty of the various exhibits: barrels, casks, and vats from the earliest of times to the present day next to harvest carts and an antique vertical wine press.

This museum does not just bear witness to the history of the vineyards and wines of Alsace, it is a vibrant tribute to the generations of winegrowers who have forged the reputation and unique personality of the wines of Alsace.

TOURISM

The wines of Alsace are also celebrated by other wine brotherhoods of their area, among them:
   La Confrèrie du Haut-Koenigsbourg,
   Les Amis du Kaëfferkopf,
   Les Bienheureux du Frankstein,
   Les Rieslinger de Scherwiller,
   Les Hospitaliers d'Andlau,
   La Confrèrie des Quatre Bans.

La Maison des Vins d'Alsace in Colmar has an information center and a reception area with an interactive map of the vineyard region and activities concerning wine and food matches. Regular tasting sessions are held there, either as an introduction to the wines of Alsace or in greater detail, both for the public and for the professionals.

The wine harvest, in Alsace, usually takes place from late September to late October, the dates varying each year according to the evolution of the ripeness of the grapes. At that time of year, due to the pressure of the harvest work, it is not always possible to visit some wine cellars, it is then recommended to make an appointment in advance.

The vineyards of Alsace, lining the eastern flank of the foothills of the Vosges Mountains, enjoy maximum sunshine all day long. Facing mainly south and southeast, they benefit from the autumnal sunny weather which ensures that the grapes ripen slowly to full maturity.

Protected from the oceanic rain and windstorms by the natural barrier of the Vosges Mountains, the Alsace vineyards have practically the lowest rainfall in France (450 to 500 mm of precipitation per year). Warm summers, followed by sunny days in the fall, and sometimes harsh winters are the characteristics of a semi-continental climate; however, the weather cycle can change through the seasons and through the years, and nobody can predict a superb vintage year all the time.

The diversity of the soils in Alsace has no equivalent anywhere in France. There are soils of clay, limestone, marl, granite, gneiss, schist, and even soils of volcanic origin. These soils are intermingled for one easy-to-understand reason:

Approximately ten million years ago, both the Vosges Mountains and the Black Forest Mountains located across the Rhine River were a single massif, and when it collapsed, the plain of the Rhine was formed. As the Alsace vineyards are situated along the fault line between the remaining massif of the Vosges and the plain, it is logical that their soil is a mosaic of the collapsed ancient upper layers.

For the same reason, all fifty geographic locations that have been granted the status of *Alsace Grand Cru* vary in size, some being extremely small, as each one possesses its own homogenous geological characteristics.

When one speaks about the elaboration of the wines from Alsace, it is in general to bring to mind the vinification in white, but it is above all to consider what characterizes them in relation to wines from other regions, especially their fruitiness or their characteristic aromas linked to the different vinestock from which they issue.

What represents the originality of the vineyard of Alsace is the cultivation of the Pinot Noir stock which produces either rosé or red wine. This recent production is rather small, four percent, compared to the white. Also the variety of Edelzwicker is found in some areas, and it produces a white wine used for blending and constitutes the everyday wine for consumption.

The two prime wines produced in Alsace are:

Riesling: This vinestock variety is of German origin. Distinguished, lively, and subtle, I would call it the king of Alsacian wines.

Gewurztraminer: The grape variety is Traminer, of German origin. With its distinctive perfumed bouquet, pungent and spicy flavor, the Gewurztraminer wine stands out as one of the unique wines found anywhere in France and perhaps the world. Therefore, I would call it the queen of Alsacian wines.

Wine growing and production suffered a lot under the occupation during the Second World War. At that time, the German wine growers did not desire a better quality of wine made in Alsace to compete with their own Rhine and Mosel wines, so they requested inferior wines to blend with their production. Therefore, the Alsacian wine industry had to produce inferior-quality wines. In 1945, however, despite many Alsacian wine villages destroyed and a great loss of lives, the hard-working Alsacian wine growers made sure they would survive. They started replanting the better varieties as what existed before WWII.

The Alsacian wine bottle has the shape of a flute made of a dark green glass, while its counterpart in Germany is amber in color, also made in a flute shape, for the region of the Rhine only. The Mosel wine bottles, however, are of green color.

The three appellations d'origine contrôlées (AOC)

All Alsace wines enjoy one of three appellations d'origine contrôlées (AOC):
1- Alsace AOC wines
2- Alsace Grand Cru wines
3- AOC Crèmant d'Alsace

ALSACE AOC WINES

If the name of a grape variety appears on the label of an AOC Alsace wine, it is made from one hundred percent of that grape variety. If no grape variety is named, then the wine is made from a blend of several white wine varieties and is either called Edelzwicker or by a brand name.

From the 1999 vintage onwards, the currently authorized annual yield per hectare for white Appellations Alsace Contrôlée wines is eighty hectoliters per hectare plus ten percent PLC (Plafond Limite de Classement), a reserve calculated annually by the INAO, and seventy-five hectoliters per hectare plus ten percent PLC for the red Pinot Noir wines.

The minimum ripeness levels currently in force, expressed in degrees of potential alcohol, are 9 for Sylvaner, Pinot Blanc, and Edelzwicker; 9.5 for Riesling and Muscat; 10 for Pinot Noir; and 11 for Tokay Pinot Gris, Gewurztraminer, and Klevener de Heiligenstein.

ALSACE AOC GRAND CRU

Introduced in 1975, Alsace AOC Grand Cru wines can only be made from the Riesling, Gewurztraminer, Tokay Pinot Gris, or Muscat varieties. Besides the varietal name and the vintage, it is compulsory for its origin, in one of the fifty named vineyards delineated by law, to be shown on the label.

These fifty vineyards were delineated under the authority of the INAO (Institut National des Appellations d'Origine Contrôlées), according to very strict criteria of geology and micro-climate.

ALSACE GRAND CRU WINES

While Alsace wines are traditionally known by their familiar grape names like Riesling, Sylvaner, Pinot Blanc, Muscat d'Alsace, Pinot Gris, Gewurztraminer, and Pinot Noir, the Appellation Alsace Grand Cru gives an added dimension, known as *Terroir* (type of a particular soil). It gives the unique influence of the vineyard itself on the wine. Fifty sites have been delineated and selected according to strict criteria of geology and microclimate, to make up the mosaic of Alsace Grand Cru vineyards.

These exceptional vineyards vary in size from three to eighty hectares, each having its own specific character and personality, according to its geology, aspect, and slope.

With an annual average of almost 45,000 hl, Alsace Grand Cru wines represent only four percent of total Alsace wine production. In order to appreciate Alsace Grand Cru wines under optimum conditions, it is best to follow a few simple hints on storage and serving.

Although Alsace Grand Cru Wines are agreeable to enjoy when they are young, they will gain from being kept for much longer (five to ten years, or sometimes more in the finest vintages), preferably in a dark, well-ventilated cellar with a constant temperature (45° F to 55° F). The bottles should be stored on their sides so that the wine is in permanent contact with the cork. Alsace Grand Cru wines should be served cold but not chilled (at about 45° F), in a slender, long-stemmed, clear, crystal glass. These are gastronomic wines by excellence, and they can accompany every course on the menu.

Muscat d'Alsace is an ideal apéritif. Riesling Grand Cru is the perfect partner for all seafood, fish and shellfish. Tokay Pinot Gris is perfect with white meats, game, and goose liver terrine, while Gewurztraminer is unrivalled with ethnic food, cheese, and dessert. Alsace Grand Cru wines are entitled to this appellation since the last decree of January 24, 2001.

Each, vineyard must be planted with a minimum density of 4,500 vinestocks per hectare. In addition, the vines must be pruned back to from eight to ten buds per square meter, according to the grape variety. Grapes must be harvested by hand. The basic yield is limited to 55hl/hectare per grape variety and per vineyard. This basic limit may be increased by a variable annual amount of from zero to twenty percent depending on conditions in each vineyard. The minimum potential alcohol levels are 12.5 for Pinot Gris and Gewurztraminer, and 11 for the other grape varieties. In order to enjoy the status of AOC Alsace Grand Cru, each wine must pass an "agreement" tasting, supervised by the INAO. Besides its varietal character, equal or even greater importance is given to the specific personality that is unique to each Grand Cru vineyard.

AOC CRÈMANT D'ALSACE

Sparkling AOC Crèmant d'Alsace wines are made from selected Alsace grape varieties, allied to the traditional technique of fermentation in bottle. Crèmant d'Alsace wines, the vast majority of which are white, are vinified from one or more grape varieties. Only the following varieties are authorized: Pinot Blanc, Riesling, Pinot Gris, Pinot Noir (the only *blanc de noirs*) and Chardonnay.

Whenever a specific grape variety is mentioned on the label, then that Crèmant d'Alsace is made with one hundred percent of the variety named.

The annual yield per hectare for AOC Crèmant d'Alsace must not exceed eighty hl/ha plus ten percent PLC with a minimum potential alcohol content of 8.5 percent.

Besides the French consumption, the province of Alsace has fourteen major foreign markets. Production and sales for 2002 are shown below:

Figures are shown in hectoliters
One hectoliter = 100 liters = 26.4 U.S. gallons

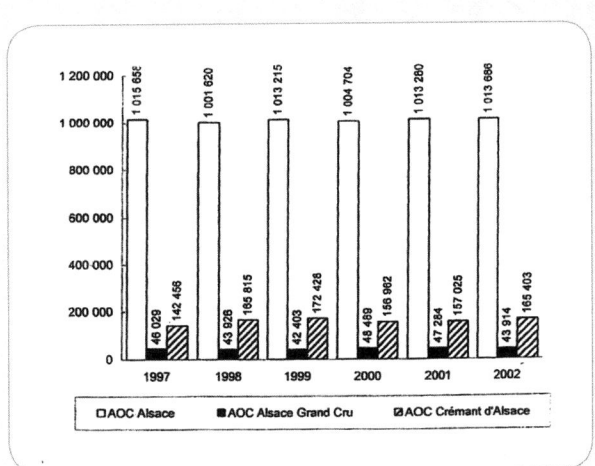

BACKGROUND TO ALSACE GRANDS CRUS WINES

To be entitled to the Appellation d'Origine Contrôlées or AOC Alsace Grand Cru according to the decree dated January 200 wines must be produced from grapes harvested by hand and grown in strictly-defined vineyard areas inside the delineatation of the AOC Alsace region.

Experts designated by the Institut National des Appellations d'Origine des vins et eaux de vie (INAO) have defined a total of fifty Grand Cru vineyard sites, where each one is protected by strictly enforced legislation.

In order to produce AOC Grand Cru wines, each winegrower must declare before March 1 of each year which grape varieties are to be destined for the production of these wines.

AOC Alsace Grand Cru wines may only be produced from four grape varieties: Riesling, Gewurztraminer, Tokay Pinot Gris, and Muscat d'Alsace.

To be entitled to the appellation AOC Alsace Grand Cru, the wines must have a minimum natural potential alcohol of 11° for Riesling and Muscat d'Alsace and 12.5° for Gewurztraminer and Tokay Pinot Gris.

Each vine planted since September 1, 2000 must be cultivated according to the new regulations that govern the density of plantation, the spacing between rows, and the maximum height of vegetation. At the same time, new pruning regulations, applied throughout the region, define the distance between the supporting wires and limit the number of buds per vine.

As a result of the new decree, the role of the local *Syndicat Viticole* (winegrowers' association) in the administration of each Grand Cru vineyard is reinforced (specific choices for grape varieties, harvest starting date, annual PLC limit). It is compulsory for the label of each AOC Alsace Grand Cru wine to mention not only its appellation, but also the name of the vineyard, the grape variety, and the vintage.

VINIFICATION OF THE WHITE WINES OF ALSACE

The main characteristic in the white vinification consists of the quick separation of the must from the coloring matters of the grapes which are the skin parts of the pulp, the peeps, and the raffles. The maceration of solid matters must be kept from the liquid that the grape allows to escape.

This initial precaution is primordial, it will prevent the oxidations of the constituents of the must which is a condition leading to the brown color of the liquid. Too much coloration of the must will create slightly colored or tinted wine (see coloring matters in the chapter of degustation).

LABELING

The wines of Alsace are labeled with the name of the grape variety used to make that particuliar wine. For instance "Meursault" is the name of a village in Burgundy, all the wines produced around that village must bear the name "Meursault". On the other hand, Riesling is the name of the variety and is followed by the name "Alsace". The appellation "Alsace" controlee with the name "Riesling" will guarantee the variety and its origin.

An extra guarantee of quality has been developed in the last thirty years namely adding the site of the parcel of that particular vineyard (the name of the terroir), with either Appellation Alsace Controlee or Alsace Grand Cru, which represent the unique influence of the vyneyard itself on the wine.

Fifty sites have been delimited according to strict criteria of geology and micro-climate, to make up the mosaic of Alsace Grands Crus vineyards. These exceptional vineyards vary in size fromthree to eighty hectares. However, with an annual average of almost 45,000 hectolitres production, Alsace Grand Cru wines represent only 4% of total Alsace wine production.

The appellation status for the wines of Alsace were granted in 1962, based on the continued use of the varietal name such as Riesling, Gewurztraminer, Sylvaner, Pinot Blanc, pinot Noir or Muscat.

Ninety five per cent of wines produced in Alsace are white and as I said previously, is the second white wine producer in France, after the white wine production of the region of Bordeaux. Twelve million cases are produced every year and are mostly exported to England, the Scandinavia countries, Germany, Belgium, Holland and Switzerland. All the better restaurants in Alsace are of course proud to list their famous bottles on their wine-lists, not to mention all the good eating places in Paris and all over the country of France.

Less than one per cent is exported to the United States due perhaps to the fierce competition of other Riesling type producers from other countries or from California. But in general the American public have never heard about Wines from Alsace.

Some individual wine growers also feature bottles of Alsacian wine bearing the words "Grand Vin" or "Grand Cru", or "grande Reserve" or "Late Harvest". These are legally defined guarantees that the wine has met a higher standard of quality as I will explain next page.

The Alsacian wines in the United States are known by brand name because it is the shippers rather than individual domains that cont??? the Alsacian wine trade. Alsace is quite unusual among French wine district in that most of the growers either bring their grapes to cooperative cellars or sell them directly to the large shipping houses, rather than vinifying the wines themselves. In order words the shippers do not only buy wine but also grapes at the time of the harvest and can then vinify the wines from each grape variety to their own specifications. Therefore the Alsacian shippers have much more control over the way they sell than do shippers in other French viticultural regions.

ALSACE EXPORTERS TO THE UNITED STATES

Jean-Baptiste Adam	Gewurztraminer, Alsace "Reserve"
Léon Beyer	Gewurztraminer, Alsace "Cuvée de Comtes d'Eguisheim"
Dopff & Irion	Alsace Riesling "Château de Riquewihr", "Les Murailles"
Marcel Deiss	Pinot Gris, Alsance Grand Cru "Mambourg"
Joseph Meyer	Riesling Alsace, "Les Pierrets"
Domaine Schlumberger	Pinot Blanc, Alsace "Les Princes Abbés"
Trimbach	Riesling, Alsace "Clos Ste Hune"
Willm	Gewurztraminer, Alsace Grand Cru "Clos Gaensbroënnel"

ALSACE WINES COMPATIBLE WITH FOOD COURSES

Crèmant d'Alsace: Crèmant d'Alsace sparkling wines are an ideal partner for all celebrations. They match the finest dishes like caviar, fish, and white meats, and they brighten cocktail parties and informal get-togethers. Can also be served with fresh fruit or desserts of any type.

Gewurztraminer: Richly aromatic, Gewurztraminer matches all cheeses and is also perfect with all desserts that are not too sweet. Unusual matches with Gewurztraminer are the exotic cuisines of Asia, India, and Morooco.

Muscat d'Alsace: Not to be confused with the varieties from Italy and the South of France. Also, the Muscat grape is often compared to Muscatell, a completely different type of vinestock. Muscat d'Alsace is a semi-dry wine and is a good wine to be consumed as an aperitif thanks to its unique fruit aroma.

Pinot Blanc: Soft and delicate, the Pinot Blanc goes will with fish, poultry, and white meats.

Pinot Noir: Produces a rosé and light red wine. It can be served with a wide range of dishes.

Riesling: Riesling is a dry and delicate white wine. It is usually given the name of King of Alsacian wines due to its outstanding character of distinction.

Sylvaner: Light, crisp, and refreshing, Sylvaner is at its best when consumed young. After two years, it reaches its peak. It is an excellent value for retail wine shops and on restaurant wine lists.

Tokay Pinot Gris: The Tokay of Alsace is a local name for an agreeable white wine made from the Pinot Gris grape. It bears no relation to the sweet and rich Tokay of Hungary.

Traminer: Bottles labeled only as Traminer are simply less pungent white wines as compared to spicy Gewurztraminer with its highly-perfumed bouquet.

ALSACE: EXPLANATION OF THE NAME

The name "Alsace" is derived from the Latin word "Illsuës". When the Romans invaded Alsace in the third century and established themselves in this land, they called Alsace the land of the river Ill.

The river indeed flows all the way north, almost parallel to the bigger River Rhine until above Strasbourg, then turns to the right and flows into the Rhine River.

Over half a dozen tributaries coming from the Vosges Mountains connect with the Ill River. The main ones are:

The "Lauch" which flows through the wine town of Turkheim
The "Fecht" passes in Colmar, the Capital of the wine region
The 'Andlau" passes through the village of Andlau
The "Bruche" passes through the city of Molsheim.

Needless to say that this region is well irrigated and where the frogs are numerous which is a delight for the storks coming every years migrating there until the cold weather moves in.

THE ALSACIAN WINE PRODUCTION

Comparison of the year 1969 and the year 2002

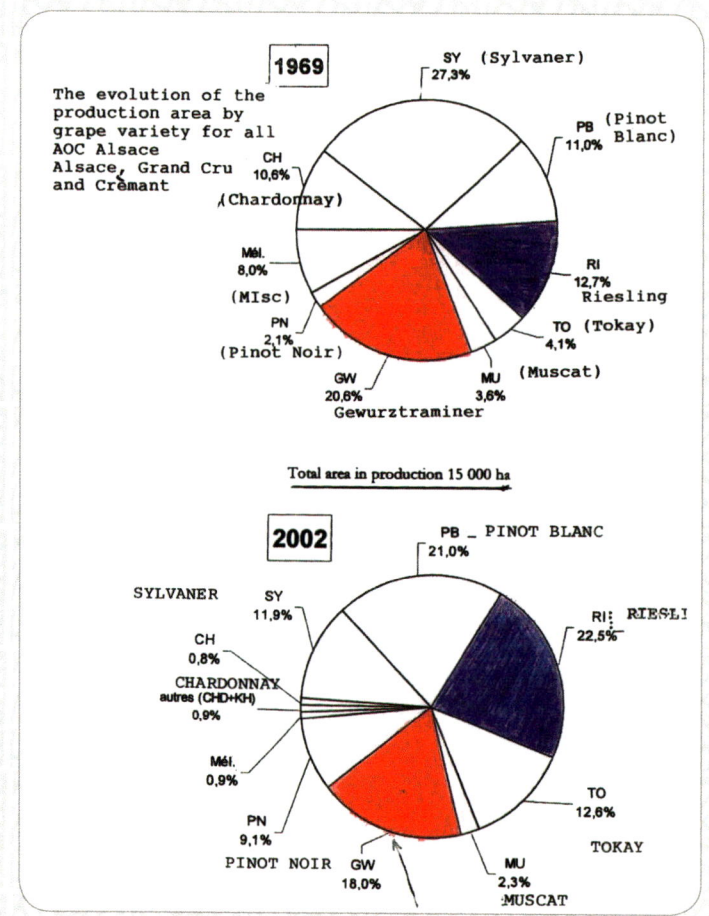

The area planted with Sylvaner has declined considerably over the past decades, having been replaced notably by Pinot blanc and Tokay Pinot Gris. During the same period, the area planted with Riesling has risen significantly.

SECTION B

The Wines of Bordeaux

BORDEAUX

THE BORDEAUX WINE AREA

CHATEAU LAFITE-ROTHSHILD, PAUILLAC ....

CHATEAU MOUTON-ROTHSHILD, PAUILAC .....

THE WINE DISTRICT OF SAINT-ESTEPHE .....

THE WINE DISTRICT OF SAINT-JULIEN ....

THE WINE DISTRICT OF MARGAUX ....

THE WINE DISTRICT OF GRAVES ....

THE WINE DISTRICT OF SAUTERNES ......

THE WINE DISTRICT OF POMEROL ....

THE WINE DISTRICT OF SAINT-EMILION ....

THE IMPORTANCE OF FRENCH WINES

MORE GREAT GRAPE VARIETIES HAVE REACHED THEIR PEAK IN FRANCE THAN ANY OTHER COUNTRIES. THESE VINESTOCKS WERE SELECTED AND IMPROVED TO PERFORM BEST IN FRENCH VINEYARDS OVER A PERIOD OF MANY CENTURIES.

MANY WINEMAKING TECHNIQUES STILL USED TODAY HAD THEIR ORIGINS IN FRANCE, LIKE "RAKING", "BARREL AGING", METHODS USED TO MAKE CHAMPAGNE AND ALSO FOR THE PRODUCTION OF BEAUJOLAIS WINES IN THE CARBONIC MACERATION.

THE FRENCH WINEMAKERS ORIGINATED THE CONCEPT OF "TERROIR", THE UNIQUE COMBINATION OF THE INTERACTION OF THE SOIL WITH THE VINE PLANT. FROM THERE, THE CLIMATE TOPOGRAPHY AND GRAPE VARIETIES OF ANY NAMED SITE PUT ITS STAMP ON THE WINE PRODUCED.

THE WINES FROM BORDEAUX ARE ABOVE AVERAGE IN QUALITY, BREED AND DISTINCTION:

1) THEY ARE SUBTLE, REFINED AND HAVE AN ELEGANT FLAVOR.

2) THEY ARE FRAGILE AND HAVE A BRILLIANT COLOR.

3) THEY ARE DELICATE IN BOUQUET AND INCOMPARABLY SMOOTH.

4) THEY ARE POWERFULL WITHOUT BEING TOO HEAVY OR TOO STRONG.

5) THEY ARE THE ARISTOCRATES OF WINES AND THEY GROW OLD GRACEFULLY.

WHEN YOU WILL CONSUME THESE "APPELLATION CONTROLÉE" WINES, THEY WILL CAPTIVATE YOU FOR LIFE. BY CHOOSING AN "A.C." PLEASE READ CAREFULLY THE LABEL.

THERE ARE ABOUT 3,000 CHATEAU ESTATES NAMED IN THE BORDEAUX WINE DISTRICT. HOWEVER, THE TOP BEST OR "CRÈME DE LA CRÈME" ARE LIMITED TO 300 FINE ESTATES. THE NAME "CHATEAU" TRANSLATES AS "CASTLE" BUT IT APPLIES MOSTLY TO LARGE AND ELEGANT COUNTRY MANSIONS. THESE HIGH-CLASS HOMES BUILT IN THE EARLY 20TH CENTURY HAVE AN ENGLISH FLAIR, BUT ARE ELABORATED HOMES WITH WAREHOUSES NEXT TO IT.

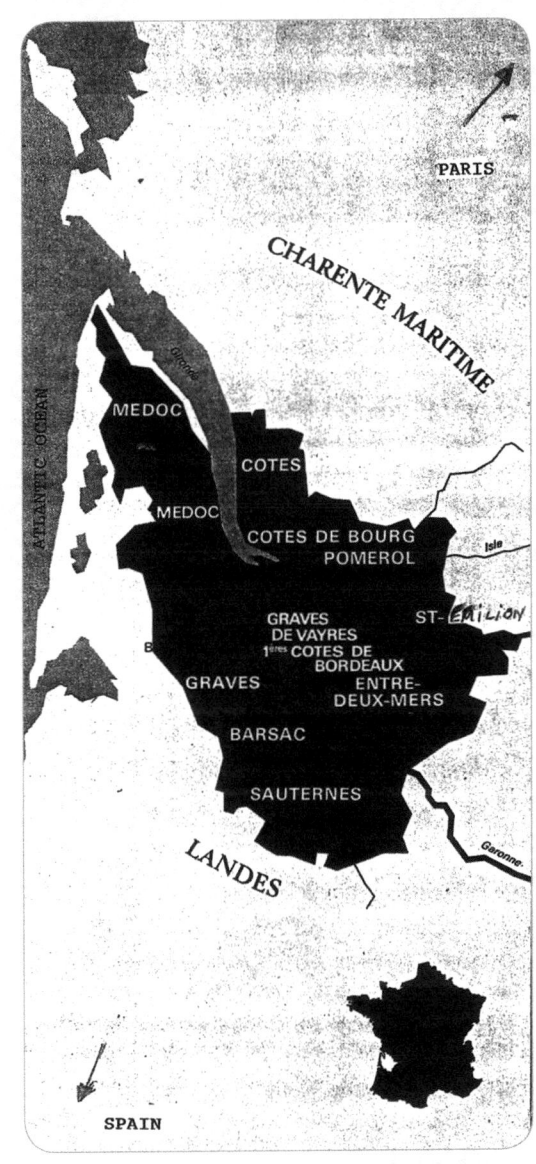

HISTORY OF THE BORDEAUX WINES

THE BORDEAUX WINE TRADE HAS BEEN SHIPPING ITS WINES IN BARRELS TO ENGLAND AS EARLY AS THE TWELVE CENTURY.

AT THAT TIME, IN 1154, THE KING HENRY II, ALSO KNOWN AS HENRY PLANTAGENET, ALSO WAS COUNT OF ANJOU FROM THE LOIRE VALLEY, MARRIED ELEANOR OF AQUITAINE, FORMERLY THE WIFE OF LOUIS VII, KING OF FRANCE.

AQUITAINE WAS THE NAME OF THE SOUTHWESTERN PART OF FRANCE, ALSO CALLED THE "BASSIN D'AQUITAINE, CONSISTING OF THE VAST AREA SURROUNDING BORDEAUX UNTI THE BOUNDARY WITH SPAIN.

KING HENRY II ANNEXED THE REGION OF BORDEAUX AND DECLARED IT A PART OF HIS EMPIRE.

THE COUNTRIES OF HOLLAND AND SCANDINAVIA WERE ALSO IN THE SHIPPING BUSINESS OF BORDEAUX WINES. THE BORDEAUX WINE WAS THEN CALLED "CLAIRET" (PRONOUNCED "KLAARAY") AND THE NAME EVOLVED INTO "CLARET". IT WAS A PALE RED WINE AND IT EVENTUALLY BECAME A SNOBBISH NAME. FURTHER ON, THE EARLY MOVIES OF HOLLYWOOD FEATURED THE NAME "CLARET".

IN THE LATE 1950'S, ALL BORDEAUX WINEGROWERS DECIDED TO BOTTLE THEIR PRODUCTION THEMSELVES AND IN THEIR OWN CELLARS, RATHER THAN SHIPPING THE WINE IN BARRELS, AS IT WAS THE CUSTOM.

IT WAS ALSO A GUARANTEE THAT THE WINE BOTTLE LABEL WAS A PROOF OF AUTHENTICITY. AN EXTRA CARE WAS ALSO PROVIDED TO THE CORK, BESIDE ITS TOP QUALITY, IT HAS A STAMP WITH THE NAME OF THE CHATEAU. IT ALSO READ "MIS EN BOUTEILLE AU CHATEAU", MEANING FILLED IN BOTTLES AT THE ESTATE,

ONCE THE FERMENTATION IS OVER, THE WINE IS TRANSFERED IN OAK BARRELS (CALLED BARRIQUES), FOR A PERIOD OF 27 TO 30 MONTHS (2½ YEARS). THIS PROCEDURE CALLED "AGING" CONTRIBUTES A LOT TO THE COMPLEXITY, THE DEPTH OF FLAVOR AND GIVES A DISTINCTIVE CHARACTER OF HIGH QUALITY WINES. THESE BARRELS HOLD 55 GALLONS, THE VALUE OF 24 CASES OF WINES.

THE MEASURE OF TRADE IN BORDEAUX WHEN WINES ARE BOUGHT IS CALLED A "TONNEAU", A MEASURE EQUIVALENT TO FOUR BARRELS OR 250 gallons, the total of 96 cases.

THE BORDEAUX VINEYARDS ARE USUALLY THE EASIEST TO UNDERSTAND IN COMPARISON WITH VINEYARDS LOCATED IN THE LOIRE, BURGUNDY OR ALSACE. EACH PROPERTY BELONGS TO ONE OWNER AND PRODUCES ONLY ONE TYPE OF WINE. (EXEMPLE: SAINT-JULIEN, MARGAUX OR SAINT-EMILION.

TO THE OPPOSITE, MOST BURGUNDY OR ALSACIAN VINEYARDS HAVE SEVERAL OWNERS, SOMTIMES IN DIFFERENT COMMUNITIES, EACH ONE MAKING A DIFFERENT TYPE OF WINE EACH YEAR AND ALSO ACCORDING TO THEIR SKILLS.

NOT EVERYBODY TODAY IS HOWEVER ABLE TO AFFORD THE HIGH PRICE OF THE BORDEAUX CHATEAU WINES, BUT YOU STILL COULD LOOK FOR THE REGIONAL BORDEAUX BLENDS, PRODUCED BY WINE-BROKERS OR NEGOCIANTS.

THESE WINES ARE SIMPLY SOLD AS BORDEAUX APPELLATION CONTROLEE MEDOC A.C. OR SAINT-EMILION FOR EXEMPLE. THEY ARE A BLEND OF MANY PROPERTIES WITHIN THE PARTICULAR APPELLATION AND ARE CONSISTENT IN QUALITY AND FIRST OF ALL ARE AFFORDABLE.

THE BORDEAUX WINES CLASSIFICATION

WHENEVER YOU WILL HAVE AN OPPORTUNITY TO TALK ABOUT BORDEAUX WINES, THE SUBJECT WILL BE TO RECOLLECT THE SIX PRINCIPAL WINE DISTRICTS WHICH ARE AS FOLLOW:

1) THE MEDOC:

   IS SUBDIVIDED BY THE BAS--MEDOC LOCATED CLOSE TO THE JUNCTION OF THE GIRONDE ESTUARY AND THE ATLANTIC OCEAN AND THE HAUT-MEDOC, SLIGHTLY MORE ELEVATED.
   THE MEDOC AREA IS THE LARGEST PRODUCER OF RED WINES.

2) THE GRAVES DISTRICT:

   LOCATED WEST OF THE CITY OF BORDEAUX IS A PRODUCER OF MOSTLY WHITE WINES, BUT THE MOST OUTSTANDING ARE RED WINES, WHERE THE CHATEAU HAUT-BRION ESTATE IS THE KING.

3) THE SAUTERNES AND BARSAC DISTRISTS:

   IS PRODUCING WHIT WINES ONLY, FROM VERY DRY, SEMI-DRY AND SWEET DESSERT WINES.
   AMONG THE BEST IS THE QUEEN: THE CHATEAU D'YQUEM.

4) THE POMEROL DISTRICT:

   IS THE SMALLEST WINE AREA BUT IS IMMENSE IN FAME.
   THE CLASSIFIED GROWTHS OR CRUS, ARE NOWADAYS FETCHING THE SAME PRICE THAN THE MEDOC WINES.
   THE MOST OUTSTANDING RED WINE COMES FROM CHATEAU PETRUS. NO WHITES ARE PLANTED IN POMEROL.

5)   THE SAINT-EMILION DISTRICT:

THE VINEYARDS OF THIS AREA GO BACK TO THE ROMAN TIMES, AND ENJOY PROMINENCE SINCE MANY CENTURIES, THE BEST RENOWNED WINES ARE FROM CHATEAU AUSONE AND CHATEAU CHEVAL BLANC.

6)   THE "ENTRE-DEUX-MERS" DISTRICT:

LITERALLY MEANS "BETWEEN TWO SEAS", AND SHOULD BE MORE LOGICALLY BE CALLED "ENTRE DEUX FLEUVES" OR BETWEEN TWO RIVERS: THE GARONNE AND THE DORDOGNE RIVERS. THIS AREA PRODUCES A HUGE AMOUNT OF WHITE WINES; TEN MILLION GALLONS A YEAR.
THESE WINES ARE RATHER LIKE EVERY DAY WINE AND INEXPENSIVE. A SMALLER RED WINE PRODUCTION IS NOT ENTITLED TO AN APPELLATION CONTROLÉE AND IS COMMERCIALIZED AS BORDEAUX AND BORDEAUX SUPERIEUR.
WHITE WINES PRODUCTION FROM THIS AREA AND OF A HIGHER QUALITY ARE MADE AROUND LOUPIAC, ST. CROIX DU MONT AND VEYRES WITH A RECOGNIZED APPELLATION.

(SEE COMPLETE CLASSIFICATION PAGE ....

REPRESENTATIVES OF THE BORDEAUX WINE TRADE FROM THE MEDOC AND SAUTERNES DISTRICTS WERE CHOOSEN TO DRAW-UP A LIST OF THE BEST WINES FROM THESE TWO DISTRICTS, FOR THE INCOMING OF THE FIRST UNIVERSAL EXIBITION OF 1855 IN PARIS (SIMILAR TO A WORLD'S FAIR NOWADAYS).

AT THAT TIME, THE WINES FROM MEDOC, ALREADY WERE RATED AS EXCELLENT. THOSE OF THE GRAVES, SAINT-EMILLION AND POMEROL WERE NOT WIDELY KNOWN. HOWEVER, THE CHATEAU HAUT-BRION WINES HAD BEEN ACCLAIMED TO BE TOO IMPORTANT TO LEAVE OUT OF THIS CLASSIFICATION

THIS LIST WAS REPRESENTING THE WINES OF FIVE LEVELS OF EXCELLENCE. A FIRST RATING DID NOT CONSTITUTE THAT ONE FIFTH WAS AS GOOD AS THE FIRST RATING. IN ORDER TO RATE THE WINES, THE BEST APPROACH TO START WAS WITH THE TOP VINEYARDS, RECOGNIZING THE PRICE VALUE THEY FETCHED.

THE CLASSIFICATION TOOK IN CONSIDERATION THE RELATIVE PARTICULIARITY OF THE LOCATION, THE RICHNESS OF THE SOIL COMPOSITION

THE RATING THEN CAME GRADUALLY. THE CLASSIFICATION DID NOT EXPRESS MALVEILLANCE TO ANY WINEGROWER NOR TO ANY TYPE OF SOIL.

THE COMMUNES OF THE MEDOC ARE RESPONSIBLE FOR NAMING THE BEST GROWTHS FOR THIS DISTRICT, NAMELY THE COMMUNES OF:

SAINT-ESTEPHE; BEST WINES ARE COS D'ESTOURNEL AND CHATEAU MONTROSE

PAUILLAC; BEST WINES ARE CHATEAU LAFITE-ROTHSCHILD
                          CHATEAU LATOUR
                          CHATEAU MOUTON-ROTHSCHILD
                          CHATEAU PICHON-LALANDE
                          CHATEAU PICHON-LONGUEVILLE

SAINT-JULIEN; BEST WINES ARE

                          CHATEAU LEOVILLE-POYFERRE
                          CHATEAU LEOVILLE-BARTON
                          CHATEAU GRUAUD-LAROSE
                          CHATEAU DUCRU-BEAUCAILLOU
                          CHATEAU BEYCHEVELLE

MARGAUX; BEST WINES ARE CHATEAU MARGAUX

CHATEAU LASCOMBES

CHATEAU KIRWAN

CHATEAU RAUZAN-SEGLA

CHATEAU CANTENAC-BROWN

CHATEAU PALMER

THE WINES GROWN IN BORDEAUX ARE:

FOR RED WINES; CABERNET-SAUVIGNON, MALBEC, MERLOT, CABERNET-FRANC AND PETITS VERDOTS.

FOR WHITE WINES; SAUVIGNON BLANC, SEMILLON, AND MUSCADELLE.

NOTE: THE WINEMAKERS ARE BLENDING THESE SPECIES ACCORDING TO THE PRACTICES DONE FOR YEARS OF RESEARCH.

THE FIRST GROWTHS-PREMIER CRUS

THE FIVE AND ONLY FIRST GROWTHS, CLASSIFIED IN 1855

PRODUCE OF FRANCE

SPÉCIMEN

1947

CHATEAU HAUT-BRION

PREMIER GRAND CRU CLASSÉ

APPELLATION GRAVES CONTRÔLÉE

MIS EN BOUTEILLES AU CHATEAU

S.A. DU CHÂTEAU HAUT-BRION, PROPRIÉTAIRE A PESSAC (GIRONDE)
DÉPOSÉ

GRAND VIN
DE
CHATEAU LATOUR

PREMIER GRAND CRU CLASSÉ

APPELLATION PAUILLAC CONTRÔLÉE

PAUILLAC-MÉDOC

1959

MIS EN BOUTEILLES AU CHATEAU

SOCIÉTÉ CIVILE DU VIGNOBLE DE CHÂTEAU LATOUR
PROPRIÉTAIRE A PAUILLAC-GIRONDE

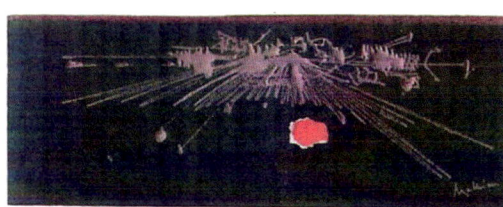

1961

1961

Cette récolte a produit :
Bordelaises et 1/2 B^{les} de à
Magnums de à
Grands Formats de à
double-magnums, jéroboams, impériales
"Réserve du Château" marquées
Ci, N°

Philippe de Rothschild

Château
Mouton Rothschild

BARON PHILIPPE DE ROTHSCHILD PROPRIÉTAIRE A PAUILLAC

APPELLATION PAUILLAC CONTRÔLÉE

TOUTE LA RÉCOLTE MISE EN BOUTEILLES AU CHATEAU

HISTORY OF CHATEAU LAFITE-ROTHSCHILD
PAUILLAC, HAUT-MEDOC

FIRST GROWTH- PREMIER CRU

THE VINEYARDS OF LAFITE HAVE NINE CENTURIES OF HISTORY BEHIND IT. SEVERAL NOBILITIES CULTIVATED THIS PROPERTY UNTIL THE FRENCH REVOLUTION OF 1789, WHEN IT BECAME A PUBLIC PROPERTY.

IN 1868, THE BARON JAMES DE ROTHSCHILD ACQUIRED THIS ESTATE FOR A MODEST SUM OF $43,000.00. THIS WOULD BRING TODAY EASILY A 100 TIMES THAT PRICE.

THE NAME LAFITE IS DERIVED FROM THE OLD MEDOC WORD "LAHITE", MEANING THE HIGHEST KNOLL OF THE PAUILLAC AREA.

THE PRESENT OWNER OF LAFITE IS ELIE DE ROTHSCHILD, A COUSIN OF PHILIPPE DE ROTHSCHILD OF CHATEAU MOUTON-ROTHSCHILD.

THE VINEYARDS OF LAFITE ARE PLANTED WITH CABERNET-SAUVIGNON, CABERNET-FRANC, PETITS VERDOTS AND MERLOT, WHICH GIVE THE SOFTNESS FOR WHICH LAFITE IS FAMOUS. THE ESTATE OF MOUTON HAS ONLY 30% MERLOT AND 70% CABERNET-SAUVIGNON AND PRODUCES A HARDER WINE.

THERE ARE MANY MAGNUMS AND DOUBLE-MAGNUMS IN THE LAFITE CELLARS SINCE WINE AGES MORE SLOWLY IN LARGE BOTTLES.

IN GREAT VINTAGE YEARS, THE WINE OF LAFITE IS SUPREME, IT HAS A GREAT FINESS AND SOFTNESS DUE TO THE MERLOT VARIETY.

THE VINEYARD AREA CONSISTS OF 80 HECTARES (200 ACRES) AND THE AVERAGE PRODUCTION IS 250 TONNEAUX (22,000 CASES) PER YEAR.

A VISIT TO PAUILLAC WITHOUT SEEING THE ESTATE OF CHATEAU LAFITE IS LIKE COMING TO PARIS WITHOUT VISITING THE EIFFEL TOWER!

THE MOST IMPRESSIVE SIGHT AT LAFITE ARE THE CELLARS OF THE CHATEAU: A RANK OF BINS, EACH WITH ITS WOODEN VINTAGE PLAQUE.

HISTORY OF PAUILLAC, HAUT-MEDOC

PAUILLAC WAS YEARS AGO A HAMLET AND A SMALL HARBOR, IT IS FROM THIS HARBOR THAT THE MARQUIS DE LAFAYETTE, A NOBLE ARMY MAN, SET SAIL WITH HIS MERCENARY ARMY TO NORTH AMERICA. THEY LANDED ON THE EAST COAST OF THE STATES TO HELP THE CONTINENTAL ARMY TO DEFEAT THE COLONIALISM OF ENGLAND AND HELP THE CAUSE OF THE NEW INDEPENDANCE OF THE UNITED STATES.

THE NAME LAFAYETTE IS RECOGNIZED IN MANY AMERICAN STATES AS THEY NAMED THEIR TOWNSHIPS LAFAYETTE, FAYETTE AND FAYETTEVILLE.

A VERY IMPRESSIVE BROTHERHOOD OF WINE-FELLOWS IS ALSO HEADQUARTERED IN PAUILLAC, IT IS CALLED THE "COMMANDERIE DU BONTEMPS DE MEDOC".

HISTORY OF CHATEAU MOUTON-ROTHSCHILD

THE CHATEAU MOUTON-ROTHSCHILD IS ONE OF THE MOST IMPRESSIVE ESTATE IN PAUILLAC, THE MEDOC AREA.

THOUSAND OF TOURISTS VISIT AND LOVE TO SEE THE REMARKABLE WINE MUSEUM EVERY YEAR.

THIS UNIQUE MUSEUM IS COMPOSED OF ART MASTERPIECES RELATED TO WINE FROM 2000 YEARS B.C. TO THE 20TH CENTURY.

BARON PHILIPPE CREATED THIS MUSEUM WITH THE HELP OF HIS AMERIC WIFE, IN 1962. THE LOCATION OF THE MUSEUM WAS FORMERLY A WINE-CEL AND ITS MAKES IT EVEN MORE MYSTERIOUS TODAY.

THE COLLECTION INCLUDES PERSIAN GOBLETS, ANTIQUE FURNITURE WITH GRAPE-PATTERNED UPHOLSTERY, SOME OF THE FINEST GLASS FLASKS AND "FLAGONS" IN FRENCH MEANING "BONBONNE", WHICH ARE LARGE GLOBA TYPE GLAS CONTAINERS.

PAINTINGS FROM PICASSO AND DUTCH MASTERS DECORATE THE ROOMS. TAPESTRIES AND OBJETS D'ART FROM FROM DISTANT COUNTRIES CAN ALSO BE SEEN. THEY ARE FROM TIBET, RUSSIA AND EGYPT.

THE EXIBITS ARE ELOQUENTLY AND CLEVERLY DISPLAYED.

THE VINEYARDS OF MOUTON COVER SEVENTY-TWO HECTARES, SOME SIXTY OF WHICH ARE UNDER PRODUCTION, THE AVERAGE YIELD IS ABOUT 180 CASKS A YEAR.

BORDEAUX WINES ARE USUALLY STORED IN THESE SMALL OAK BARRELS HOLDING FIFTY-FIVE GALLONS OR TWENTY-FOUR CASES OF 12 BOTTLES,

THE WINE REMAINS IN BARREL FOR TWO TO THREE YEARS. THIS METHOD OF AGING GREATLY CONTRIBUTES TO THE COMPLEXITY, DEPTH OF FLAVOR AND DISTINCTIVE CHARACTERISTIC FOR THE FINE RED WINE.

THE MEASURE OF TRADE IN BORDEAUX WHEN NEW WINES ARE PUT ON THE MARKET IS CALLED "TONNEAU", A MEASURE EQUAL TO FOUR CASKS.

THE WINEGROWERS IN CALIFORNIA ALSO SWITCHED THEIR METHOD AND INSTEAD USE LARGE REDWOOD VATS FOR THE SAME REASON.

BARON PHILIPPE CAME TO THE IDEA OF A MOTTO FOR HIS WINE-LABELS AS A PROTEST AGAINST THE LONG TIME CLASSIFICATION OF 1855.

THE MOTTO SAID: "FIRST I CANNOT BE, SECOND I WILL NOT BE, I AM MOUTON".
                   TRANSLATED AS:
                   "PREMIER NU PUIS, SECOND NE DAIGNE, MOUTON SUIS"

AFTER THE VINEYARDS HAD BEEN ELEVATED TO FIRST GROWTH IN 1973, BARON PHILIPPE CHANGED THE MOTTO AS FOLLOW:

                   "FIRST I AM, SECOND I HAVE BEEN, MOUTON REMAINS THE SAME"
                   TRANSLATED IN FRENCH AS:

                   "PREMIER JE SUIS, SECOND JE FUS, MOUTON NE CHANGE".

THE VINEYARDS OF MOUTON WERE BOUGHT IN 1853 BY THE BARON NATHANIEL DE ROTHSCHILD IN A DILAPIDED STAGE. THIS TOOK PLACE TWO YEARS BEFORE THE FIRST UNIVERSAL EXIBITION IN PARIS.

THE WINE PRODUCTION THEREFORE COULD NOT BE CLASSIFIED AT THAT TIME DUE TO THE LACK OF RECORDS, INCLUDING THE INCONSISTENCY OF THE PRODUCTION.

THE ESTATE WAS AT THAT TIME JUST A FARM-HOUSE BUILT NEXT TO THE VINEYARDS. IT TOOK FORTY YEARS BEFORE MOUTON BECAME A GENUINE "CHATEAU". AN ELEGANT MANSION WAS BUILT IN THE EARLY 20TH CENTURY ALONG THE CHAIS (WINE-STORAGE BUILDING).

IN 1920, BARON PHILIPPE ONLY 21 YEARS OLD, TOOK COMMAND OF THE WINERY. HIS FATHER HENRI HAD OTHER BUSINESS OPPORTUNITIES, SO THE YOUNG SON WANTED TO ACCOMPLISH TO UPGRADE MOUTON TO A FIRST GROWTH ESTATE, IT IS SAID THAT FROM THAT TIME ON, THERE HAS BEEN A FEUD BETWEEN BARON PHILIPPE AND THE LAFITE-ROTHSCHILD FAMILY. THEY WERE DIRECT COUSINS AND THE LAFITE'S HAD TO ENDURE RIVALRY OF MOUTON-ROTHSCHILD.

BY 1934, BARON PHILIPPE CAME FORWARD WITH NEW IDEAS. MOUTON HAD TO BECOME THE AVANT-GUARDE OF THE WINE INDUSTRY. HE DECIDED THAT THE WINE PRODUCTION SHOULD BE BOTTLED AT THE CHATEAU. HE ALSO DIRECTED THAT THE MOUTON LABEL HAD TO MENTION THE NUMBER OF BOTTLES PRODUCED PER YEAR AND EACH BOTTLE HAD TO BE NUMBERED AND PRINTED ON THE LABEL.

AN INTERESTING THOUGHT IS HELD THAT THE YEARLY ILLUSTRATION OF THE LABEL DESIGN MUST INDICATE THE STYLE THAT NATURE HAS GIVEN TO THE VINTAGE. FOR EXEMPLE, THE PAINTER CHAGALL WHO DESIGNED THE 1970 COLORFUL GOUACHE, SYMBOLISES THE EXUBERANCE OF THAT VINTAGE.

THE NAME "MOUTON" IN FRENCH MEANS "SHEEP". IT IS BELIEVED THAT IT WAS THE ORIGINAL NAME OF THE GRAZING LAND FOR THE SHEEPS, BEFORE IT BECAME THE VINEYARDS OF MOUTON.

THE VILLAGE OF PAUILLAC, LOCATED AROUND TWO MILES FROM THE ESTATE OF MOUTON, HOLDS THE OFFICES AND CELLARS OF "LA BERGERIE" MEANING IN FRENCH THE SHEEP-PEN.

THE LINE OF MOUTON-CADET WINE BOTTLING TAKES PLACE THERE. THE WINE, HOWEVER HAS NO APPELLATION RANKING, JUST APPELLATION "BORDEAUX". IT IS A COMMON WINE AND IS A BLEND OF SEVEN VARITIES OF WINES. MOUTON-CADET MEANS THE JUNIOR WINE AND IT IS SHIPPED BEHOND FRANCE AND ALL OVER EUROPE AND NORTH AMERICA, IT COMES IN RED, WHITE AND ROSÉ WINES, THEY ARE MOSTLY SEEN ON SUPER-MARKET SHELVES.

SAINT-ESTEPHE DISTRICT, HAUT-MEDOC

CHATEAUX COS D'ESTOURNEL AND MONTROSE WERE SECOND GROWTHS CLASSIFIED IN 1855 AND THE LEADING CLASSIFIED GROWTHS OF SAINT-ESTEPHE.

THE WINE DISTRICT OF SAINT-ESTÈPHE
SAINT-ESTÈPHE, HAUT-MEDOC

SAINT-ESTÈPHE IS LOCATED ON THE NOTHERMOST MAIN WINE-GROWING TOWNSHIPS OF THE HAUT-MEDOC, DIRECTLY ADJOINING THE TOWNSHIP OF PAUILLAC.

ITS BEST WINES ARE SLIGHTLY HARSH, FULL-BODIED, GENEROUS AND VERY AGREABLE. THEY HAVE LESS FINESSE AND BREED THAN COMPARABLE THE MEDOC WINES.

THE TOP RANKING GROWTHS ARE THOSE OF CHATEAU COS D'ESTOURNEL, CHATEAU MONTROSE, CHATEAU CALON-SÉGUR, CHATEAU LAFON-ROCHET AND CHATEAU COS LABORY. THE FIRST TWO WERE GIVEN A SECOND GROWTH CLASSIFICATION. WHILE THE THREE OTHERS RECEIVED A RANK LOWER IN THE THIRD, FOURTH AND FIFTH CLASSIFICATION.

THERE ARE MANY EXCELLENT LESSER WINES CALLED SIMPLY REGIONAL AND LABELED AS SAINT-ESTÈPHE. THEY ARE IN GENERAL OF A GOOD VALUE.

THE ANNUAL PRODUCTION IS 50,000 HECTOLITERS (1,325 US GALLONS). SOME LESSER SAINT-ESTÈPHE WINES ARE TRANSITIONAL BETWEEN THE BAS-MEDOC AND THE MORE FAMOUS MEDOC. THIS IS NO SURPRISING, SINCE THE VILLAGE OF SAINT-ESTÈPHE STANDS ON THE BOUNDARY OF TWO DISTRICTS.

CHATEAU BEYCHEVELLE
ST. JULIEN
FOURTH GROWTH OF THE MEDOC
(but actually very superior to its classification)

-0-

Achille Fould, former agriculture Minister of France and his heirs are now the owners.

-0-

The Château Beychevelle is one of the most important and one of the most ancient property of the Medoc.

Its site facing the Gironde Estuary is outstanding. The dwelling was built in 1757 by Mr. De Brassier, a former owner, in the style "Louis XV".

The name of Beychevelle (meaning in old French language -"Baisse-Voile", (lower the sails), comes from the "Salute" which was formerly given by the ships passing by, along the Château of the Duc d'Epernon, at that time Grand Admiral of France, and owner of Château Beychevelle.

The production of this Estate averages 150 Tonneaux, a quality wine, full of fragrances and very delicate. It is very appreciated in foreign countries as well as France as a wine of great reputation.

One tonneau = 900 liters or 4 pieces of 225 liters.

THE WINE DISTRICT OF SAINT-JULIEN
SAINT-JULIEN-HAUT-MEDOC

WHEN ENTERING THE COMMUNE OF SAINT-JULIEN-BEYCHEVELLE, A LARGE BILLBOARD ANNOUNCES: "PASSERS-BY, YOU ARE NOW ENTERING THE ANCIEN AND FAMOUS VINEYARDS OF SAINT-JULIEN; BOW LOW!

A SPECIAL RECOGNITION WAS GIVEN BY THE OLD CUSTOM OF THE SAILORS WHO USED TO LOWER THE SAILS OF THEIR SHIPS WHEN PASSING BY THE ELEGANT MANSION OF THE DUC D'EPERNON, AN ADMIRAL OF FRANCE IN THE 17th CENTURY.

THE CUSTOM GAVE THE NAME TO THE CHATEAU BEYCHEVELLE (MEANING LOWERING THE SAILS OR IN OLD FRENCH LANGUAGE: BAISSE VOILE.

ACHILLE FOULD, THE FORMER AGRICULTURAL MINISTER OF FRANCE AND HIS FAMILY ARE NOWADAYS THE OWNERS OF CHATEAU BEYCHEVELLE.

CHATEAU BEYCHEVELLE HAS BEEN CLASSIFIED AS A FOURTH GROWTH OF THE MEDOC IN 1855. SAINT-JULIEN HAS NEITHER FIRST NOR FIFTH GROWTH.

THE WINE OF BEYCHEVELLE IS ALWAYS AN OUTSTANDING QUALITY WINE, FULL OF FRAGRANCES, SOFT AND VERY DELICATE.

THE PRODUCTION AVERAGES 150 TONNEAUX. (A TONNEAU EQUALS 900 LITERS), OR FOUR OAK BARRELS OF 225 LITERS.

THE MAJOR SAINT-JULIEN GROWTHS ARE:

SECOND GROWTHS:
- CHATEAU LEOVILLE-LAS-CASES
- CHATEAU LEOVILLE-POYFERRE
- CHATEAU LEOVILLE-BARTON
- CHATEAU GRUAUD-LAROSE
- CHATEAU DUCRU-BEAUCAILLOU

THIRD GROWTHS:
- CHATEAU LAGRANGE
- CHATEAU LANGOA-BARTON

FOURTH GROWTHS
- CHATEAU SAINT-PIERRE
- CHATEAU TALBOT
- CHATEAU BRANAIRE
- CHATEAU BEYCHEVELLE

OUTSTANDING BOURGEOIS GROWTH:

- CHATEAU GLORIA

CHATEAU LASCOMBES
SECOND GROWTH OF MEDOC
MARGAUX DISTRICT
-0-

This well known estate from Margaux enjoys its fame from its fineness and distinguished wines.

Noble types of growths and meticulous care given to the vinification, gave Château Lascombes the right to compete with the famous Château Margaux, the number one ranking Margaux of the first growth classification. The property has 90 hectares of vineyard, producing around 40,000 gallons of wine.

THE WINE DISTRICT OF MARGAUX
MARGAUX, HAUT-MEDOC

THE NAME MARGAUX IS DERIVED FROM "MAROJALLIA," NAMED BY AUSONIUS THE FOURTH CENTURY FAMOUS LATIN POET, AFTER WHOM THE CHATEAU AUSONE IN THE SAINT-EMILION AREA WAS ALSO NAMED.

FIVE COMMUNES IN THE AREA OF MARGAUX HAVE THE RIGHT TO THE PLACE-NAME MARGAUX. IN THE EARLY 20TH CENTURY, A FEUD TOOK PLACE WITHIN SEVERAL WINEGROWERS, OWNERS OF PROPERTIES AROUND MARGAUX. IT FINALLY WAS SETTLED TWENTY FIVE YEARS LATER. NEW REGULATIONS DEFINED THE MARGAUX WINES. THEY STATED THAT THE VINES MUST BE GROWN FROM SOILS CERTIFIED BY THE EXPERTS OF THE APPELLATION CONTROLEE. THE COMMITTEE INSURED THAT THE WINES FROM THE FIVE COMMUNES BE CALLED MARGAUX A.C., THAT THE YIELD MAY NOT BE MORE THAN FORTY HECTOLITERS TO THE HECTARE (424 US. GALLONS), THAT THE METHODS OF PRUNING AND CULTIVATION MUST REACH A HIGH QUALITY STANDARD FOR ALL FIVE COMMUNES.

CHARACTERISTICS OF THE CHATEAU MARGAUX WINES:

CHATEAU MARGAUX PRODUCES THE MOST ELEGANT AND DELICATE FEMININE WINES. THEY ARE PERFECTLY BALANCED AND QUICK TO DEVELOP. THEY SOMETIMES SURPASS IN EXCELLENT VINTAGE YEARS THE WINES FROM CHATEAU LAFITE AND CHATEAU LATOUR, FROM PAUILLAC.

CHATEAU MARGAUX ALSO YIELDS A SMALL AMOUNT OF DRY WHITE, A REAL EXCEPTION FOR THE MEDOC DISTRICT. IT IS CALLED "PAVILLON BLANC DU CHATEAU MARGAUX", ALSO A DELICATE EXCEPTIONAL WINE. IT IS FOUND IN THE TOP RESTAURANTS IN FRANCE AND THE UNITED STATES.

VINEYARD AREA: 66 HECTARES (165 ACRES).
AVERAGE PRODUCTION: RED WINES-175 TONNEAUX (16,000 CASE
WHITE WINES-4,000 CASES

(SEE COMPLETE CLASSIFICATION OF THE MARGAUX VINEYARDS, PAGE ...)

CHATEAU RAUSAN-SEGLA
SECOND GROWTH OF MEDOC
MARGAUX DISTRICT

-0-

By the volume of wines sold since many centuries under the name of Château Margaux, there was one of the vineyards which a wine-broker gave his name in 1661. It was Mr. de Rausan.

After the revolution of 1789, the Domain became the ownership of the heirs of Baronne de Segla. The property is known nowadays as Rausan-Segla and belongs to the Holt's family business, which is managed by the House of Louis Eschenauer from Bordeaux.

The vineyard lies over 50 hectares of land and is adjacent to the one of Chateau Margaux. This estate has wine-cellars dating from 1661. The actual production is around 130,000 bottles per year. The Chateau Rausan-Segla, classified in 1855 as a top 2nd Growth from Margaux, was placed immediately after the Chateau Mouton-Rothschild, Pauillac, which has been amended in 1973 to a First Growth of the Medoc.

THE GRAVES WINE DISTRICT

LOCATION OF
CHATEAU HAUT-BRION

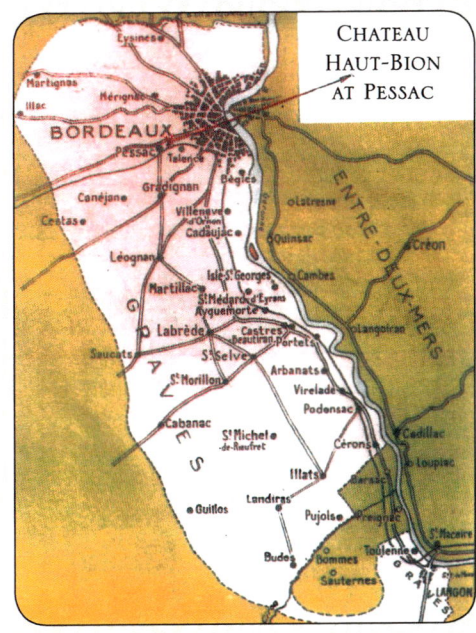

THE GRAVES DISTRICT.   AREA OF THESE TOP OUTSTANDING WINES AS:
CHATEAUX HAUT-BRION, LA MISSION HAUT-BRION, CHATEAUX
LAVILLE HAUT-BRION, HAUT BAILLY.

THE BORDEAUX GRAVES WINE DISTRICT LIES DIRECTLY TO THE SOUTH WEST OF THE CITY OF BORDEAUX.

IT WAS TRADITIONALLY KNOWN AS A LARGE WHITE WINE PRODUCER, WHILE THE RED WINE PRODUCTION WERE IN THE PAST, OVERSHADOWED WITH SOME EXCEPTIONS BY MORE WELL KNOWN RED WINES FROM THE MEDOC.

THE RED GRAVES WINES ARE NOWADAYS OF A HIGHER QUALITY. THEY HAVE MORE BODY BUT ARE LESS REFINED COMPARED TO THE MEDOC WINES. THEY ARE NEVERTHELESS VERY MUCH IN DEMAND DUE TO THEIR RICHER TEXTURE. THEY ARE TREMENDOUSLY APPEALING CLARETS.

THE WHITE GRAVES WINES ARE DRY WINES WITH A TRACE OF SOFTNESS OR "MOELLLEUX" AND THEREFORE ARE RATED LESS THAN THE BIG WHITE BURGUNDIES.

THE WORD GRAVES IN FRENCH SIMPLY MEANS GRAVEL OR GRAVELLY SOIL IT ALSO MEANS A SPECIFIC, DEFINED AREA ON THE LEFT BANK OF THE GARONNE RIVER.

THE RED GRAPES ARE PRODUCED FROM CABERNET SAUVIGNON, CABERNET FRANC, MERLOT, MALBEC AND PETIT VERDOT.

THE WHITE GRAPES FROM SEMILLON, SAUVIGNON AND A SMALL QUANTITY OF MUSCADELLE.

THE BEST VINEYARDS OF THE GRAVES DISTRICT, PRODUCING RED AND WHITE WINES, WERE CLASSIFIED IN 1953. THE RATING, HOWEVER, HAS BEEN OVERLY CRITIZED AND HAS BEEN REVISED IN 1959.

RELATING TO THE CHATEAU HAUT-BRION ESTATE, IT REMAINED A FIRST GROWTH OF THE MEDOC CLASSIFICATION OF 1855. IT IS ALSO RATED AS A CLASSIFIED GROWTH OF THE RED WINES OF THE GRAVES DISTRICT.

TO MAKE IT A LITTLE MORE COMPLEX WAS AN ERROR MADE IN THE ORIGINAL GRAVES CLASSIFICATION, WHERE THE WHITE WINE OF HAUT-BRION WAS NOT MENTIONED IN THE 1953 CLASSIFICATION.

THE WHITE WINE OF THE HAUT-BRION ESTATE HAD BEEN RECOGNIZED AS AN OUTSTANDING DRY WHITE WINE AND HAD BEEN AMONG THE FINEST WHITE IN THE WORLD. THE ERROR HAS BEEN RECTIFIED IN 1960.

AVERAGE PRODUCTION PER YEAR AT HAUT-BRION:
RED WINE: 130 TONNEAUX OR 11,000 CASES OF 12 BOTTLES
WHITE WINE: 9 TONNEAUX OR 800 CASES.

VINEYARD AREA:
RED WINE: 39 HECTARES OR 98 ACRES
WHITE WINE: 3 HECTARES OR 7.5 ACRES

CHATEAU LA MISSION HAUT BRION
DISTRICT OF GRAVES

Explanation of the label:

"LA MISSION HAUT BRION" stands for the commercial name of the vineyard and winery.

The mention "grand cru classe", immediately makes you aware that you are dealing with a wine of great stature. Nevertheless, the name Mission Haut Brion should not be confused with the famous growth of the Chateau Haut Brion, which is a "First Great Groth".

APPELLATION GRAVES CONTROLLEE, means the wine comes from the site or the district of Graves (origin).

As the Graves region produces white and red wines, La Mission Haut Brion, however harvests only red wines.

The bottle labeled is from the vintage 1964.
Below the illustration of the castle is the name of the proprietor, a company of several share holders, which also has acquired several other vineyards years ago, as Chateau La Tour Haut Brion, Chateau Laville Haut Brion, all adjoining the Chateau La Mission Haut Brion. The wine comes from the Bordeaux Province, France and has been bottled at the estate itself. (Mis en bouteilles au Chateau).

The vineyard of La Mission Haut Brion is located between the communities of Talence and Pessac.

Its origin, its name and its reputation is due to a religious congregation, that used to be called "The Preachers of the Mission". It was founded in the 17th century by Saint Vincent of Paul.

These Preachers, beside their religious duties, possessed a highly degree of knowledge in viticulture, choosing the exposures of their vineyard and also giving it great care of the culture of the vine. They researched the finest growth to be planted there. Their marvelous wines produced at that site became famous world wide.

Around that time, the production of these red wines were strictly reserved for the tables of the Princes of the Church.

It was also remembered in history that Maréchal Richelieu enjoyed this wine of predilection. Richelieu played a brilliant political role under the Regency area. He used to pleasantly say, "If God forbade to drink, how could He allow to work such a miracle of a good wine"!.

The monks were dispossessed of their property in 1792, by the French Revolution and the land was disposed as a national welfare. It was later sold to a civilian for a huge price at that time.

The acreage remains at 20 hectares. The site is located on a splendid crest, the best in this area, has an outstanding exposure to the sun. These factors contribute to a wine production of full vigor, an extreme fineness and a noticeable good robe (velvety color).

The Jury of the 1st Universal exhibition of wine in London in 1862, awarded a gold medal to Château La-Mission Haut-Brion. In the last 50 years, the vintage years of 1947, 49, 55, 59, 61, 64, 66, 70, 73, 75; 81, 85, 88, were outstanding. The universal reputation of La Mission Haut Brion will not be forgotten soon.

CHATEAU D'YQUEM
PREMIER GRAND CRU DE SAUTERNES

HISTORY:

THIS PROMINENT VINEYARD HAS REMAINED IN THE SAME FAMILY OVER FOUR CENTURIES. VERY FEW ESTATES CAN HOLD THAT TITLE ESPECIALLY DURING UPRAISINGS, WARS AND THE REVOLUTION OF 1789.

A CERTAIN JACQUES DE SAUVAGE, AN ANCESTOR OF THE PRESENT HEIRS, ACQUIRED THE DOMAIN FROM THE ROYAL FAMILY IN 1593.

THE OUTSTANDING QUALITIES OF YQUEM, WHICH EVERYONE HAS HEARD OF BUT THAT A FEW HAVE TASTED, HAD ITS ORIGIN IN A 16TH CENTURY PACT BETWEEN A FAMILY OF THE VILLAGE OF BAZAS, A SMALL COMMUNITY SOUTH OF SAUTERNES. THIS FAMILY'S NAME IS LUR-SALUCES.

THE MYTHICAL CHARACTER OF YQUEM OWED ITS EXISTENCE FIRST AND FOREMOST TO THE "BOTRYTIS CINERA", CALLED THE FAMOUS NOBLE ROT. THIS MYSTERIOUS FUNGUS OCCURS WHEN THE GRAPES ARE LEFT TO WITHER ON THE VINE BRANCHES. IT WORKS ITS MAGIC ON THE WINE LIKE AN ALCHEMIST TRANSMUTING VULGAR METALS INTO GOLD. ONCE THE FUNGUS IS AT WORK, THE GRAPES SHRIVEL AND THE FRUIT TAKES ON A RATHER UNAPPETISING APPEARANCE.

BETWEEN SEPTEMBER AND DECEMBER, EACH ROW OF VINES ARE HARVESTED UP TO A DOZEN TIMES. PICKERS CAREFULLY CHOOSE INDIVIDUAL GRAPES THAT HAVE REACHED OPTIMUM MATURITY AND THE SUGAR CONTENT THAT DERIVED FROM IT, BRINGS IT TO AN ALCOHOL PROOF OF 18 TO 20% per volume.

THE ACTUAL HEIR, MR. ALEXANDRE de LUR-SALUCES, LIKES TO SAY THAT THE "GLORY OF YQUEM" IS ITS RENUNCIATION, THE RENUNCIATION OF A SMALLER CROP.

OWNERS OF THESE VINEYARDS HAVE HISTORICALLY BEEN DRIVEN NOT BY PROFIT BUT BY AN OBSESSION OF EXCELLENCE.

ALTHOUGH THIS GREAT SWEET WINE IS PROPERLY APPRECIATED, THE PRESENT FASHION FOR MORE DRY WHITE WINES IS SO IRRESISTIBLE THAT YQUEM IS NOW MAKING SOME FAIR DRY WHITES CALLED "Y". AROUND 8,000 BOTTLES OF "Y" ARE SHIPPED EVERY YEAR.

DESPITE SOME GREEDY FOREIGN COMPETITORS WHO TRYED TO IMITATE THE NAME SAUTERNES TO THEIR WINES, THEY HAVE POORLY SUCCEDED AND FINALY HAVE DISAPPEARED FROM THE MARKET FOR LACK IN DEMAND AND LACK OF QUALITIES OVERALL. LOOK AT ONE OF THESE LABELS, "SAUTERNE" IS WRITTEN WITHOUT AN "S".

THE CHATEAU D'YQUEM IS RATED AS A GRAND PREMIER CRU LIKE HAUT-BRION, THE LAFITE'S, MARGAUX AND PETRUS.
THEY ARE THE ONES TO BE REMEMBERED AS THE TOP WINES FROM FRANCE AND THE WORLD.

VINEYARD AREA: 90 HECTARES (225 ACRES)
AVERAGE PRODUCTION PER YEAR: 100 TONNEAUX.
                                 ONE TONNEAU EQUALS 225 LITERS.
TYPE OF VINES GROWN: TWO VINE GROWTHS ARE PLANTED AT THIS DOMAIN.:
1) THE SAUVIGNON: ONE QUART OF THE ACREAGE.

2) THE SEMILLON: THREE QUARTS OF THE ACREAGE.

THE FIRST IS THE MOST PRODUCTIVE IN ALCOHOL, AND GIVES TO THE WINE A VERY SPECIAL AROMA WHICH CHARACTERIZES THE BOUQUET OF ALL THE GREAT WHITE BORDEAUX.

THE SECOND IS BETTER KNOWN FOR ITS EXTREME FINENESS AND BRINGS TO THE WINE ITS BREED AND ITS LEGENDARY ELEGANCE.

NATURE OF THE SOIL: THE SOIL IS SILICEOUS, GRAVELLY AND SHAPED OF QUARTZ STONES WHICH GIVE A BRILLIANT APPEARANCE AND ARE SCATTERED ALL OVER THIS REGION.

SAUTERNES: CHATEAU RIEUSSEC (sweet white)

PREMIER GRAND CRU OF THE SAUTERNES

The vineyard of Château Rieussec is adjacent to the Château d'Yquem. Its wines are of a very high quality gold, luscious with a very delicate aroma.

The nature of the soil is gravelly, on slight slopes of the area of Sauternes;

The types of wine-growths are: Sauvignon, semillon and Muscadelle.

The acreage is planted over 112 acres.
The average yearly production is 2,000 gallons.

NOTE: In the Sauternes area, the wine-growers are entitled to call their ratings as PREMIER GRAND CRU, and then Deuxieme Cru.

CHATEAU PETRUS
DISTRICT OF POMEROL

CHATEAU PETRUS IS THE RENOWNED ESTATE OF THE DISTRICT OF POMEROL (....), ADJACENT ON THE WEST FROM THE SAINT-EMILION AREA. THE RED WINES PRODUCED AT PETRUS BECAME AS MUCH PRAISED AS THE GREAT MEDOC WINES. DUE TO THEIR GEORGOUS VINOSITY, THEIR VELVETY QUALITY AND THE FULL-BODIED STYLE, THEIR REACH ALMOST PERFECTION.

PERHAPS TO THE LACK OF TRANSPORTATION A COUPLE OF CENTURIES AGO AND THE SHORTAGE FOR PURCHASE, THE WINES FROM POMEROL WERE NOT CLASSIFIED IN 1855. HOWEVER, THEY ARE CLOSE TO THE CHARACTERS OF MEDOC WINES.

IT IS IN MY OPINION THAT CHATEAU PETRUS RANGES WITH THE TOP WINES OF BORDEAUX. I DID TASTE ONE DAY A PETRUS FROM THE 1964 VINTAGE AND IT WAS ABSOLUTLY SUBLIME.

OTHER INTERESTING FACTS:

THE POMEROL WINES ARE RECOMMENDED AS A MEDICINE WINE. THE SOIL OF THIS AREA NOURISHES THE VINESTOCK WITH A FERRUGINOUS ELEMENT.
THE REGION OF POMEROL PRODUCES ONLY RED WINES. THE NATURE OF THE SOIL IS GRAVELLY, SANDY AND FERUGINOUS.

THE AVERAGE PRODUCTION AT PETRUS IS AROUND 4,000 BOTTLES YEARLY.
NOWADAYS VERY HIGHLY IN DEMAND A BOTTLE OF PETRUS FETCHES ALMOST THE SAME PRICE THAN THE GREAT GROWTHS WINES WINES OF THE MEDOC.

THE POMEROL DISTRICT

The vines of Pomerol are LIMITED IN SURFACE BUT IMMENSE IN FAME.

The land situated on a plateau is shaped sometimes with a silicon soil or a gravelly and sandy soil. It is said that such a formation of soil, in general rules, gives rise to wines of great fineness. There are also trances of iron and clay. It has a beautiful country side shaped with hills and slopes.

This area is also known as "Le Libournais", derived from the City of Libourne, an important harbor, along the affluent of the Dordogne which flows into the Gironde River.

The vine growths are cultivated in such order of varieties and consist of; 17% of Cabernet Sauvignon

17% of Cabernet Franc
66% of Merlot

This is approximatly the blend used for Chateau Petrus. The varieties of vine growth used for the production at Chateau Lafite-Rothschild, located in the Medoc District is exactly the opposite blend:

66% Cabernet Sauvignon
17% Cabernet Franc
17% Merlot

Three different Appellations Controllees are given to the area of Pomerol. They are Pomerol AC
Lalande de Pomerol
Neac

The production of Pomerol is around 45,000 Hectoliters or 12,000 US Gallons. Lalande de Pomerol and Neac are the extension of the North-West of the vineyards of the Pomerol area. The type of wine produced there is the same without reaching completly the elegance and the harmonious nuances of the Wine of Pomerol.

If during your life time, should you have the opportunity to taste a Chateau Lafite, a Medoc wine and a Chateau Petrus from Pomerol, your palate and your sense of tasting, will give you an extraordinary level of higher education in the knowledge of fine wines.

Please note that the wines from Pomerol and the wines from St. Emilion have both a similarity, they are called masculin wines, while the wines from the Medoc are known as feminine. Both areas are producing a wine which is vigorous and fleshy. The wine of Pomerol however is copious, full of muscle and smooth at the same time. It is also more refined and more elegant than the wine of St. Emilion.

A fine example of a neat label, described as follow:

This wine comes from Bordeaux:
Top of the label says "Grand vin fin de Bordeaux"
                              (actually "grand Vin fin does not mean too much).
The vintage year is 1970. The logo is the copy right of the firm
The name "Chateau Lafleur-Gazin" is the commercial name coming either from former owners or name given to this vineyard.

The wine is from Pomerol.

It has the appellation Pomerol Controlée. (very important).

At the left it has the seal that the wine was bottled at the premises of the Château.

And last and finally the name of the Château's owner:

                              "Maurice Borderie"
                              Proprietor at Pomerol Gironde.
                              (name of the County)

CHATEAU CITRAN
CRU BOURGEOIS SUPERIEUR
WINE FROM THE MEDOC

Château Citran is an ancient Lordship manor, which was owned for 600 years to a family de Donnissan and their heirs. It was in 1832 that the large Domain was acquired by the family Clauzel, who kept it for one hundred years and set-up in 1905, "The Society Civile de Château Citran. (a Civil Status Company).

From the Château of the 13th century, there is only some moats left. The actual Château was built in the 18th century.

The Château Citran actually dominates a Domain of 500 hectates approximately, composed with pine forests, acacias and poplars.

The vineyard is divided in two territories:
The one which is the most extended is adjacent to the Château, is composed of pure gravels of the same nature than those of the area of Margaux.
The other one is located around the village of Avensan is of argillaceous and calcareous soil like the area of Moulis.

Château Citran formerly was one of the most important producer from the Medoc.
These wines have been particularly appreciated for years by Great Britain and the Scandinavian countries.
The production is 100 tonneaux (225 liters per tonneau.).

THE WINE DISTRICT OF SAINT-EMILION

MOST OF THE BEST VINEYARDS LAY AROUND THE TOWNSHIP OF SAINT-EMILION, BUT SEVEN ADJOINING COMMUNES ARE ALSO ENTITLED TO THE APPELLATION SAINT-EMILION. THE FINEST WINES ARE GROWN FROM THE STEEP, CHALKY SLOPES OF THE ESCARPTMENT ITSELF (VINS DES CÔTES) OR FROM THE HIGH, GRAVELLY PLATEAU BEHIND.

IT IS NOWADAYS STILL RECOGNIZED THAT THE CHÂTEAU CHEVAL BLANC AND THE CHATEAU AUSONE HOLD THE POSITION NUMBER ONE IN THE CLASSIFICATION OF THE "PREMIERS GRANDS CRUS", CLASS (A) OF THE SAINT-EMILION DISTRICT.

AS PER THE HEIRS OF CHEVAL BLANC THE VINEYARD OF OLD VINESTOCKS HAS NEVER BEEN GRAFTED WITH THE AMERICAN VARIETY (PART OF THE VINEYARD). THIS ALSO IS THE REASON FOR THE EXCEPTIONAL QUALITY OF THE WINE PRODUCED WHICH HAS A DELICATE VELVETY NATURE.

THE SAINT-EMILION 1970 VINTAGE OF CHÂTEAU BALESTARD LA TONNELLE HAS BEEN AWARDED THE GOLD MEDAL AT THE WINE FAIR OF BORDEAUX IN JUNE 1971.

SITUATION OF THE VINEYARD: LOCATED ON TOP OF THE SAINT-ÉMILION HILLS.
VARIETIES OF VINESTOCKS GROWN: CABERNET FRANC, CABERNET SAUVIGNON MERLOT AND MALBEC.
NATURE OF THE SOIL IS ARGILLACEOUS AND CHALKY.
THE PRODUCTION IS ONLY IN RED WINES.
THE ACREAGE IS 25 ACRES.
THE YEARLY AVERAGE PRODUCTION IS 6,500 GALLONS OR APPROXIMATLY 31,312 BOTTLES.

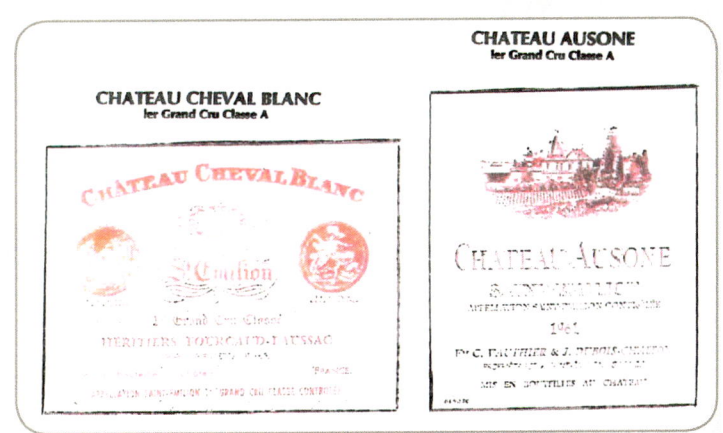

The wines of Saint-Emilion are called wines of the hills. Slightly more elevated than along the Gironde Estuary, the vineyards are also cultivated inland. They grow on a variety of soil and sub-soil from limestone to chalk to gravel and to ferruginous terrain.

Moreover the vineyards exposed to the wind coming from the sea and facing southwest, have more heat in the afternoon from the sun while the other vineyards lying on the flat of the plateau take the baking heat of the full sun.

It is therefore recognised that the red wines of Saint-Emilion with its neighbor from Pomerol produce a fuller-bodied wine than the wines from the Medoc or the Graves areas. They are however not as full-bodied as the red Burgundies and much less robust than the red wines from the Rhône Valley.

The vine-growths species grown in Saint-Emilion are: Cabernet Franc, Cabernet Sauvignon, Merlot and Malbec.
The district produces only red wines.

The properties of Château Cheval Blanc and of Château Ausone still hold today the number one position in the classification of the Premier Grand Crû classé of the Saint-Emilion district.

Another interesting fact about Cheval Blanc, according to the heirs of the property is that in one part of the vineyard the old French vines have never been grafted with the American support-Graft done after the philoxera invasion. This is to be the reason for the exceptional quality of the wine produced which has a delicate velvety nature.

The township of Saint-Emilion located on top of a hill is a picturesque medieval village with a lot of history.

The Sain-Emilion wines show in general the classic qualities of Bordeaux wines, despite the fact that they tend to mature more quickly than the wines of the Medoc.

SECTION C

The Wines of Burgundy

BURGUNDY

MAP OF THE DISTRICT OF BURGUNDY

CHABLIS DISTRICT
ONLY WHITE WINES

CÔTE DE NUITS DISTRICT
MOSTLY RED WINES

CÔTE DE BEAUNE DISTRICT
RED AND WHITE PRODUCTION
BEAUNE
POMMARD
VOLNAY
MEURSAULT, CHASSAGNE
AND PULIGNY-MONTRACHET

MÂCONNAIS DISTRICT
AREA OF MACON AND
POUILLY-FUISSE

THE BEAUJOLAIS DISTRICT

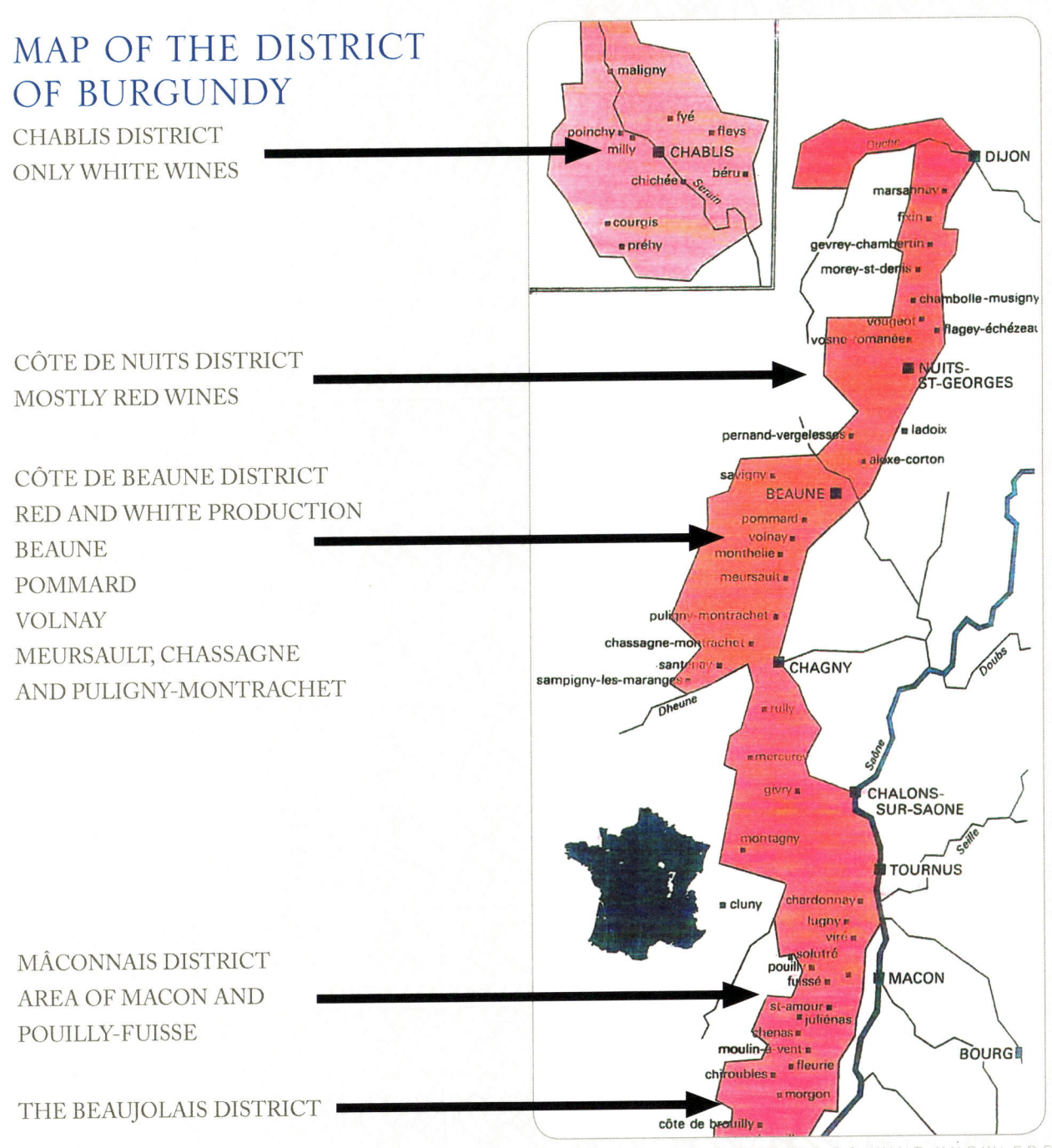

The region of Burgundy is called the "CÔTE D'OR" or translated from the French "Golden Slope". This name had been given for the appearances of the hillside vineyards when they have taken their foliage of the fall.

The most unusual quality of the red and white wines of this region lies in its spirituosity. Its wines are full and robust with an alcohol content of 12% proof, sometimes more.

They also have a sumptuous robe (or gown) and after a few years of aging, develop a whole range of the red color for the red wines and a delicate golden color for the white wines.

The two major wine producing areas in Burgundy are:

1)   THE CÔTE DE NUITS
      Between Dijon and Nuits St. Georges
      See map ...page

2)   THE CÔTE DE BEAUNE
      Between Beaune and Chalons-sur-Saône
      See map ...page

Three more districts are included in the Burgundy region, further South.
They are: THE CÔTE CHALONNAISE, THE MÂCONNAIS AND THE BEAUJOLAIS.
See map ... pages

The CÔTE DE NUITS has only, around 1500 hectares of vineyards, while the CÔTE DE BEAUNE contains 3000 hectares. The later produces more red wines than white wines, but is more famous for its outstanding white wines.

HISTORY ABOUT CHAMBERTIN:

In the 13th century, a winegrower named Bertin had the idea to break new ground in the adjacent field and planted a vineyard. It was called the "CHAMP DE BERTIN." for a long time. It became legally known as the "CHAMBERTIN. (field of BERTIN).

Five centuries later, CHAMBERTIN became the favorite wine of Napoléon.

THE CÔTE D'OR

A - THE CÔTE DE NUITS

B - THE CÔTE DE BEAUNE

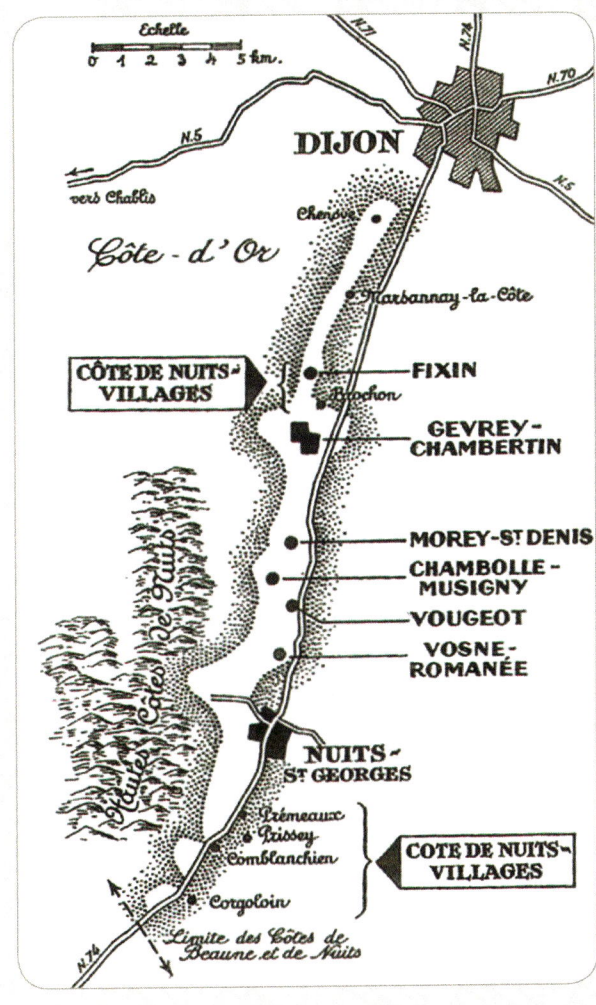

The most unusual quality of the red wine of the Côte d'Or lies in their spirituosity (full and robust- alcohol 12.5% +) their firmness and the somptuous "gown" which according to aging unfolds their pomp in all the range of the red color: cherry, rubis, garnet, bright red and purple red.

All of these conditions are soothing and become shades of tiles, shades of topaz, shade of musk when the aging process sets to work.

The third district is the Chalonnais or Côte Chalonnaise

Geographicaly the Côte de Beaune continues its way South toward the Valley of the Saône-et-Loire with the three growths of Sampigny, Cheilly and Dezize-les Maranges. A little further down, the same relief remains and the vineyards are located on a chain of hills with the villages of Rully, Mercurey, Givry and Montagny, all cousins of the wines of the Gold Coast which however don't have the same famous qualities.

Most of these hills through Burgundy are facing east and southeast over only 40 miles from Dijon to Chagny and form the ultimate border of the chain of mountains called the Massif Central, a well known region of the primary age and dotted with a lot of health resorts.

The dazzling range of vinegrowthes in the Côte d'Or answer to the complicated puzzle of the differents soils.

The wine pathes are not necessarily the delimitations of the vineyards itself but the shades of the soil which have imposed its layout to the whimsical network of the pathes and cartways.

THE CÔTE CHALONNAISE

The wines issued from this area are less delicate. They don't have the tenderness of their neighbors. However they possess an excellent perfume.

Major wines produced here are: the "MERCUREY", the "RULLY" and the "GIVRY" for the red.
For the white: "RULLY", MONTAGNY" AND "GIVRY".

CLASSIFICATION OF THE RED WINES FROM THE CÔTE DE NUITS

Village Name	Grands Crus	Premiers Crus
Fixin		Clos de la Perrière Clos du Chapitre Les Hervelets Les Arvelets
Gevrey-Chambertin	Chambertin Chambertin Clos de Bèze Latricières-Chambertin Mazys-Chambertin Ruchottes-Chambertin Chapelle-Chambertin Charmes-Chambertin Griotte-Chambertin	Clos Saint-Jacques Varoilles Les Cazetiers Combe au Moine
Morey-Saint-Denis	Clos de Tart Clos Saint-Denis Clos de la Roche Monnes Mares (part)	Clos des Lambrays Clos Bussière
Chambolle-Musigny	Musigny Bonnes Mares (part)	Les Amoureuses Les Charmes
Vougeot	Clos de Vougeot	
Flagey-Echézeaux	Grands Echézeaux Echézeaux	
Vosne-Romanée	Romanée-Conti	La Grande Rue
	La Romanée La Tâche Richebourg Romanée Saint-Vivant	Les Gaudichots Les Beaumonts Les Malconsorts Les Suchots Aux Brulées Clos de Réas
Nuits-Saint-Georges (including the adjacent village of Premeaux)		Les Saint-Georges

CÔTE DE NUITS

1 - MAP OF THE AREA OF GEVREY CHAMBERTIN

2 - LABEL OF A GEVREY CHAMBERTIN WINE

The area of Gevrey Chambertin is spread over 300 Hectares of vineyards which are divided as follows:

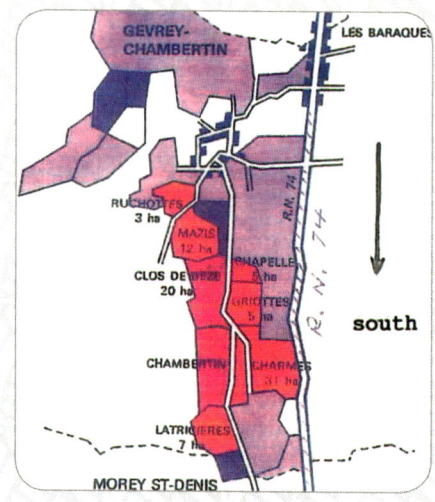

1 - The district of GEVREY CHAMBERTIN (in gray color)

2 - The area of the first grows (in dark gray)

3 - The area of the top vineyards (in red color)

4 - The area of the vineyards of "LE CHAMBERTIN" AND THE ADJACENT "CLOS DE BEZE" (in dark red color)

COMMUNE OF VOSNE-ROMANÉE

VOSNE-ROMANÉE PRODUCES WINES OF VERY HIGH STANDARDS AS IN THE ESTATE OF ROMANÉE-CONTI. THE DOMAIN OF ROMANÉE-CONTI OWNS THE PARCEL OF LA TÂCHE, RICHEBOURG, ÉCHÉZEAUX, GRAND-ÉCHÉZEAUX AND A PART OF LE MONTRACHET VINEYARDS. IT IS SAID THAT THIS PARTICULIAR AREA HAD BEEN SPARED FROM THE DEVASTATION OF THE "PHYLLOXERA" AND THE "OIDIUM" DUE TO THE HIILS SURROUNDING THESE PARCELS. THEREFORE NO VINESTOCKS NEEDED TO BE GRAFTED.

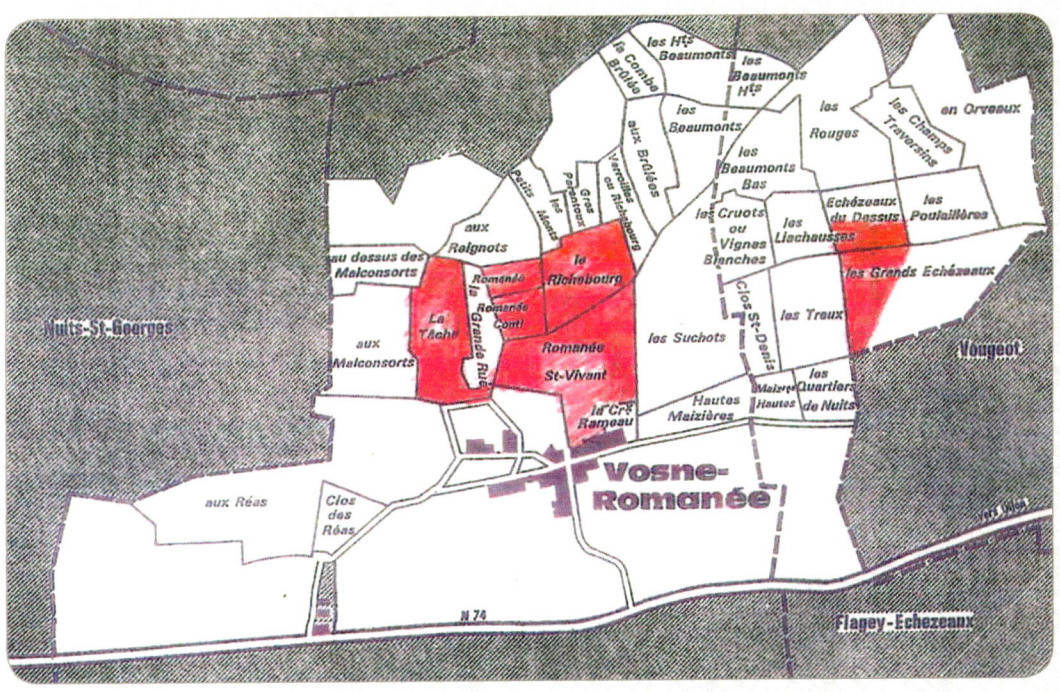

MAP OF THE VILLAGE OF VOSNE-ROMANEE AND ITS SPLENDID SURROUNDING OF GREAT GROWTHS.

THE VINEYARDS OF THE ROMANÉE-CONTI ESTATE ARE IN RED COLOR.

THE CÔTE D'OR

B - THE CÔTE DE BEAUNE

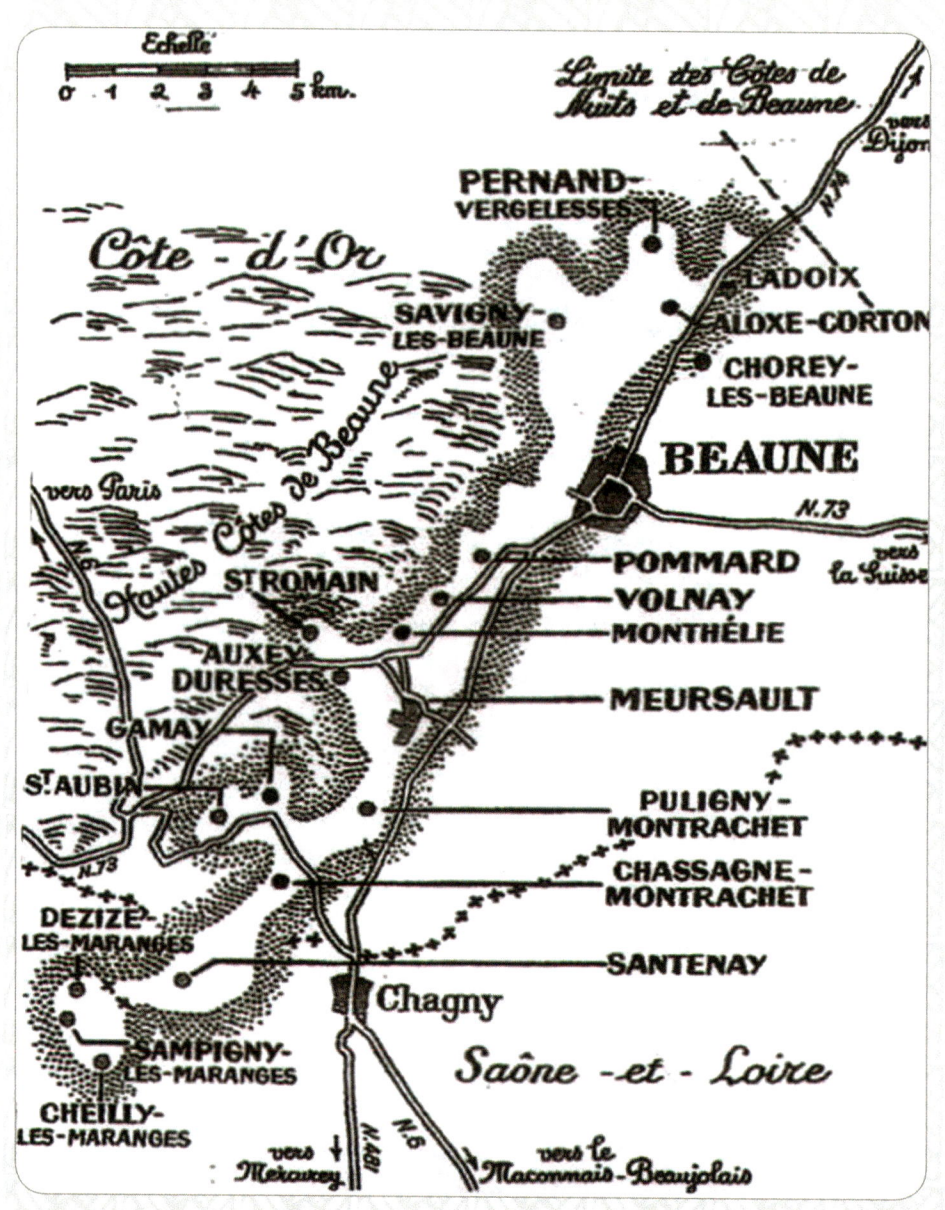

ASSORTED LABELS OF THE MAJOR WHITE WINES
FROM THE CÔTE DE BEAUNE

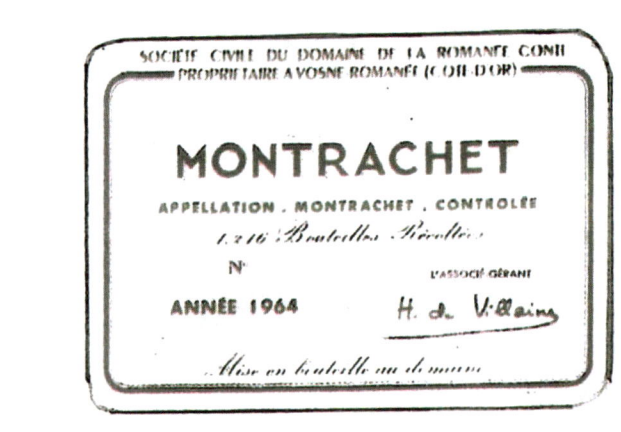

CLASSIFICATION OF THE WHITE WINES FROM THE CÔTE DE BEAUNE

Village	Grand Cru	Premier Cru
Aloxe Corton	Corton-Charlemagne Charlemagne	
Beaune		Les Clos des Mouches
Meursault		Charmes La Goutte d'Or Les Genevrières Les Perrières Blagny Poruzot Santenots
Puligny-Montrachet	Montrachet (part) Batard-Montrachet (part) Chevalier-Montrachet Bienvenue-Batard-Montrachet	Les Combettes Les Caillerets Les Chalumeaux Le Champ Canet Les Pucelles
		Clos des Ducs Les Fremiers Le Clos des Chênes Santenots
Monthelie		Les Champs Fuillots
Auxey-Duresses		Les Duresses Clos du Val
Chassagne-Montrachet		Clos de la Boudriotte Clos St. Jean Les Caillerets La Maltroie Morgeot
Santenay		Clos Tavannes Gravières

THE CÔTE DE BEAUNE

THIS DISTRICT PRODUCES WINES WHICH ARE NEITHER TENDER NOR VERY DRY, LESS POWERFUL AND LESS MASCULIN. THEIR REACH THEIR PEAK FASTER THAN THE ONES FROM THE CÔTE DE NUITS.

THE CÔTE DE BEAUNE AS IT WAS SAID BEFORE, IS ALSO THE AREA OF THE MOST FAMOUS WHITE WINES FROM BURGUNDY. See page ...

THE WINE NAMES TO BE RETAINED ARE:
FOR THE WHITE
THE WHOLE FAMILY OF MONTRACHET, THE MEURSAULT, THE CORTON CHARLEMAGNE, BATARD-MONTRACHET, CHEVALIER-MONTRACHET AND THE BIENVENUE-BATARD-MONTRACHET.

FOR THE RED:
ALOXE CORTON, BEAUNE, POMMARD, VOLNAY, AUXEY-DURESSES, SAVIGNY-LES-BEAUNE.

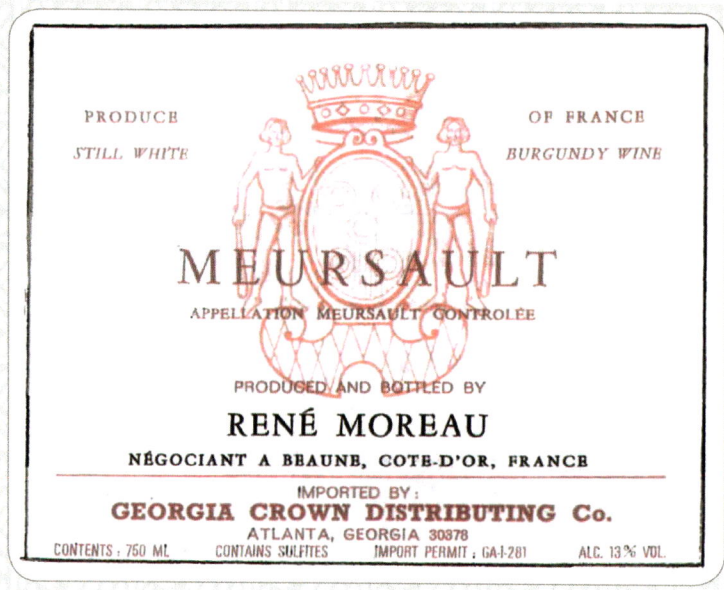

CLASSIFICATION OF THE RED WINES
FROM THE CÔTE DE BEAUNE

Name of Village	Grand Cru	Premiers Crus
Pernand-Vergelesses		Ile-des-Vergelesses
Aloxe-Corton	Le Corton	Corton Bressandes Corton Clos du Roi Corton Marechaudes Corton Renarde Corton les Meix
Savigny-les-Beaune		La Dominode Les Vergelesses Les Marconnets Les Jarrons Les Lavières
Beaune		Les Fèves Les Grèves Les Marconnets Les Bressandes Les Clos des Mouches Les Cent Vignes Clos du Roi Les Avaux

Pommard		Les Clos Blanc Les Epenots Les Rugiens La Platière Les Pezerolles Les Chaponnières
Volnay		Les Caillerets Les Champans
		Clos des Ducs Les Fremiers Le Clos de Chênes Santenots
Monthelie		Les Champs Fuillots
Auxey-Duresses		Les Duresses Clos du Val
Chassagne-Montrachet		Clos de la Boudriotte Clos St. Jean Les Caillerets La Maltroie Morgeot
Santenay		Clos Tavannes Gravières

LABEL OF THE HOSPICES DE BEAUNE

PRODUCT OF FRANCE
TABLE WINE
CONTENTS 3|4 QUART

HOSPICES DE BEAUNE

1961

BOUTEILLE № 000735

Grand Vin
des
Hospices de Beaune

Pommard

Cuvée Billardet

APPELLATION POMMARD CONTROLÉE

ESPECIALLY SELECTED BY FRANK SCHOONMAKER
AND PURCHASED AT THE HOSPICES AUCTION

AUCTION NOVEMBER 1961

HISTORY OF THE HOSPICES DE BEAUNE PARTICULIAR APPELLATION

THE HOSPICES DE BEAUNE was built to become a Charity Hospital for the sick and poor people of the region.

It was founded in 1443 by a Tax Collector, named Nicolas Rolin. He also was proprietor of 60 Hectares of vineyards around the town of Beaune, the main City at that time in Burgundy.

During the Revolution period of 1789, most of the large domains were confiscated by the State, but The Hospices de Beaune was spared, being part of a Lay Organization.

THE HOSPICES DE BEAUNE became famous every year with the celebration of the auction of the wines, not only from the production of the Hospices but from a large number of Wine-grower of the region giving away some of their wines to the auction.

This celebration is still vibrant nowadays. The wines are sent to the Hospices in barrels and are bottled and labeled at the Hospices. A private and special label is used to honor the bottles with the name of the donnor. Therefore all wines are sold under the original donor, and not the name of the vineyard where the wines are issued from.

These sales are creating recognition and a good advertisement for the Wine-growers of this Burgundy region.
At the conclusion of the auction, a dinner is held in the cellars of the Hospices during three days. It is called the dinners of the "THREE GLORIEUSES".

Here is an example on how these wines from Burgundy are given to the Hospices for auction:

BEAUNE: NICOLAS ROLIN gave 40 pièces

(a pièce is equivalent to a barrel of 224 liters or 24 cases of 12 bottles).

CORTON: DOCTEUR PESTE gave 33 pieces

VOLNAY: GENERAL MUTEAU gave 33 pièces

CORTON CHARLEMAGNE: FRANCOIS DE SALINS - 4 pièces

MEURSAULT-GENEVRIERES: PHILIPPE LE BON - 11 pièces

THE BEAUJOLAIS DISTRICT: the two most trusted shippers to the United States.

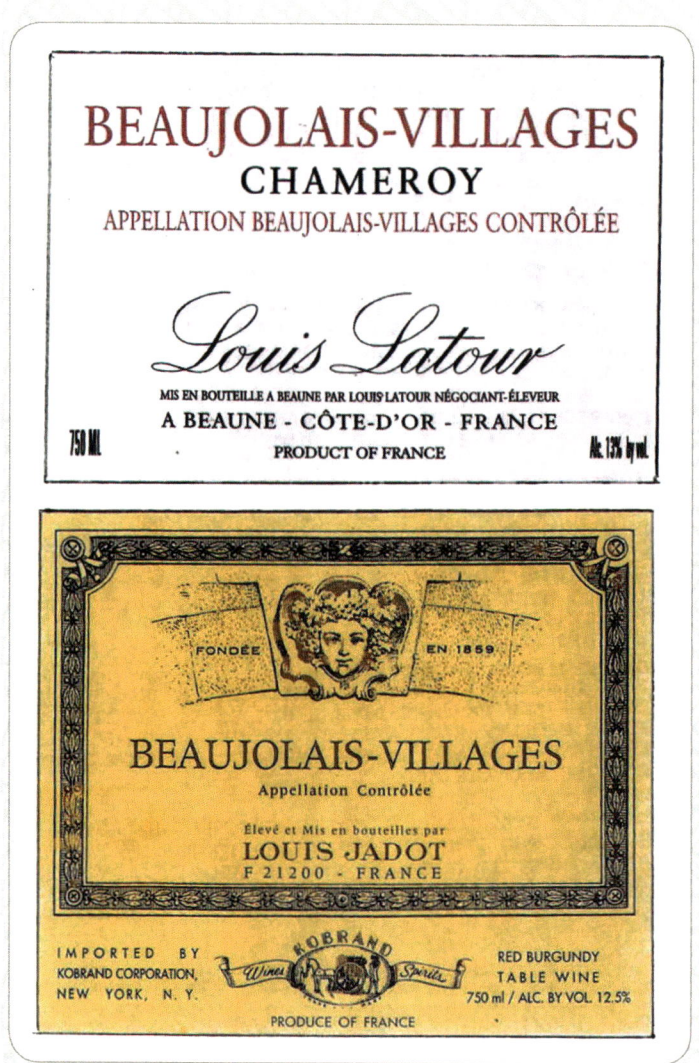

WINES FROM THE BEAUJOLAIS DISTRICT

THE BEAUJOLAIS-VILLAGES AREA CONSISTS OF 35 COMMUNES AND IS LOCATED IN THE NORTHERN PART OF THE COUNTY OF THE RHÔNE, SOME FIFTY MILES AWAY FROM THE CITY OF LYON. LYON IS THE SECOND LARGEST AGGLOMERATION IN FRANCE.

THE WINE AREA IS A KIND OF SQUEEZED-IN HILLY REGION BETWEEN THE AREA OF MÂCÒN IN THE NORTH AND THE AREA OF THE RHÔNE VALLEY TOWARD THE SOUTH.

THE APPELLATION "BEAUJOLAIS-VILLAGES" WAS GIVEN AND FOLLOWS THE APPELLATION OF THE GREAT GROWTHS OF THE BEAUJOLAIS WINES. (page 162)

ALL BEAUJOLAIS WINES ARE ISSUED FROM THE GAMAY VARIETAL. THE NAME GAMAY HAS BORROWED ITS NAME FROM A HAMLET LOCATED IN THE VICINITY OF THE VILLAGE OF PULIGNY-MONTRACHET, FURTHER NORTH, AS PER THE TEXTS OF THE FOURTEEN CENTURY.

THE GAMAY VARIETAL IS ALSO CALLED GAMAY NOIR (DARK RED SKINS) AND GAMAY "À JUS BLANC" (WHITE GRAPE JUICE).

IT IS SAID THAT THE WINEGROWERS OF THE MÂCON AREA (CALLED LE MÂCONNAIS) AND THE ONES IN BURGUNDY ARE A LITTLE JEALOUS OF THIS VARIETAL, BECAUSE IT IS PLANTED IN THE CLAY-LIMESTONE OF BURGUNDY, IT PRODUCES ONLY ORDINARY WINES.
AGAIN THE SOIL IS THE BIG FACTOR IN THE BEAUJOLAIS AREA. IT CONSISTS OF GRANITE, SHIST AND SLATE. THE AVERAGE PRODUCTION OF THE BEAUJOLAIS-VILLAGES AREA IS 4,200,000 GALLONS. VERY LITTLE BEAUJOLAIS BLANC (WHITE) AND ROSÉ IS PRODUCED IN THIS AREA.

IN GENERAL THE WINES OF BEAUJOLAIS ARE DELICATE QUICK TO MATURE AND LIGHT, BUT NOT AS RICH IN SCENT AS THE GREAT WINES FROM THE BURGUNDY "COTE D'OR".
BEAUJOLAIS WINES ARE RECOGNIZED THROUGHOUT FRANCE AND THE WORLD. HOWEVER, MOST OF THE FRENCH PEOPLE DO NOT KNOW THE GREAT GROTHS AND OUTSTANDING WINES THEMSELVES, FROM OTHER AREAS IN FRANCE, BEAUJOLAIS WINES ARE LIKE A BIG RIVER FOR THIRSTY DRINKERS AND ARE SERVED IN DECANTERS (CARAFE) AT ALL THE POPULAR RESTAURANTS IN FRANCE. THE GRAND CRUS ARE MOSTLY RESERVED FOR EXPENSIVE PLACES AND HOME, FOR THOSE WHO ARE ABLE TO AFFORD THEM.

THE PRODUCTION OF BEAUJOLAIS WINES VARIES AND IS AROUND 900,000 HECTOLITERS. THE WINE OF BEAUJOLAIS IS ONE OF THE BEST KNOWN OF ALL RED WINES. IT OUTSELLS ANY FRENCH WINES FROM ANY DISTRICTS IN THE UNITED STATES.

BEAUJOLAIS / BURGUNDY

The Beaujolais wines give us echoes or resonances which arouse only reassuring thoughts. Beaujolais is made from the Gamay vinestock and reflects a perfect marriage with its terroir which is composed of clay and decomposed granite.

This district produces seven million cases of wine per year. A great amount, however is never bottled for the reason that the wine is served directly from small barrels to the large cities bars and restaurants like Lyon and Paris.

The Beaujolais grape fermentation is limited to three days, so that a minimum of tanin is imparted to the grape-juice.
Beaujolais wine needs to be consumed when young, within one to two years, in order to maintain its freshness and fruitiness.

One more matter to remember is when you taste a Beaujolais, look for a fruity and dry red wine rather than a wine with deep flavor and complexity which are the characteristics of good Bordeaux wine.
Beaujolais wines also taste better when served slightly chilled or at a cellar temperature of 50°F.

It became a popular affair in recent years to taste the Beaujolais of the year (or Beaujolais Nouveau) in all restaurants in France by mid-November. The trent, even went overseas to America and a large supply of Beaujolais-Nouveau can be seen displayed in supermarkets for shoppers to complement their Thanksgiving Dinners. Unfortunately, lighter wines don't always travel well and have a shorter lifespan while they are on the shelves. It has therefore been authorized to add one degree of pure alcohol per bottle for the exportation. This authorization decree is also valid for the exportation of French wines.

The area of Beaujolais can be divided into three parts. The production is entitled to the appellations Beaujolais, Beaujolais-Villages and Beaujolais Grands Crus.
The southern portion produces lighter wines and are entitled simply as Beaujolais. About twenty-five percent of all Beaujolais wines are entitled as Beaujolais-Villages.

The finest and most appraised Beaujolais Grand Cru comes from ten villages located in the northern part of the district.
They are listed by alphabetic order on page ...

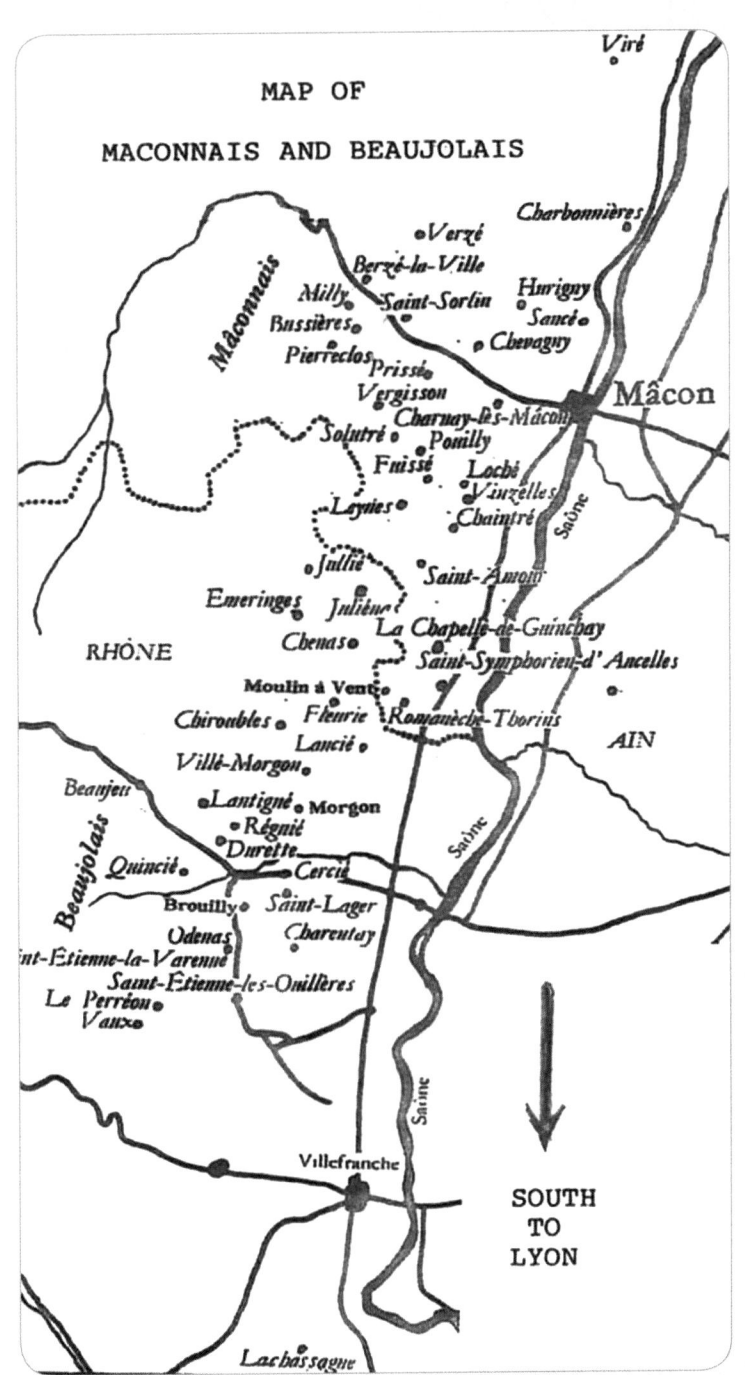

MAP OF

MACONNAIS AND BEAUJOLAIS

LISTING OF THE GRANDS CRUS OF BEAUJOLAIS
THEIR CHARACTERISTICS

BROUILLY -   has a scent of prune and peony

CHÉNAS -   almond, violet (also sold legally as Moulin à Vent)

CHIROUBLÉS -   red currant, prune

FLEURIE -   iris, violet, amber, musk, réséda

JULIÈNAS -   peach, raspberry

MORGON -   apricot, red currant, kirsch

MOULIN A VENT -   prune, violet, musk

CÔTE-de-BROUILLY -   scent of raspberry, prune and peony

SAINT-AMOUR -   peach, réséda

RÉGNIÉ -   black currant, cherries, peony

(this later appellation was given in the 1980s)

BEAUJOLAIS / BURGUNDY

The slopes and hills of the Beaujolais wine district form the most picturesque vineyards in France. Also mentioning is the famous tourist attraction of the Abbaye of Cluny, a must-see visit. Part of this monastery is the large church built during the Roman times, it is a marvel of architecture. Many other Roman edifices and churches can still be seen in that region, like in Autun, Charlieu and Paray-le-Monial.

Where does the amazing success of the Beaujolais wine comes from? It has by no means like other famous wines, any outstanding characteristics. To the contrary of a great Medoc wine for example the Beaujolais wine does not ask any questions, it is direct frank, jovial and with no problems.

In order to describe the Beaujolais wine, one must define its charm. To explain its success is to accept, to bet, to comment upon the harmony or to discover the mystery of the emotion, it is like being willing to estimate the pleasure.

The word BEAUJOLAIS takes its name from the village of Beaujeu which used to be a Barony is a Noble'man domain, created a thousand years ago.

Nowadays, the center of the Beaujolais wine trade is Villefranche, a town forty miles from the city of Lyon.

ABBAYE OF CLUNY, BURGUNDY
(Saône et Loire)

Pure Roman architecture

LABELS OF THE CHABLIS GRAND CRU

THE WINES FROM THE CHABLIS DISTRICT

The region of Chablis, located seventy miles northwest of Dijon is properly a part of Burgundy. The name Chablis is known and use all over the world, but true wine produced from the Pinot Chardonnay vinestock grows in a chalky soil like in the Champagne area. Most of the vineyards are located on the banks of the Yonne river, which flows northward toward the Seine River passing through Paris while the rest of the vineyards lie along the Saône River which flows south to the Rhône Valley.

The northerly vineyards are subject to a particular climatic condition which results in an average year with rich-bodied flavor and refreshing wines and with a touch of acidity. occasionally years with too warm summers do not produce a typical Chablis and tend to be a little heavy and flabby in character. there is also the appellation "Petit-Chablis" grown from sites farthest from the village of Chablis which produces fairly good wines. These wines however, need to be consumed young and will decline a after three years of age.

A more important aspect of the geological soil in chablis is found in the chalky soil which also contains flint. Flint imbedded in chalk in some parcels will produce a clean and dry taste of Chablis wine. It is sometimes referred as a flinty wine.

The best wines of Chablis are grown in semi-circle of hills facing south where the fruit can bask in the sun. The locations of the Grands Crus or great growths vineyards are as follows:

Blanchots, Les Preuses, Bougros, Les Clos,
Grenouilles, Valmur, Vaudesir, La Moutonne.

These eight Grands Crus represent 5% of the total production. These Chablis wines will generally have more depth of character and a very subtle taste of dryness. Ninety percent of the product in Chablis represent the plain Chablis, the Chablis Premiers Crus and together with the Grands Crus are recognized as equal to their southern Burgundy Chardonnay.

The word Chablis is one of the most duplicated in the world and winegrowers of Chablis outside France produce a wine completely different than the French Chablis.

LISTING OF THE BETTER WELL-KNOWN WINEGROWERS AND SHIPPERS.

BACHELET-RAMONET

BIZE

BONNEAU DU MARTRAY

CHANDON DE BRAILLES

CHEVALIER

CHOPIN-GROFFIER

DOMAINE DE LA ROMANEE CONTI
(mostly exclusive producer of the inimitable wines of 'LA TACHE", "LA ROMANEE" "ROMANEE CONTI", "MUSIGNY" AND "LA ROMANEE SAINT-VIVANT"

DOMAINE RAMONET

DOMAINE ROULOT

JOSEPH DROUHIN

FAIVELEY

GRIVOT

LOUIS LATOUR

LOUIS JADOT

COMTE LAFON

LA GUICHE (MONTRACHET)

LABOURE-ROI

LAFARGE

LEROY

LUPE-CHOLET

DUC DE MAGENTA

MANCIAT-PONCET

MEO-CAMUZET

MOILLARD

MOREAU

MOROT

MUGNERET

PAVELOT

PRUNIER

JOSEPH ROTY

ROUNIER

RAPET

REMOISSENET

ROBERT VOCORET

VOARICK

SECTION D

The Wines of
Champagne

CHAMPAGNE

THREE MAJOR SITES DIVIDE THE CHAMPAGNE AREA

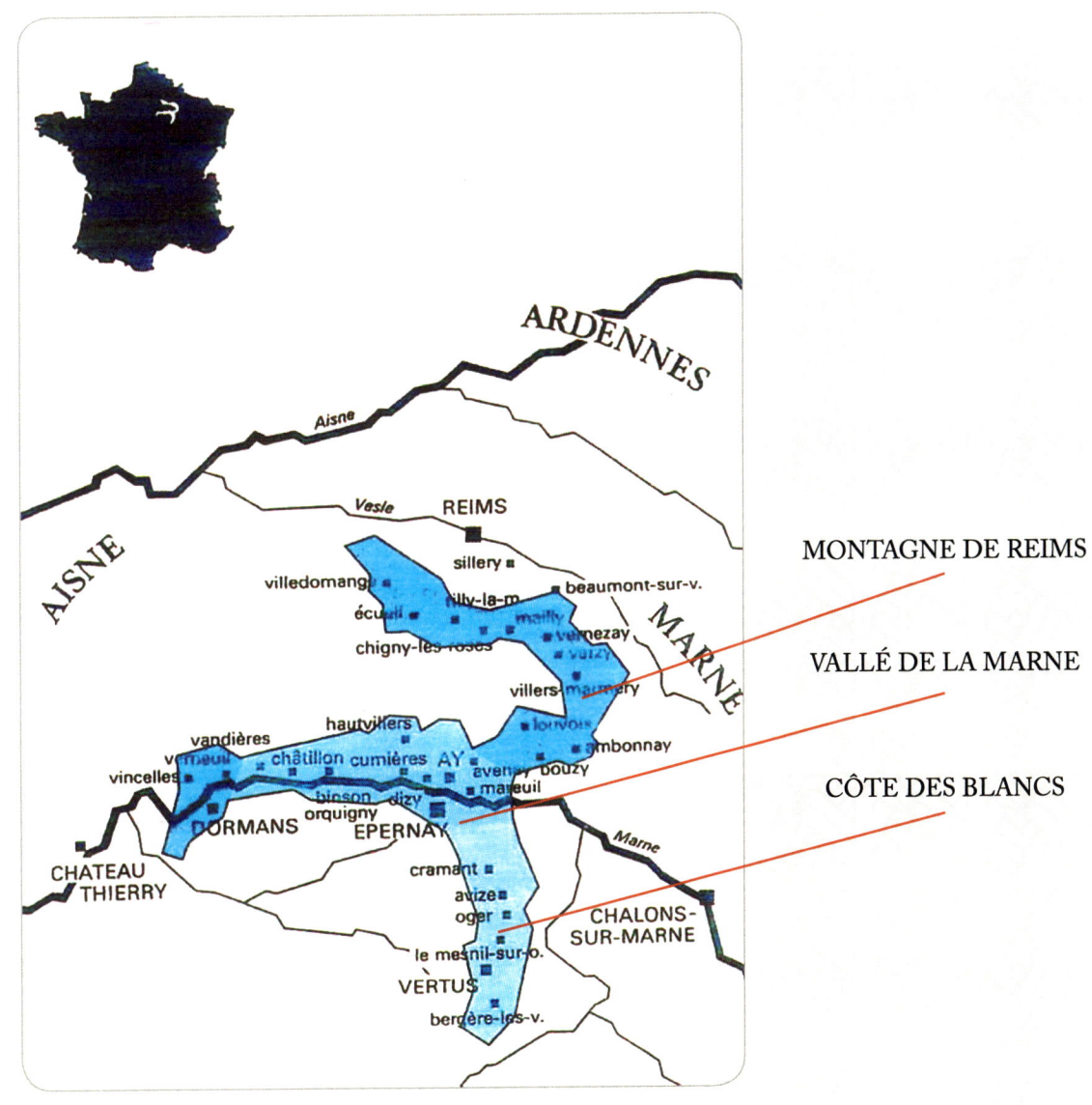

MONTAGNE DE REIMS

VALLÉ DE LA MARNE

CÔTE DES BLANCS

LABEL OF CHAMPAGNE NICOLAS FEUILLATTE

BRUT - ROSÉ

Champagne has launched ships, blessed weddings, christened newborn babies, and showered down on graduates. Thus we can say that Champagne has long been the centerpiece of celebration. The toast that has come to be associated with happy times was discovered by a French monk named Dom Perignon in 1688. This pious Benedictine monk was the master cellarman of the Abbey of Hautvilliers. He is the one who succeeded in domesticating the wine foam to which the Champagne is congenially predisposed. The success of the wine of Champagne proceeds from the spontaneous adhesion of men to the exterior manifestations of this exuberant wine.

The wine of Champagne has been created for the delight because it personifies it—by the explosion of its cork, by the unruliness of its foam, and by the plume of its fireworks of bubbles.

All this exuberance was discovered when carbon dioxide, the natural gas formed by fermentation, became trapped in a bottle the monk that had begun to ferment a second time. From there on, the tradition was born. The effervescent wine from the Champagne area in France was eventually exported to the world and, in particular, to the United States of America where a legend says that George Washington drank one of the supplies at a Senate dinner in 1790.

After World War II, exports of Champagne skyrocketed to the States as Americans enjoyed this light effervescent wine they have seen propped in the movies, among them *Bonnie and Clyde*, featuring Dom Perignon Champagne. It is even rumored that Marilyn Monroe once bathed in three hundred bottles of Champagne.

Cheers! This coming New Year's Eve, when you will toast with real French Champagne, you will be part of a three-hundred-year-old tradition.

HISTORY AND GEOGRAPHY

At the time of the Roman conquest, vines were already being cultivated in the valley of the Marne. In A.D. 92, Emperor Domitian ordered all vines in Gaul destroyed, especially those in Champagne, so that the wines of Champagne would not become a serious rival to the wines of Italy. Two centuries later, Emperor Probus abolished this strict decree and, according to legend, the people of Champagne then built the triumphal arch of the Porte Mars at Reims to honor him; however, in those days and in succeeding centuries, the wines of Champagne were still wines, and it wasn't until the latter part of the seventeenth century when the pious Benedictine monk, Dom Perignon, who was then the head cellarer of the Abbey of Hautvillers near Epernay, first put bubbles in Champagne and gave us Champagne as we know it today. Dom Perignon was also the first to use the bark of the cork tree as a stopper, replacing the bits of tow soaked in oil, thereby retaining the sparkle for a much longer period. He also observed that wines from different vineyards differed as to dryness, fullness of body, and finesse. Consequently, he introduced the blending of wines from different vineyards in order to produce a more balanced and uniform wine. This learned monk quite definitely did more for Champagne than any man before him.

By French law, Champagne is defined as a sparkling white wine produced by a secondary fermentation in the bottle and produced solely from grapes grown in a delimited geographical area which is roughly equivalent to the old Duchy of Champagne. The Champagne region, which is the most northerly wine-producing area of France, lies about seventy miles east of Paris, mainly in the Department of the Marne. To the east is Alsace, and to the south is Burgundy, with the Marne River forming an important line of division. North of the Marne only black grapes are grown around the towns of Ay and Hautvillers and in the Montagne de Reims section. South of the Marne lies the Côte des Blancs where white grapes are grown around the towns of Cramant, Avize, Le Mesnit, and Vertus. Pinot Chardonnay and Pinot Noir are the two grape varieties used in Champagne, but the chalky soil gives the grapes a special quality, so that the wine made from the same Pinot grape used in Burgundy is quite different.

THE CHAMPAGNE VINTAGE

Since Champagne is a blend of wines made from grapes grown in a number of different vineyards, no vineyard name appears on the label making the shipper's name all-important. While each important shipper owns vineyards in the various districts, his own vineyards do not produce enough grapes; therefore, he buys additional quantities from the smaller vineyard owners.

Vintage operations usually begin around the end of September when a veritable army of pickers harvests the grapes throughout the region. The picking of the grapes is carried on under strict supervision in order to make certain that only sound and fully-ripened grapes are harvested. The pickers place the grapes in baskets called *paniers* carried on their backs. When the paniers are full, they are taken to the side of the road where experienced sorters cull out any green, overripe, or defective grapes. This selection process is called *épluchage* and is only practiced by the great firms in Champagne who exercise this special care to make certain that they use only sound and fully-ripened grapes. This process applies not only to their own vineyards, but particularly to the additional grapes they buy from the small vineyard owners. Thus, right at the very beginning of the process, there is room for considerable differences in quality. By law, all wine produced from grapes grown in the Champagne region may be called Champagne, but quite obviously, wine produced from sound, fully-ripened grapes is of a considerably higher quality.

PRESSING THE GRAPES

The grapes are brought to the pressing house in old-fashioned horse carts and then, after each basket has been marked and weighed to determine the exact quantity being pressed, the grapes are loaded onto the large hydraulic presses. One loading is called a *marc*, totaling four tons, and each marc produces about 572 gallons of juice, filling thirteen casks of forty-four gallons each. Four pressings are made from each marc; the cuvée, the première taille, the deuxième taille, and the rebêche. Of the thirteen casks of juice produced from each marc, the first ten constitute the cuvée and the balance of three casks constitutes the première and deuxième taille. The remainder of the marc is then removed to a smaller press to produce the rebêche. Only the casks containing the cuvée, the première taille, and the deuxième taille can be called Champagne while the rebêche is used to make vin-de-table which is not entitled to any district designation.

The great Champagne firms, who are so prideful of the quality of their wines, use only the cuvée and première taille pressings, selling off as bulk wine the deuxième taille and the rebêche. Here again, at this stage of production, there are understandable reasons for the difference in quality and price of various brands of Champagne. Although the wine produced from the deuxième taille is entitled to the designation Champagne and also the vintage year designation, it is not equal in quality to that from the first two pressings. In the third pressing, the pips and stalks get crushed in the process; therefore, the juice cannot be the pure juice of the grape. Quite obviously, it is more expensive to produce Champagne from only the first two pressings.

Both black and white grapes are grown in Champagne, but about two-thirds of the grapes are of the Pinot Noir variety; however, Champagne is nevertheless a white wine because the fruit of both Pinot Noir and Pinot Chardonnay grapes is white with the skin containing all the coloring matter. The juice is run off immediately, so that during pressing, the skins are not permitted to give their color to the wine. As the juice runs out through the bottom of the press, it is gathered in a cistern and is then transferred into small casks holding about forty-four gallons where the must ferments into wine.

At this stage of production, there has been no blending and each cask is carefully marked with the name of the vineyard where the grapes were grown. The casks are not completely filled and the bung is left open so that the carbon dioxide created during fermentation may escape. After the first violent fermentation, the wine becomes quiet and the bung is driven home so that the wine rests quietly throughout the winter months. Normally, fermentation should continue until all the sugar is fermented out, but in Champagne, the cold weather arrests the fermentation prematurely, leaving some of the sugar unfermented which will later produce the second fermentation—the secret of Champagne.

BLENDING THE WINES

In the spring, before the fermentation starts anew, the head cellar-man and the heads of the firm taste the wines and decide what proportion of different wines will go into the cuvée or blend. This is probably the most important and exacting task in the production of Champagne. Years of experience are necessary in order to judge how the new wine, barely six months old and not completely fermented, will taste some five years hence. It is on this judgment that the proportion of wine from different vineyards is established to produce the desired overall taste. The art of making the cuvée is truly the highest art of the Champagne producer.

Once this decision has been made, the new wines are blended in the established proportions in large blending vats where they are thoroughly married. At this point, the wine is given the *dosage de tirage*, a small quantity of the finest rock sugar dissolved in old wine which assures a uniform secondary fermentation. Then the wine is fined and immediately bottled. The cork is firmly secured in the neck with a heavy metal clip, known as an *agrafe*, strong enough to withstand the pressure created by the secondary fermentation in the bottle which gives the sparkle to Champagne.

THE WINE BECOMES SPARKLING

There are various ways of making a wine sparkling; but the traditional champenoise method requires secondary fermentation in the bottle, and this is the only method which can legally be used in France if the wine is to bear the designation Champagne. The great advantage to producing the sparkle through secondary fermentation in the bottle is that the sparkle is natural and much finer in texture; therefore, it lasts longer once the bottle is opened. When the cold weather arrested the fermentation, some unfermented sugar remained in the wine. With the coming of the warmer spring weather, the remaining sugar begins to ferment and is transferred into alcohol and carbon dioxide gas. This secondary fermentation must take place very slowly if fine, light, continuous bubbles are to be obtained, the desirable signs of quality in a great Champagne; therefore, the bottling must be completed before the warm spring and the bottles are stored in below-ground cellars, carved out of the natural chalk subsoil of the Champagne district which remains at a constant temperature of about ten degrees centigrade. The bottles are stored on their sides and are constantly examined for any breakage or leakage because the pressure developed during secondary fermentation can be as high as 110 pounds per square inch. In the old days, breakage was as high as every other bottle but today, with improved bottle manufacture and scientific measuring of the sugar content in the wine, this breakage has been reduced to a minimum.

French law requires that the wine must be aged for at least one year from the time it becomes sparkling, but the great Champagne firms age their wines from three to six years. Here is another variable in the process of production which has a considerable effect on the quality and price of various brands. Obviously, a five-year aging period is costlier, but it will also produce a considerably better quality wine than aging for just one year.

DISGORGING

During secondary fermentation and aging, a certain amount of natural sediment develops which must be removed so that the wine will be perfectly clear. In other types of wine, sediment is eliminated before bottling by fining and drawing off the clear wine. In Champagne, it is a very complicated process because it must be accomplished after bottling, without losing any of the natural effervescence.

The sediment which has formed during secondary fermentation and aging lies along the side of the bottle and must first be gotten down onto the cork before it can be removed. To do this, the bottles are placed cork down in slanting racks called *pupitres*. Over a period of three to four months, an experienced workman rapidly jiggles each bottle every few days, turning it clockwise an eighth turn each time, thus loosening the sediment and causing it to settle down on the cork. Once this process, called *remuage*, is completed, the bottles are placed cork down in wicker cellar baskets and carried to the *salle de dégorgement*.

Here the neck of the bottle is frozen, imprisoning the sediment in a small block of ice. Then comes one of the most ticklish jobs in the whole process: the *dégorgement*—the removal of the cork together with the frozen sediment, but done in such a manner that very little effervescence and very little wine escape. A highly-skilled workman grasps the bottle while wearing a leather apron and often a wire-covered mask to protect his face from an exploding bottle. Standing opposite the barrel and protected by a shield, he releases the *agrafe* with a pair of pliers and the cork flies out, taking with it the frozen bit of sediment. He gives the neck of the bottle two or three sharp raps to loosen any remaining sediment and in doing so, a small amount of wine foams out which he examines to be sure it has a perfectly clean bouquet. He then hands the bottle to another workman who adds the *liqueur d'expédition* (shipping dosage) which consists of wine from bottles which have been previously disgorged, in order to replace the wine that has escaped. When somewhat sweeter Champagne is required for a particular market, the *liqueur d'expédition* also includes a small amount of rock sugar dissolved in old wine, with the amount of sugar depending on the degree of sweetness required.

The *liqueur d'expédition* also involves another quality differentiation. While the amount of sugar added basically depends on the requirements of the market, the dosage can also indicate the quality of the wine. The finer the wine, the less dosage is needed, while a heavier dosage is often used in lesser quality wines to disguise what they may be lacking.

After the dosage the shipping cork is driven home and secured in place by the wired cap and then follows a further aging period to let the wine rest from the strain of "degorgement". Finally, after five years and all these delicate operations, the wine is ready to be labeled, packed, and shipped, and at this point, the role of the importer enters as a final determination of quality.

Champagne is the most delicate of all quality wines; thus, it suffers the most from the turmoil of the ocean voyage. Importers of the finer Champagnes let the wine rest in warehouses for three or four months before shipping it to the trade. This again is ano costly procedure which only the importers of finer Champagnes can afford.

THE IMPORTANCE OF BRAND NAMES

Looking back, it is obvious that the process of producing French Champagne requires an unusual amount of hand labor and a large immobilization of capital. In every step of the process, there is considerable room for variations in procedure and quality and, consequently, in cost.

1. The quality of the grapes used and the care with which they are picked and selected.
2. The use of only the juice of the first two pressings, the cuvee and the premiere taille, as opposed to using all three pressings which gives a 10% greater yield.
3. The care and skills with which the wines of the various vineyards are blended together.
4. The aging of the wine before disgorging which can vary from a minimum of one year to a maximum of five to six years.
5. The shipping dosage which while dictated by the market requirements can also be use to disguise lesser-quality wine.

In every type of product, there is a large variance in quality between the brands marketed by different producers; hence, the brand name is always of paramount importance. This is more true in Champagne than in any other wine because Champagne is not the product of a single vineyard but is a blended wine produced by a delicate and demanding process. There is also a great difference between the minimum legal standards and the higher standards observed by the great Champagne firms. Therefore, it is the shipper's brand name which is all-important and not merely a particular designation such as Brut or Extra Dry or a given vintage year.

VINTAGE AND NON-VINTAGE WINES

Every Champagne producer markets its wine under vintage and non-vintage labels. The non-vintage wines are a blend of wines produced from grapes grown in various years, while a vintage wine is produced from grapes grown in a single year. It is a mistake to assume that simply because a wine is of a certain vintage year that this is a guarantee of quality. Nothing could be further from the truth. The quality of a particular shipper's brand is no better or worse than the reputation and standards of that shipper. There are both good and poor wines produced in every year, and a shipper can bottle an inferior wine and still label it with the vintage date.

Many people believe that the vintage wine of a given shipper is always superior to their non-vintage wine. Actually, a great many of the leading Champagne firms use wines of the same quality, produced under the same high standards, for both their vintage and non-vintage wines. To clarify this statement, it is important to realize that there is a considerable difference between the meanings of the words "quality" and "taste". The great Champagne firms only bottle as vintage wines those years which produce wines that are sufficiently well-balanced and individualistic to meet their own exacting standards for a vintage wine. On the other hand, when a given year does not produce this sort of wine, it is blended with wines of other vintage years so as to produce the desired well-balanced wine. The principal distinction between vintage and non-vintage is that while there may be a family resemblance between the various vintage wines of a given shipper, each vintage year has its own characteristics of taste and nose. The shipper's goal in producing its non-vintage wine is to blend their wines so that they have the same taste year in and year out.

DESIGNATIONS AS TO DRYNESS

Every bottle of Champagne bears one of the following designations: Brut, Extra Dry, Sec, Demi-Sec, with Brut being that shipper's driest wine and Demi-Sec his sweetest. In the United States, only the designations Brut and Extra Dry are generally used, while wines labeled Sec and Demi-Sec are usually found in Latin American countries. These designations are not definitive terms since there are no prescribed standards as to what degree of dryness constitutes a Brut Champagne or what degree of sweetness constitutes a Demi-Sec Champagne. Here again, each shipper establishes his own standards for these designations, and, consequently, the Brut wine of a given shipper may be drier or even less dry than the Extra Dry wine of another shipper. Again we see why it is important to rely on the reputation of the shipper.

BOTTLE SIZES: NAMES AND EXPLANATIONS

The traditional names, explanations, and contents of the various bottle sizes of Champagne are as follows:

Split, Baby, or Nip	6 1/2 oz.
Pint	13 oz.
Bottle or quart	26 oz.
Magnum (two quarts)	52 oz.
Jeroboam (double Magnum)	104 oz.

In ancient times, Jeroboam was the son of Nebat. It is said that he lifted up his hand against the king.

Rehoboam   156 oz. or six bottles

Rehoboam literally means "enlarger of the people". He is in the Bible as the king of Judah.

Methuselah   208 oz. or eight bottles

In the Hebrew language, means the man of Shelah (a Babylonian deity). Methuselah also became a king. He was one of the patriarchs who lived for 969 years (Genesis 5:27)

Salmanazar	312 oz.
Balthazar	416 oz. or sixteen regular bottles
Nebuchadnezzar	520 oz. (the largest bottle) or twenty bottles

Some 3,000 years ago, Nebuchadnezzar was the king of Babylonia. He conquered Jerusalem and destroyed the Temple. His death was in 562 B.C.

Only the first five sizes are typically sold commercially which means that the Jeroboam is normally the largest size available.

Champagne is fermented in only four bottles sizes: the half bottle or pint, the regular bottle of twenty-six ounces, the magnum, and the Jeroboam. All larger sizes are refilled from bottles and consequently in the large sizes. Champagne does not always retain its sparkle and flavor quite so long.

It is also important to remember that the larger the bottle in which Champagne is fermented, the finer the quality.

OPENING AND SERVING CHAMPAGNE

The final step before drinking Champagne is opening the bottle and here, too, this is an art. Since there is a great deal of pressure in the bottle, care must be taken that the cork does not fly out with a big pop and possibly injure someone. The Champagne cork is tightly held in the neck of the bottle, making it particularly hard to remove without breaking the cork. To avoid these pitfalls, this is the accepted way to open and serve Champagne:

1   Remove the wire cap and with the bottle slightly tilted, hold the cork in your left hand and the bottom of the bottle in your right hand. Slowly turn the bottle (not the cork) and gradually ease out the cork while pressing the cork into the bottle so that it will not pop out.

2   Before serving, make sure the cork smells clean to determine if the wine is corky. When a cork is unsound, it smells earthy and gives the wine a musty odor and taste which is known as a corky bottle.

3   When you are ready to serve, wipe the lip of the bottle clean before pouring. Do not wrap a napkin around the bottle. Just wipe the bottle so that it does not drip and pour so your guests can see and read the label. Wrapping the bottle can only mean that you are shamed of the brand name of the Champagne and want to hide the label.

4   The traditional tulip-shaped long-stemmed glass is the best to use because the bouquet can be better appreciated. Champagne should be poured slowly so that it won't foam up and lose its effervescence. The glass should be filled only halfway, so that the wine can be swirled around to permit you to appreciate the bouquet.

5   Champagne should not be served too chilled because the true taste and bouquet will be hidden if it's too cold.

THE WINES OF CHAMPAGNE

The major Champagne houses exporting to the United States, by alphabetic order and with the top of the line in parenthesis are:

Bollinger

Veuve Clicquot Ponsardin (La Grande Dame)

Nicolas Feuillate

Charles Heidsieck

Heidsieck (Piper Heidsieck)

Lanson

Mercier

Moet et Chandon (Dom Perignon)

Mumms

Laurent Perrier

Louis Roederer (Crystal Roederer)

Ruinard

Taittinger (La Française)

About the names, several houses of Champagne bear a Germanic name. Remember, the Province of Alsace in 1870 had been annexed to Germany. During this period, some Alsacian vintners emigrated to the Province of Champagne and set up their wine-making business there. Their heirs still continue the making of Champagne their ancestors had begun.

HISTORY OF CHAMPAGNE

Madame Clicquot: Her peaceful conquest of Russia

Here is a story from a great family of wine growers of champagne. It begins in the early nineteenth century. This is a true narration of the conquest of Russia by Madame Veuve Clicquot-Ponsardin, a peaceful conquest achieved by popping corks! At the same time, a conquest requiring astuteness, boldness, and an iron will to overcome difficulties as varied as they were dangerous.

It was written by Count Bertrand Vogue, President of the National Academy in Reims, in the early sixties.

The story begins in 1805. In October of that year, the husband of Madame Clicquot died suddenly of a malignant fever. His father had given him charge of the family business four years earlier. He was just thirty years old.

Mr. François Clicquot was aware of the immense possibilities offered by the wine of Champagne, then in its infancy, and had decided to export it across the borders of France, largely ruined by the revolution of 1789.

With the Heidsiecks, the Moets, and the Ruinart families, he was one of the pioneers of the Champagne export trade. He was a good judge of men and surrounded himself with outstanding teams who travelled the roads of Germany, Poland, and Bohemia. Among them and most remarkable of all, was a certain Mr. Bohn, a German from the Rhine area, who is the hero of this adventure, as the Veuve Clicquot herself is the heroine.

The birth of the Napoleonic Empire produced an international climate distinctly unfavorable for the trade of Champagne. Europe communications were difficult and payment almost impossible. Voices were more accustomed to war cries than anything else.

In spite of the grief she felt at the loss of her husband, Madame Clicquot was undaunted by these obstacles. She was adamant about carrying out her husband's plan and instructed Mr. Bohn to capture the Russian market, a plan which nobody had even thought of, let alone attempted. It was a bold decision, and we can still follow its course today in their massive correspondence.

Shrewd salesman that he was, Mr. Bohn kept his eyes and ears open. "I am reliably informed that the Czarina is with child. What a blessing it will be if it is a prince! Oceans of Champagne will be drunk in this immense country. Please do not say a word to anyone, otherwise our competitors will arrive in droves."

An important client proposed to visit France. Mr. Bohn advised Madame Clicquot to shower on him all the good things and pleasures that Reims and the neighborhood could offer. "Take possession of him entirely. Do not give him a chance to think. Either you or your friends must invite him for every meal so that our competitors never get near him."

Sometime later, in 1808, a great lover of Clicquot Champagne arrived in Reims. "He is a man of no education, a boilermaker by trade. I recommend him to your closest attention. Take him, lodge him, feed him, flatter him, let him see the cellars (but not the work) and make him feel at home in a great house. He will tell you many things that are true and many that are not, he will yawn, he will be bored, but he will buy. You know well how to encompass him in an amiable way as the spider does the fly."

Mr. Bohn knew how to look after a client and could channel greediness into profit. The wines of Madame Clicquot became fashionable in Russia. "You have the same renown here as Maille in Paris with his mustards and vinegars," wrote Mr. Bohn in 1808. "I am quite happy with what we have, a good solid trade, with the most respected houses of their kind in the north and throughout Europe, famous as a concern in the first rank of your profession, the terror of all your competitors by the very size of your shipments and all for foreign accounts. These are the rare advantages which give you a marked ascendancy over your colleagues and only await a general state of peace to flourish exceedingly. I am not talking of your own virtues and insight nor of the favorable prejudice for Clicquot which exists in foreign countries, these are invariable and indeed are the foundations of your establishment. Nobody can deny that with these assets, which few of your countrymen have had the skill to build up, you can expect something very splendid when peace returns to Europe."

This prophecy would not come true for six long years, full of disappointments and fruitless effort. The war was devastating Europe. England was applying the blockade and all sea transport was subject to search. Mr. Bohn was not pleased with the British: "May the genius of our great emperor rid humanity of these harpies of the sea and give the world peace once more!

"May they pass the winter at the bottom of the sea rather than in their wicked islands, the home of the assassins of prosperity and of the happiness of the human race." He even worked out a special personal revenge for them. "The more I detest the English, the more I want to corrupt their habits. May the good God give us peace so that we can take vengeance on their throats for the evil they have done us, by giving them over to total drunkenness!" Mr. Bohn did not know how near the truth he was. The English of our day are the most faithful friends of Champagne.

In 1812, the situation worsened. Napoleon had set off on his Russian adventure. The frontiers were closed. The fruits of so many years' efforts had been lost. People still hoped for a quick and easy victory. The rest is well known. The prestige of the emperor was hard hit. In the eyes of Mr. Bohn, he is no longer the great emperor but the evil genius who has tormented and ruined the world for five or six years. Mr. Bohn was lucky, in those far-off days, there was no censorship, and imprisonment for subversive talk had not yet been conceived!

Events were moving quickly. At the beginning of 1814, invasion threatened Reims itself. The empire was crumbling. On the 26 of January, Madame Clicquot's father, Baron Ponsardin, who was at that time the first magistrate in Reims, was ordered to leave the town. Madame Clicquot did not follow him and even sent for her daughter who was at school at a convent in Paris. Madame Clicquot stayed put in the hope that her presence might help to protect her wines. "All is going very badly," she wrote to her cousin in Paris. "I have been busy for several days walling up my cellars, but I am afraid that this will not stop me from being robbed and pillaged. Well, if I am ruined, I am, and I must resign myself to it and to working for a living. I shall not regret losing my comfortable life except for my child since it should have happened five or six years earlier and then she should not have known the enjoyments which she is losing. This will certainly be painful, but I shall try to get over it and will sacrifice everything, and I mean everything, that she should be spared unhappiness."

The days which followed were full of tragedy. Reims was at the very center of the war in its final stages. Then in April came the news of the fall of the emperor. Madame Clicquot was relieved, "Thanks be to heaven, I have suffered some loss, but it is not fair to complain of something that happens to everybody. It is in this way that we become purified by misfortune and privations and thus become once again worthy to be governed by the ancient Royal House of France, and peace and happiness will return amongst us."

Now was the moment to carry out a plan thought up two years before by Mr. Bohn. Load a vessel as quickly and as secretly as possible full of Champagne and be the first to land it in Russia long before the slow and timid competitors have recovered from their surprise. Mr. Bohn added: "They will suddenly realise that you have made a shipment. Everybody will be intrigued. They will write around and maybe even try and follow the shiop to discover its destination. In the end, they will discover where. Then they will all come clattering in. If after that we can do nothing, at least we shall have been the first, and our wine will have been well and truly sold before the great crowd of sheep have arrived to lower the price."

This operation was in fact carried out with mathematical precision. Madame Clicquot's Champagne was the first to arrive in a thirsty Russia. It was dispatched in a "small sailing ship of seventy-five tons even before peace was signed, and from that moment, the prestige and popularity of Clicquot in Russia was established during the nineteenth century.

Mr. Bohn had come back to Reims following the happy turn of events. Mr. Rondeaux, a large shipowner in Rouen, was warned. He was an old friend of the business and there were some bold decisions to take. Russia had still not lifted the embargo. Should they wait and be safe? This would sacrifice the vital element of surprise. The ship would touch at Koenigsberg. It should be possible somehow to slip the wine over the frontiers. Speed was the essence. The cellars were unwalled, the bottles were prepared, the *remuage* completed. Everyone was in a hurry. There were not enough hands, not enough carters.

At the end of April, one month after the abdication of the emperor, the heavy carts had carried ten thousand bottles over the rough roads to Rouen. Mr. Bohn took the mail coach from Paris. He had decided to join the precious shipment to Russia in person. He arrived in Rouen at the end of May. The ship, the Dutch *Gebroeders*, commanded by Captain Cornelis, was alongside. "My berth on board defies description, not even a bed! The cabin is no bigger than a bedroom cupboard." Mr. Bohn had to feed himself and bought hams, biscuits, tea, vinegar, lard, and apples. Among the cases delivered to the ship was one addressed to him by Madame Clicquot containing eighteen bottles of red wine from Cumière, five bottles of Cognac, and six volumes of *Don Quixote*!

On the sixth of June, the ship slipped down the river to Le Havre. Mr. Bohn went by road and wrote a final letter to Madame Clicquot, "Goodbye and on to Koenigsberg, where I shall hope to have good news for you. If I fall out of bed and perish, I recommend to your kindness, my good wife and your little godson. Nothing has been neglected to get off quickly, and Mr. Rondeaux has done everything possible while I was there. The big trouble has been the Customs. None of them knew their job, and they are quite unused to business. They seem in a sort of devilish, nagging harassment, only out to tie one up in knots and victimize one—it has been a real Jewish christening!"

A month later, news arrived from Elsinore in Denmark of the first stage of the crossing. "After winds from every point of the compass, nothing remarkable has happened to us except in the Channel one night when we tore an English fishing net to ribbons and were profoundly cursed for this kindness. In the Kattegat, we were stopped by a large Danish frigate towing a Norwegian vessel seized as prize, and they examined us then they let us go. Finally, the ticks as big as sixpence have drunk half my blood. The roadstead is full of ships, and we cannot get off until tomorrow when, if the wind is favorable, we hope to set sail. Our ship is the first for many years to go north from Rouen with a cargo of Champagne.

In the meantime, news reached Reims that Russia had thrown open her frontiers. At once, Madame Clicquot decided without reference to her colleagues to make a second shipment, this time direct to St. Petersburg. She took the same precautions as before and forbade the captain to carry any wines other than her own.

On the third day of July, Mr. Bohn arrived without incident in Koenigsberg in East Prussia. "The good God, knowing that my son still has need of his father to keep him in order, has willed that this miserable weed should not perish."

Immediately on landing, he learned that the wine could enter Russia freely. "This is what I have decided. As people have seen both me and my wine arrive with obvious pleasure, I am going to sell a part of it here to cover expenses and try to make a little money, then, as the freight charges from here to St. Petersburg are nothing, I am sending the rest straight there. While I am waiting, I shall make it known that the whole consignment has already been sold and is destined elsewhere and that only if I am offered an enormous price, will I consider obliging anybody.

"I have looked at our samples with unspeakable pleasure. Spring water is not as clear as the wine samples are and the whole consignment is dry. Oh! How cruel and severe I am going to be! All their tongues are hanging out to taste it, and if it is as good as it is beautiful, they will all finish by having a favorable attitude toward me."

These first pieces of news delighted Madame Clicquot. "Heaven be praised! You have arrived there safe and sound. Honestly, I have been so used to bad news for so long, that what you have told me is like a dream."

The prodigious success of this sparkling wine of Champagne will be forever legendary. Two centuries ago the Russian Army crossed the Rhine River and occupied the city of Reims, capital of the Champagne. In full view of the Russian officers who were gulping down Champagne from the Clicquot's cellars, the grand lady contented herself with these words: "Let them drink, they will have to pay one day."

In truth, Russia appreciated the Champagne of France long before the sack of Reims by the Russian Army; therefore, Madame Clicquot owed her fortune not to the libations of a few soldiers, but to the bold stroke which she carried out in 1814.

SECTION E

The Wines of the Côtes Du Rhône

CÔTES DU RHÔNE

MAP OF THE VINEYARDS OF CÔTES DU RHÔNE

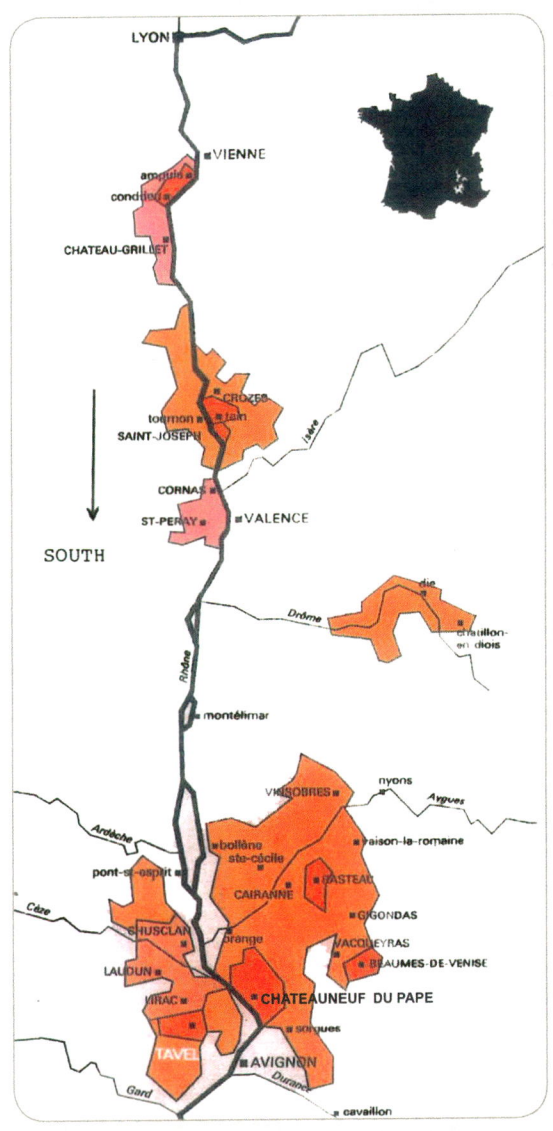

THE WINES OF THE RHÔNE

The appellation Côtes du Rhône includes the vineyards located on the hills along the two shores of the Rhône River between the cities of Vienne and Avignon. The wine region begins twenty miles south of the city of Lyon and continues its course along the Rhône, 120 miles until reaching Avignon.

In the first part of its stream, the valley, which is very steep, forbids the vines to grow on the left bank, while on the right bank, the vineyards of the Côte-Rôtie (translated as roasted slope) produce the wines of Condrieu and Château Grillet, both white wines issued from the vinestock *Viognier*, a genus existing nowhere else; however, some cuttings have been planted in the Sonoma Valley in California for a trial.

The Côte-Rôtie is followed by the district of Hermitage until the city of Valence, all along the Rhône River Valley which becomes much wider. The slopes of Hermitage produce red and white wines, both quite rich in flavor. Croze-Hermitage produces almost three times as much wine as Hermitage. The appellation Côtes-du-Rhône's production is huge, about twelve million cases per year and is ninety-nine percent red wine.

A Côtes-du-Rhône wine is a red wine with no pretentions, it is known as a dependable every day wine, with a lower alcohol content.

There are some villages with a higher rating, like Gigongas for its fleshy and robust flavor, bearing their own village name on the label, the same goes for the village of Chusclan for its production of rosé wines.

Châteauneuf-du-Pape is the most famous wine of all the Rhône coming from a village bearing the same name (translated as Castle of the Pope).

During most of the fourteenth century, the popes were French, the city of Avignon was the papal seat, and the summer residence was called Châteauneuf or new castle. A few thousand cases a year of white Châteauneuf-du-Pape are produced, but it is for the red wines that Châteauneuf-du-Pape became world famous.

Over the years, winemakers have discovered that the very high heat of the Rhône Valley does not favor the growth of any of the finest grape varieties. Therefore in Châteauneuf-du-Pape, a dozen grape varieties are used, each one contributing a particular characteristic to the finished wine. In general, the wines from that district will vary from domain to domain. This variation in wine style is affected by the different vinification methods. Châteauneuf-du-Pape used to be known as a wine that needed several years of bottle age to reach its maturity. Some producers continue to employ the long vatting and long maturation in barrel which produces long-lived wines. The increasing demand for well-known wines have created a number of producers to vinify these wines in the style of Beaujolais in order to have a full-bodied but fast-maturing wine that will be ready to drink sooner.

The Châteauneuf-du-Pape and Côtes-du-Rhône Districts

Here are some topics to complete this dazzling array of special wines not mentioned before. Along the tributary of the Drome River flowing into the Rhône, there is a particular small wine district along both banks producing the Clairette de Die, which is a sparkling wine (pétillant) resembling the Asti Spumante of Italy, but with more freshness and distinction. The Clairette de Die, due to the limitation of culture, is not exported, and the production is entirely consumed locally between Lyon and Marseille.

Coming south to the district of Vaucluse, which is also the name of a tributary, around forty small wine villages have the honor to be counted as producing Côtes-du-Rhône. To name a few:

Red wines, light: Villages of Vinsobres, Sainte-Cécile-les-Vignes

Red wines, robust: Gigondas

Vintage red wines: the whole area of Châteauneuf-du-Pape located along the east of the Rhône River.

Sweet wines: the little enclosure of Rasteau well known for its dessert wines; the area of Beaumes-de-Venise which produces a wonderful white muscat wine.

Wines elevated to the appelation V.D.Q.S. (wine of superior quality) are:

Vaucluse area: Côtes du Ventoux (red and rosé)

Côtes du Luberon (red, rosé, white)

Basses-Alpes: Côteaux du Pirrevert (red, rosé, white)

Bouches-du-Rhône: Côteaux d'Aix-en-Provence; Côteaux des Baux (red, rosé, white)

Ardeche: Côtes du Vivarais (red, rosé, white)

Drome: Wines from Chatillon-en-Diois; Haut-Comtat (red, rosé, white)

Rosé wine's specific area: The best known is Tavel Rosé, on the west of the Rhône and adjacent to Châteauneuf-du-Pape. Lesser known are Chusclan and Lirac. This rosé is issued from the grenache variety and provides a beautiful light ruby color and golden gleam. It is vinified as a dry wine and can be served with any dishes.

In the north, the region of Condrieu merits a special attention. They include Condrieu, Château Grillet, Saint-Joseph, Hermitage white, Crozes-Hermitage white, and Saint-Peray.

Condrieu, like Château Grillet, produces soft, flowery wines with a bouquet reminiscent of peaches. By the way, Château Grillet is sold largely at the world-famous restaurant, La Pyramide, in nearby city of Vienne.

LABELS OF THE CÔTE DU RHÔNE WINE DISTRICT

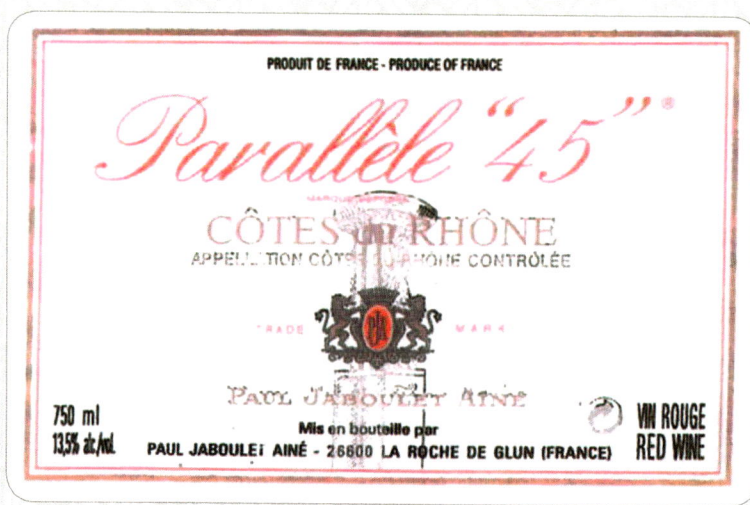

DESCRIPTION OF THE LABEL:

CELLIER DES DAUPHINS: commercial name
(translated as wine-warehouse of the oldest French King

CÔTE DU RHÔNE: appellation identifying the origin of the vineyard.

MIS EN BOUTEILLES: bottled by the United Producers in Tulle Department of the Drome

FRANCE - product of France

VINTAGE YEAR 2003

13.5 volume of alcohol

Bottle containing 0.75 centiliter or 24 oz

SECTION G

The Wines
of the
Loire Valley

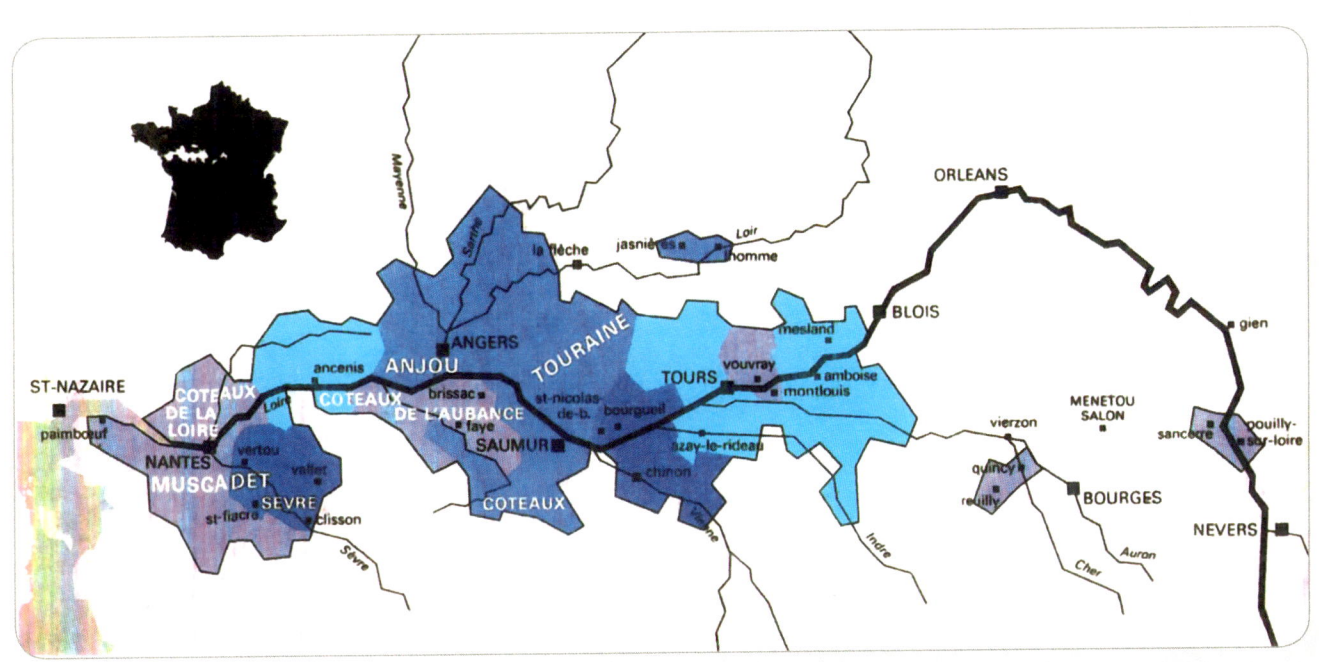

INTRODUCTION

The Loire Valley is world-renowned for its legendary castles (real châteaux) between the cities of Angers, Tours, and Orléans. Outside of France not too many people are aware of the diversity and large amounts of wine produced in that region along the Loire River and the neighbor Affluents, but many tourists visit the châteaux every year. The inhabitants of the mid-Loire area speak the purest French, it is said. Very agreeable and courteous, these people will give you a charming welcome. As for the cuisine, it is also outstanding. A good part of the French nobility comes from that region. The ancestry of the King Louis can be traced back to Orléans.

THE MUSCADET AND THE ANJOU WINES

Muscadet is the name of the vinestock, more properly known as *Melon de Bourgogne* which was introduced in the sixteenth century and cultivated along the estuary of the Loire River around the city of Nantes.

The Institution of the National Appellations Contrôlée, in short; the I.N.A.O., has singled out three varieties: the Muscadet, the Muscadet des Côteaux de la Loire (near the village of Ancenis), and the Muscadet de Sèvres et Maine (the largest of the three).

The average production is around 300,000 hectoliters. Muscadet is a dry white wine, slighlty acidic that goes well with oysters and all shelled fish. There is also an especially delightful type of Muscadet called Muscadet sur lies (on the lees). That wine has been bottled at an early stage and directly from the barrel where it had fermented but still rested on its deposits.

The next city up the Loire is Angers which has given its name to the area of Anjou. The best known of the Anjou wines is the Anjou Rosé. This popular rosé is an agreeable mellow wine made from a lesser known grape variety called *Groslot*. A second rosé, called Rosé d'Anjou Cabernet from the famous variety of Bordeaux is less sweet and has more character than the Rosé d'Anjou.

WHITE WINES FROM ANJOU

The Anjou wine district also produces white wines ranging in character from fairly dry to quiet, sweet, and robust. These wines are made from the Chenin Blanc variety, known along the Loire as the Pineau de la Loire. The color of the Pineau is a dark yellow going to a light-brownish tint. It shines like silk and fits wonderfully as an apéritif. The Pineau de la Loire is not related at all with the Pinot Blanc of Burgundy despite the same pronunciation. The last time I tasted a Pineau de la Loire, and I am able to recollect it very well, it was sublime and better than a sweet sherry. Note that there is no alcohol added to the wine, it is a beautiful natural wine. The three main producing areas are the Côteaux de la Loire, the Côteaux de l'Aubance, and the Côteaux du Layon.

The Aubance and the Layon are tributaties of the Loire River. The Côteaux du Layon produces by far the most wine, mellow and rounded in character.

THE REGION OF SAUMUR

The appellations Saumur and Côteaux de Saumur are given to wines produced around the city of Saumur; however, it is part of the Anjou district. Saumur produces still and sparkling white and red wines. A lot of rosé wine is produced there, issued from the cabernet grapes, called Rosé d'Anjou. It is quite a very decent wine and without pretence. This rosé retains a slight trace of sweetness and is really enjoyable on warm days. The consumption is largely local and for Paris and France in general. Anjou wines still can be seen in the United States. There is an area called Saumur-Champigny, also in the Anjou District, producing a famous red wine issued from the Cabernet franc grapes, a warm wine full of pep and of a deep ruby color. Its aroma recalls the scent of violets.

Below is a view of the Château de Saumur, overlooking the Loire River and the city of Saumur.

Unfortunately the Côteaux du Layon wines are not exported and are sold easily in the different regions of France.

The villages of Quarts de Chaume and Bonnezeaux make robust and luscious white wines and are considered by the growers of that region to rival the best Sauternes wines from Bordeaux.

On the left bank of the Loire River, adjacent to Anjou, grows the Chenin Blanc, rosé and red from the Cabernet Franc stock. The largest city around there is Saumur. The red Saumur is a surprise, light and dry and not expensive. If you come across a bottle of Saumur de Champigny, it's well worth trying.

LABEL OF MUSCADET FROM SÈVRE ET MAINE

SEVRE ET MAINE WINE AREA IS THE LARGEST PRODUCER OF MUSCADET.

BELOW IS PICTURED THE CHÂTEAU DE SAUMUR BUILT IN THE XIV TO XVI'S CENTURIES
FOR THE DUCS OF ANJOU. THE CHÂTEAU IS OVERLOOKING THE LOIRE.

A LABEL OF POUILLY-FUME DE LADOUCETTE,
BOTTLED AT THE CHATEAU DE NOZET.

A view of the Château du Nozet

A label of de Ladoucette Pouilly Fumé

THE WINES OF POUILLY-FUMÉ AND SANCERRE

Up the Loire River, past the city of Orléans and just before the city of Nevers, are two villages that produce the best white wine of the Loire district: the Sancerre and the Pouilly-sur-Loire whose name has been shortened to Pouilly-Fumé. The former produces two famous white wines: the Chasselas (planted also in Switzerland and known as the Pendant) and the Blanc Fumé (smoky white) issued from the Sauvignon Blanc stock. The correct name is Blanc Fumé de Pouilly-sur-Loire. The chalky soil of these two districts which face each other across the upper reaches of the Loire River is very similar to that of Burgundy nearby, so it is not surprising that the wines produced should be very similar to the white wines of Burgundy, but it is to be noted that the blowing cycle of the wind is not the same between the Loire and Burgundy. Thus nature has split the two; the Pouilly and Sancerre are not at the same level as a Meursault, for example.

Pouilly-Fumé wines are rich in flavor—very agreeable, clean, dry white wines. They are similar to the white Pouilly-Fuissé from Burgundy.

Along the Cher River are situated two more wine villages, Quincy and Reuilly. The Cher River is a tributary of the Loire River. The wines produced there are dry and crisp; similar to those of Sancerre. They are a good value for restaurant wine lists; most of their total production is sold in Paris eateries.

Clos Baudoin

VOUVRAY

Appellation Vouvray Contrôlée

MIS EN BOUTEILLE AU CLOS BAUDOIN PAR

Alc. 11,5% by vol.   PRODUCE OF FRANCE   75 cl

Prince PONIATOWSKI   Le 'Clos Baudoin'
PROPRIÉTAIRE-RÉCOLTANT   VOUVRAY (I.&L.)

THE VOUVRAY WINE

The vineyards of Vouvray in the mid-Loire grow on steep hills, four hundred feet above the river, near the city of Tours. They face directly south and, along the temperate climate of this region, give the fullness of body and tendency toward sweetness of the wines of Vouvray. A great proportion of Vouvray wines is made into sparkling wine which is consumed in the region. It is also called *mousseux* or *pétillant* wine meaning slightly sparkling.

The Chenin Blanc grape is used to make Vouvray, and in sunny years, it produces a most attractive mellow wine. When there is less sunshine, the wine will be drier in taste. In recent years however the winegrowers were encouraged to switch their vinification and completely ferment their wine in order to produce a drier wine.

The village of Vouvray is situated five miles from the city of Tours and is noted for its chalk hills. Interestingly, the inhabitants have dug caves into the slopes that are used both as wine-cellars and homes. A number of the houses built along the slopes are mere facades with the greater part of these homes situated within the hillsides themselves.

The area around Tours is one of the most frequented tourist attractions of France. It is here where the most historic châteaux are situated: the Château of Chambord, the Château of Azay-le-Rideau, the Château of Chenonceaux, and the Château d'Amboise where Leonardo Da Vinci is buried.

The Touraine district also produces two red wines in the villages of Chinon and Bourgueil. The famous poet Rabelais was born in Chinon and often praised its local wine. Made from the Cabernet grape, these two wines have some similarities with the refreshing qualities of a good Beaujolais wine.

SECTION H

The Cognac and Armagnac Wine Districts

COGNAC

MAP OF THE VINEYARDS OF COGNAC

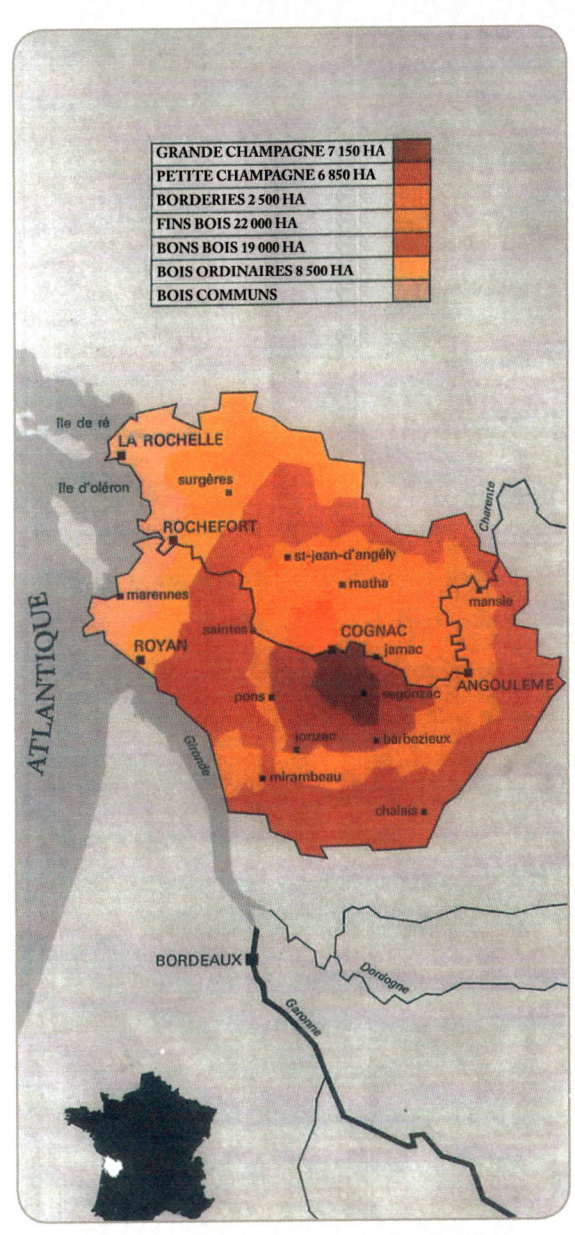

GRANDE CHAMPAGNE 7 150 HA	
PETITE CHAMPAGNE 6 850 HA	
BORDERIES 2 500 HA	
FINS BOIS 22 000 HA	
BONS BOIS 19 000 HA	
BOIS ORDINAIRES 8 500 HA	
BOIS COMMUNS	

THE WINE REGION OF COGNAC

It has been proven that the soil and the landscape of Cognac, located north of the Bordeaux area in the Charente District, are very much under the influence of a misty seaboard area, irradiated with a strange quality of ultraviolet light. Each of the smaller districts are variable to this exposure.

In 1860, a French geologist made a trip to the Charente District, also called the Bay of Biscayne. There he went to analyze different types of soil in the large area of the vineyards. He had brought with him a professional taster of brandies and wines who went from farm to farm taking notes about the area, sniffing and sipping the brandy. At the end of the day, each one compared his notes on the qualities and characteristics of each Cognac brandy, the ones he had deduced from the soil, the other he discovered in the grapes. Consequently, the geologist eventually could divide the Charente district into seven zones.

A major upswing for the sale of Cognac starting in the seventeenth century came from the English and Scandinavian seamen who used to come to the Charente, not for the wine but for the salt produced in the region. Once they were there, they bought wine as well. The next significant development was the boiling down of the wine in order to strengthen it before the North Sea voyage and to avoid taxation which was on bulk at that time.

Then came the search for good oak wood which was found nearby where the River Charente had its source (about 150 miles away), the forest district around the town of Limoges in the foothills of the Massif Central (name of these primary mountains), the land of the Limousin oak. The name of the luxury passenger cars, limousines, come from Limousin because the people of that region were the first to name these large vehicles in the nineteenth century, of course, at the time, they were wide carriages.

UNDERSTANDING THE PROCESS
OF MANUFACTURING COGNAC

It is the tranformation of the local wine of an ingrate quality through the heating process of a large still that creates the magic of Cognac. The distillation is practiced with Charente's alambic (a long still with one boiler). The grapes begin by being fermented, and the juice becoming wine. Once the wine is ready, it is distilled through the alembic, and the liquid is then called *brouillis*. The wine goes through three brouillis and is at once blended together in order to be distilled again. This process is called *la Bonne Chauffe*.

In continuing the process, the first liquids which come out are called *produit de tête* or (head product). The last liquids are called *produit de queue* (tail product). Both the head product and the tail product are eliminated. The in-between liquid produced is called the *produit de coeur* (heart product) which is the *eau-de-vie* of Cognac, also called brandy.

Only the Cognacs aged for over five years in white oak wood can carry the title of three stars, VO (very old) or VSOP (very superior old pale). The minimum aging is one year and is sold as cheaper brandy, but the best Cognacs have a much longer aging which can attain or surpass one century.

NOTES ON THE REGION OF COGNAC

The area of Cognac is located just north of the Bordeaux area and occupies two departments: the Charente (in-land) and Charente-Maritime. The main city of Charente is Angouleme, and the city of Cognac is secondary State Administrative Circonscription besides being the capital of the Cognac brandy. The main city of Charente-Maritime is La Rochelle which has been a very active harbor since the eleventh century. The port is now the biggest yachting center on France's Atlantic Coast.

What gives Cognac its superb and distinctive flavor is the interaction between the white oak wood and the brandy, as well as continuous oxidation that takes place through the porous wood. The basic elements are present in embryonic form in the raw cog, but it is the barrel aging where the brandy picks up its color and its tanin from the oak wood that refines a harsh distilled liquid into an inimitable beverage. The process of aging is quite expensive, not only for the storage of the barrels, but because Cognac evaporates while aging. Although Cognac takes on color from the oak as it matures, its pale brown color will vary according to the time it's in the barrel and is invariably blended with the addition of harmless natural caramel coloring before being bottled, so that every bottle will look the same.

A good Cognac is noted for its complex and refined bouquet, that is one of the main reason that Brandy glasses are known as snifters. A professional Cognac taster actually relies more on his nose than on his palate when making the decision for a final blend. If you take the time to inhale the Cognac before tasting it, you will be surprised at how much this will tell you about its style and its quality.

The leading Cognac firms and exporters are: Bisquit, Camus, Courvoisier, Delamain, Denis-Mounie, Pierre Ferrand, Gaston de la Grange, Hennessy, Hine, Martell, Remy Martin, Monnet, Otard, and Salignac.

The brandies of Cognac share with the wines of Champagne the merit of being the most universally-known spirit. This honor is the result of centuries of patience. It is the consecration of unrivalled merits of a product of high quality founded as much as for the soil as for the influence of man and his inspired genius through the years.

The wine which produces the Cognac comes from the following vine-growths: Cabernet franc, Cabernet sauvignon, Chenin blanc, Colombard, Folle blanche, Merlot blanc, Mourvedre, Semillion, and Ugni blanc (known in Italy as the Trebbiano). Certain vine-growths cannot be planted in more than ten percent of a vineyard. The law is very exact, and since 1955, any grower planting any part of his vineyards in unauthorized vine, has his total crop refused.

To speculate upon the unique excellence of the Cognac, one must begin with the content of chalk in the soil, the exact amount decreasing from Grande Champagne down the range of officially marked-out areas to *bois ordinaires*, the value and the quality of the Cognac decreasing with it. The geologists say that the chalk is a mother-bed for exceptional vines.

They decided, after studying these soils, to divide the regions of the Charente and the Charente Maritime into seven zones based upon variations of the layers of chalks and lime found irregularly in the soil: Grande Fine Champagne and the Fine Champagne, the Grande Champagne, the Petite Champagne, Les Borderies, Les Fins Bois, Les Bons Bois, and Les Bois Ordinaires and Les Bois Communs.

Once the grapes have been pressed and the fermentation is over, the distillation of that wine takes place in large pot stills which look like giant coffee kettles.

ARMAGNAC

THE ARMAGNAC WINE DISTRICT

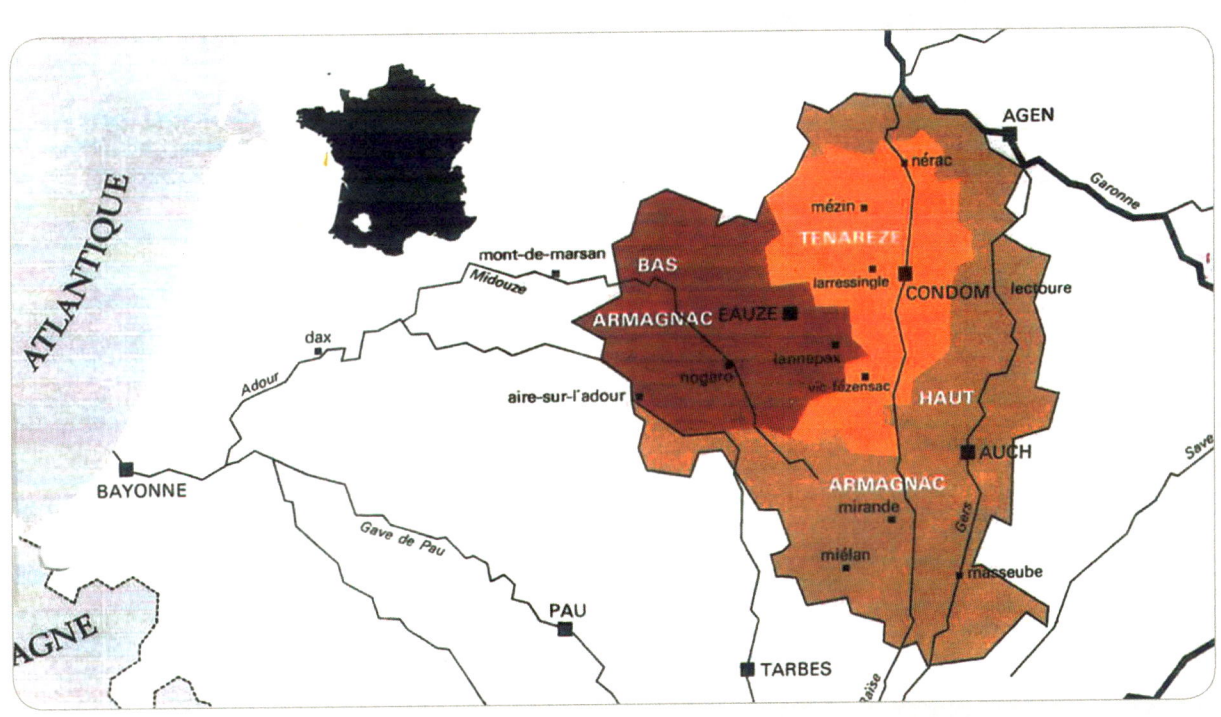

THE WINE REGION OF ARMAGNAC

Armagnac is the oldest and proudest of the French brandies. The King Henri de Navarre, the Sieur Villon (a médieval poet and writer), d'Artagnan (the chief of the Musketeers, from Gascony), Napoleon's top general, and Marshall Lannes, all appreciated Armagnac, and they made it famous, too. It is found in Gascony, the ancient name of this province. It is mostly a rural region, located more precisely to the southeast of Bordeaux, and it covers the Department of the Gers.

The *Folle blanche*, or commonly called *Picpoule* is the main grape for the production of Armagnac. Other species planted there are St. Emilion, Colombard, Jurançon, Blanquette, Mauzac, Meslier, and Plant de Grèce.

There are three natural districts which are honored to share the denomination Armagnac: the Bas-Armagnac, the district which is perhaps the best considered to produce highly regarded Armagnac, the production is concentrated around the towns of Castex, Monclar, and Monlezun; the Ténarèze Distrct with the towns of Labarrèze, Montréal, and Eauze; and the Haut-Armagnac, with the cities of Condom, Valence-sur-Baise and Vic-Fezenzac.

Armagnac is generally bottled in the Basquaise bottle, named after the bordering region of Spain called the Basque region. It is round and flattened, similar to the one used for bottling the Mateus wine made in Portugal.

The vineyards cover 47,000 hectares with total production averaging 1,500,000 hectoliters per year. Seventy-two percent of their production is appellation white wine.

The Armagnac producers are still rural artisans rather than large companies. As a result, the prices of Armagnac are usually less than Cognac. The continuous alambic invented by Edouard Adam in the mid-1800s is still in use today.

As there are many forests in the region, especially a black oak tree, the winegrowers prefer to use this type of oak wood for the maturation of the Armagnac, compared to the white oak wood used for Cognac and coming from the Limousin. Tasters of brandies in France describe the Armagnac as more fragrant than Cognac and having a "biscuit aroma". Armagnac is generally paler than Cognac due to the absence of natural caramel used as a coloring matter for the finish of Cognac. Neither Armagnac nor Cognac contains any added flavoring element as per the terms of the European Union definition of 1990.

The major exporters of Armagnac to the U.S. are: Marquis de Montequiou, J. de Mailliac (considered the best producer), Larresingle, Clos Dés Ducs and Les Domaines Grassa.

Nature of the Soil

The district of Bas-Armagnac has a siliceous sandy soil, with calcareous grounds under it. The Ténarèze soil is more argillacerous and has heavier soils despite having still sandy soil and calcareous soil. The Haut-Armagnac having a higher situation is more likely to contain calcareous soils. The entire region is interrupted by numerous valleys and by small rivers coming down from the Pyrénées Mountains. The vineyards are also mixed with oak forests.

The region of Armagnac wine production is of a very ordinary quality. The region is better known for its outstanding manufacturing of brandies issued from these grapes. As for the Cognac production, Armagnac is controlled by strict regulations as to the handling of grapes, the aging, and the marketing.

The Difference between Cognac and Armagnac

Armagnac draws its nutrition from the silicon-clay or *boulbènes* as they are called in Gascony. To the opposite, Cognac has to content itself with less perfect calcareous soils. The regions use different vinegrowths. The Folle blanche is mainly used; but other vinegrowths such as the Ugni blanc (also called St. Emilion), the Semillon, the Sauvignon, the Blanc-Ramé, and the Montils are authorized.

In Armagnac, the distillery is different from that of the Cognac alambic or still. The stills in Armagnac are not individually-owned by winegrowers as in Cognac, but are mounted on wheels and travel throughout the region, transforming wine into Armagnac from November through April. The Armagnac is distilled only once, compared to two distillations for the Cognac. The average proof coming out of the still is 104° proof. This means that more of the original taste of the wine is brought out during the distillation, ???

CHAPTER NINE

The Fortified Wines and their Areas of Production in Europe

FORTIFIED WINES

There are various types of Fortified Wines. In order to explain each of them, here is a classification but not a ranking:

A- VERMOUTH

B- MUSCAT

C- SHERRY

D- PORT

E- MADEIRA

F- MALAGA

G- MARSALA

A Fortified Wine is a wine made of red or white grapes, subjected to the addition of wine-spirit (or grape-spirits) which has between 15 to 22 proof of alcohol content.

These types of wines did not fade after long journey of sea transportation. They also have therefore a longer shelf life and don't have to be refrigerated.

Each one of them have a most complicated producing operation, which will be explained in the following pages.

A short explanation on how these wines are produced and perfected is as follow:

Most of the Sherries are grouped into three categories:

1   A "Fino" or "Manzanilla" is the driest of all Sherries.

2   An "Amontillado" is an aged "Fino" that has developed a certain depth of character. It is the most in demand for all Sherries.

3   An "Oloroso" is basically a dry Sherry of strong body and meaty which is transformed into a cream Sherry by the addition of sugar during the final stages of blending.

NOTES: SOME EXCERPTS HAVE BEEN COLLECTED FROM THE THE ENCYCLOPEDIA OF WINES AND SPIRITS WRITTEN BY ALEXIS LICHINE.

THE FORTIFIED WINE

There are various types of fortified wines. In order to explain each of them, here is a classification but not a ranking: Vermouth, Muscat, Sherry, Port, Madeira, and Marsala. A fortified wine is a wine made of red or white grapes, subjected to the addition of wine-spirit (or grape-spirits) which has between 15 and 22 proof of alcohol content. These types of wines did not fade after a long journey of sea transportation. They also have a longer shelf life and don't have to be refrigerated. Each one of them has a most complicated production operation. Fortified wines, today, are usually offered as an aperitif. For Sherry, Madeira, Port, and Marsala are also used in cooking.

The Greeks, in ancient times, were responsible for creating these fortified wines which have been in demand for centuries. It was a way for them to hide the deficiencies of poorly-made wines. There are different types of fortified wines now made around the world.

Vermouth: The word vermouth is supposedly derived from the German word wormwood which is a plant producing a bitter and dark green oil. It is also strong smelling. It is to be believed that the wormwood plant was the precursor of the vermouth and dates from the fifteenth century, but it is no longer necessary for the modern manufacture of vermouth. The base product of vermouth is wine from white or red grapes, aromatized and infused with herbs, plants, and extracts of roots. It is then blended with grape-alcohol.

INTRODUCTION

A FORTIFIED WINE IS PRODUCED WITH RED OR WHITE GRAPES, SUBJECTED TO THE ADDITION OF WINE-SPIRITS (OR GRAPE-SPIRITS). THE ALCOHOL PROOF CONTENT IS BETWEEN 15° TO 22°.

THESE TYPES OF WINES DON'T FADE AFTER LONG JOURNEYS ON SEA TRANSPORTATION. THEY THEREFORE HAVE A LONGER SHELF LIFE AND DON'T HAVE TO BE REFRIGERATED.

SHERRIES

A SHORT EXPLANATION ON HOW THESE WINES ARE PRODUCED AND PERFECTED IS AS FOLLOW:

MOST OF THE SHERRIES ARE GROUPED INTO THREE CATEGORIES:

A   A "FINO" OR "MANZANILLA" IS THE DRIEST OF ALL SHERRIES.

B   AN "AMONTILLADO" IS AN AGED "FINO", THAT HAS DEVELOPED A CERTAIN DEPTH OF CHARACTER. IT IS THE MOST IN DEMAND FOR ALL SHERRIES.

C   AN "OLOROSO" IS BASICALLY A DRY SHERRY WITH A STRONG BODY AND MEATY WHICH IS TRANSFORMED INTO A CREAM SHERRY BY THE ADDITION OF SUGAR DURING THE FINAL STAGES OF BLENDING.

SECTION A
VERMOUTH

There are various types of fortified wines. In order to explain each of them, here is a classification but not a ranking: Vermouth, Muscat, Sherry, Port, Madeira, and Marsala. A fortified wine is a wine made of red or white grapes, subjected to the addition of wine-spirit (or grape-spirits) which has between 15 and 22 proof of alcohol content. These types of wines did not fade after a long journey of sea transportation. They also have a longer shelf life and don't have to be refrigerated. Each one of them has a most complicated production operation. Fortified wines, today, are usually offered as an aperitif. For Sherry, Madeira, Port, and Marsala are also used in cooking.

The Greeks, in ancient times, were responsible for creating these fortified wines which have been in demand for centuries. It was a way for them to hide the deficiencies of poorly-made wines. There are different types of fortified wines now made around the world.

VERMOUTH: The word vermouth is supposedly derived from the German word wormwood which is a plant producing a bitter and dark green oil. It is also strong smelling. It is to be believed that the wormwood plant was the precursor of the vermouth and dates from the fifteenth century, but it is no longer necessary for the modern manufacture of vermouth. The base product of vermouth is wine from white or red grapes, aromatized and infused with herbs, plants, and extracts of roots. It is then blended with grape-alcohol.

In general, vermouth is part of a group of fortified wines called bitters which are flavored and infused as noted before, with herbs, plants, flowers, and with roots and bark extracts. Quinine is also used for the preparation of vermouth. The two largest companies in the vermouth production are: Martini & Rossi, made in Turin, Italy, and Noilly Prat, made in Marseilles, France. Other prominent producers are: Cinzano, Carpano E Mes, Gancia, Fernet Branca, all made in Italy. France also is a large producer of vermouth with Chambery, Boisset, Dubonnet, Byrrh, Lillet, and Cynar. Angostura Bitters, well known in cocktails, is made in Venezuela. From Germany comes Undergerg and from Hungary, Unicum. Vermouth is nowadays still strongly consumed specially with Vodka or Gin (the special drops of white Martini for a Dry Martini).

SECTION B
MUSCAT OR MOSCATEL

The word muscat applies to all sweet wines made of very sweet and ripe grapes. When the fermentation is restrained, the wines are blended with grape-spirit in order to retain the natural sweetness. They are mostly issued from white-kinned grapes. Moscatel is the name given to these wines growing in Spain and Portugal.

Muscat is part of a group of varietals grown where the climate and the soil are best adapted to these vines. Muscat does not bear any relationship with the Muscadet vine cultivated in the upper Loire Valley in France. Muscadet originated from Burgundy in the sixteenth century. The Muscat grape produces sweet wine with an intense aroma reminicent of perfume, delicate and refined. It is usually served as an apéritif wine or with dessert courses. The varietal group has different nuances depending on where the vine is planted. Here are the names which are always preceded by Muscat: Muscat blanc à Petits Grains, Muscat de Beaumes de Venise, Muscat of Alexandria, Muscat Ottonel, Muscat d'Alsace. In France, Muscat is also called *Vins doux naturels* (naturally sweet wines).

When shopping for Muscat or Moscatel look for the following shippers: Domaine de Coyeux and Beaumes de Venise in France; Moscatel from Setubal in Portugal; Moscatel from Valencia, Spain; Muscat de Frontignan and of St. Jean de Minervois, Languedoc; and Muscat de Rivesaltes, Roussillon, South of France. California, Australia, and South Africa also produce these sweet wines either called Muscat or Moscatel or Moscato.

SECTION C
SHERRY FROM SPAIN

Many countries have imitated the real Sherry of Spain, the original wine of this southern area of Jerez and Andalusia, but none came close to all the qualities of the Jerez. Australia, South Africa, and California are larger commercial producers. In the United States, the brand name Taylor is well known, so is the market name of the Sherries of E. & J. Gallo: Sheffield and Fairbank. They make a pale Sherry, a cream Sherry and a golden Sherry.

The name Sherry comes from *Scherisch*, the name given by the Arabs when they occupied the city of Jerez and the southern part of Spain. It had been called Sherry in English. Before, in the early centuries, the city of Jerez dela Frontera had been founded by the Phoenicians who were hardy seamen. They called the city Xera, the name then drifted in Europe as Xérès.

Many commercial Sherries are sweetened by the addition of a quantity of *mistela*, the juice of grapes, into which grape spirits have been added. However, the best type of sweet Sherry is made with grapes left to dry on the soil and the torrid heat of the Southern Spain climate. At night, they are covered so the dew does not interfere. After a while, the juice evaporates, and the sugar left is more intense. *Muy Seco* is the very driest type of Sherry.

The two major vinestocks planted around Jerez are the *Palomino* and the *Pedro Ximenez*, producing white grapes. They occupy seventy-five percent of the area. By law, the appellation of origin protects the vines and their delimitations.

Another great fortified wine is Malaga, made close to the Port City of Malaga, located along the Mediterranean Sea. Malaga is a sweet Sherry and is of a deep brown color. It was once very popular in Europe.

Wines growing in the same district will mature in varying quality. Some wines will develop a *flor* (flower) and some will not. The *flor* is a film of yeast cells covering the surface of the wine. As the wines are put in barrels which are not completely filled, the *flor* grows and gives the wines an unrivalled flavor. When these wines are attacked by the *flor*, they will become Finos. The ones not attacked by the *flor* will be set aside and held for a longer maturing period. They become known as Olorosos or sweet cream Sherries.

Olorosos

An Oloroso Sherry is completely dry when it ages in its solera, a term that will be explained in the next paragraph. Through the addition of sugar during the final stages of blending, the Sherry is transformed into a cream sherry. Because of its higher alcoholic proof, an open bottle of Sherry will last much longer than will a table wine; even so, an open bottle of Sherry will eventually start to lose its flavor. The dry Sherries are usually served chilled or with ice cubes. A lot of Sherries also are used in better restaurants and in the preparation of fine meals.

Solera

A solera is a vast warehouse facing the ocean, twenty feet or so and consists of three to five rows of barrels, all containing wines similar in style with the oldest wines at the bottom row. When wines from the bottom are drawn off to be bottled and shipped, the loss is made up from wines in the second tier which in turn are replaced with wines from the top row. As the olorosos continue to age in barrels, they are reserved for a different solera. This method is at the heart of the making of Sherry and is unrivaled to its own wines. The solera system enables the shipping firms of Jerez to maintain a continuity of the style for each of these Sherries year after year. A shipper will often combine wines from several soleras in order to blend wines from different ages and style. Because all Sherries are made by the solera method, they do not carry a vintage, nor are they identified by the name of an individual vineyard.

SECTION D
THE PORT WINES OR PORTO FROM PORTUGAL

The real Port is made exclusively in Portugal, along the River Douro. The name "Port" comes from Oporto, a city near the Atlantic Coast, far north of the Capital Lisbon.

When shopping for Ports look for these brand names: Dow's Port Warre's Port, Graham's Port, Fonseca's Port, Quinta do Noval's Port Calem's Port and Ferreira's Port.

Port is usually made with a red wine base, but there is a small amount produced with white grapes.

Port originated during the sixteen century when the English an French clashed. As a consequence, Britain put an embargo on all goods imported from France. Therefore wine-shippers had to look elsewhere and saw Portugal as an ideal provider and an ally.

In those times, Port was mostly shipped in barrels. It was also common practice to add grape spirit to the fermented wine in order to preserve th wine from torrid hot weather and choppy seas. This process is called fortification. It takes place when the normal fermentation time of the wine is not completed. In other words, the sugar level of the wine remains unconsumed by the yeast as soon the grape spitit is added. The alcohol strength varies between 18° and 22°.

There are two different Port types: First the vintage Port which is an outstanding quality port is not produced every year, only in extremely good years. It is usually kept for six years in casks where the wine will mature slowly and will change color from a dark red to amber brown. Generally, vintage Port is quite expensive but worth to try.

Second, non-vintage Port is a blend of several years and is kept for t years in casks before bottling. Non-vintage Port is widely spread around the world and is consumed either as an apéritif or an after-dinner drink; it is also used for cooking.

Many other countries are producing Port: the United States, South Africa, and Australia where the Shiraz grape variety is used. Greece also produces a fortified wine called Mavrodaphne, a dark brown wine of 15 proof which is excellent, sweet, and inexpensive.

PORT WINE - PORT OR PORTO

PORTO IS IDENTIFIED AS A FORTIFIED WINE FROM PORTUGAL. THE NAME PORTO COMES FROM ONE OF THE MOST IMPORTANT PORT IN PORTUGAL "OPORTO" ALONG THE DOURO RIVER.

"PORTO" IS A POWERFUL WINE ASSIMILATED TO THE FRENCH IDENTIFICATIONS AS SWEET NATURAL WINES OR LIQUOR WINES. ALL PORT WINES EXCEPT FOR THE TABLE WINES ARE FORTIFIED WITH GRAPE-BRANDY FROM PORTUGAL.

THERE ARE SEVEAL TYPES OF PORT WINES:
1) THE VINTAGE PORT
2) THE REGULAR NON-VINTAGE PORT
3) THE TAWNY PORT
4) THE RUBY PORT
5) THE WHITE PORT

WHEN ALL THE CONDITIONS OF GROWING HAVE MET, THE WINE-GROWERS SET MOST OF THEIR PRODUCTION ASIDE AND CAN DECLARED IT A VINTAGE YEAR. IF THE PORT SHIPPERS AGREE WITH THE WINE-GROWERS, THEY CAN DECLARE A VINTAGE YEAR, IF NOT THE WINES OF VARIOUS YEARS ARE BLENDED AND ARE SOLD AS NON-VINTAGE PORTS.

PORTUGAL IS AIMING AT PLANTING MORE VINESTOCKS PRODUCING WINE ONLY. THEY ARE THE "BUCELAS", THE "COLARES", THE "DOURO" AND THE "VERDES".

EXPLANATION FOR "RUBY PORT":

PORT IS DESIGNATED AS "RUBY" AFTER ITS RICHNESS IN COLOR ITS FRUITINESS AND SWEETNESS. THE BLEND OF THIS PORT CONSISTS OF WINES FROM SEVERAL YEARS. IT IS VERY POPULAR IN THE STATES DESPITE THE HEAVY COMPETITION OF AMERICAN PORT

EXPLANATION FOR "WHITE PORT"

WHITE PORT IS A FORTIFIED WINE ISSUES FROM WHITE GRAPES. THIS PORT ALSO IS SWEET AND HAS A YELLOWISH-AMBER COLOR. IT USED TO BE VERY POPULAR IN EUROPE.

SECTION E
THE WINES FROM MADEIRA, PORTUGAL

The geographical position of Madeira became important in the seventeenth century for the trading ships shuttling to the Middle East. It was the quickest way to make a port of call at the main harbor of the city of Funchal in order to get wines and goods supplied.

The island of Madeira is the largest of the group of tiny islands located west of the coast of Morocco. It had been claimed centuries ago by Portugal and is still a Portuguese enclave.

Due to the fact that these islands originated from volcanic soil, the wines produced there are astringent and acidic. When the pressing of the grapes is done, the wines continue to ferment in barrels which are stored in warehouses called lodges or *estufas* in Portugese. They are literally baked for several months in the heat of the tropical sun. They acquire during this process a cooked and burned flavor. This concentrated aging process is meant to approximate the beneficial effects of a long sea voyage. It was discovered in the eighteenth century that the long trips to which all cargo ships were subjected seemed to improve Madeira wines. Nowadays, there is a better method: the warehouses have central heating pipes filled with hot water.

Four basic types of Madeira are named after the grape variety from which they are made. The driest is the Sercial; the Werdelho is a little sweeter and darker; the Bual and the Malmsey or Malvasia are the other two.

In order to sum up this complicated process, do not forget that the fermentation of Madeira wines is usually interrupted by the addition of grape alcohol (wine spirit) to keep the natural sugars in the original wine.

Madeira wines are also classified according to the length of time they are kept in barrels. A Madeira wine will state on the bottle label this classification as follows: five years of barrel aging is called Reserve, ten years old is a Special Reserve, and fifteen years old is the Extra Reserve.

Madeira wines are not only consumed by the crew of ships, but they are in demand in society circles all over the world. In Europe, it is sipped as an apéritif or with desserts. It is also used a lot for the preparation of fine meals and added to soups or consommé.

SECTION F
MARSALA, ITALY

Marsala is also a fortified wine and is named after the city of Marsala in the western end of the island of Sicily. Like many of the fortified wines from Southern Europe, imitation of that wine has been practiced by many countries to produce a Sherry or a Madeira-type fortified wine. Originally, a quantity of grape-spirit was added to this white wine of Sicily. As the brand of Marsala became more and more in demand two centuries ago, the first merchant who produced and established large foreign markets was Florio. Today, the name Florio is world-reknowned for Marsala.

One of the essential conditions in obtaining a Marsala of high quality is to let it age in wood barrels for seveal years. The type of grapes used for producing Marsala is the muscat of Alexandria. In order to produce Marsala wine, grape juice which has been heated to the point of becoming a concentrated sugar juice is added to the wine. The Italian word for it is *mosto cotto*. The Marsala varies from seventeen percent to twenty percent in alcohol proof.

The latitude and the insular position of Sicily give this island a much warmer climate. Wine growing takes place not only in the coastal areas but also in higher altitudes, like on the slopes of the Etna, the famous extinct volcano.

SECTION G
THE WINES FROM MALAGA, SPAIN

MALAGA IS A SWEET WINE MADE IN THE NORTH COAST OF SPAIN, IN THE DISTRICT OF EAST ANDALUSIA.

UNLIKE THE BROWNISH SHERRIES, MALAGA IS A NATURAL WINE AND IS NOT FORTIFIED WITH BRANDY. ITS ALCOHOL PROOF, NEVERTHELESS IS BETWEEN 15° TO 23°. MALAGA IS PRODUCED BY THE "SOLERA" SYSTEM LIKE SHERRIES.

IT IS THE CUSTOM WITH THE PRODUCERS OF SHERRY TO KEEP OLD WINE IN THE OLDEST BARRELS, CALLED "SOLERA". WITH A SERIE OF CASKS OF WINE FROM DIFFERENT YEARS, THE "SOLERA" ARE REFILLED BY ORDER OF AGE. EACH REPLACEMENT POURED BACK INTO THESE OLD CASKS OVER THE YEARS WILL REMAIN THE SAME IN QUALITY. BY THIS SYSTEM, THE OVERALL CHARACTER AND QUALITY OF THE WINE WILL STAY CONSTANT AND KEEP THE WINE FROM LOSING ITS FRESHNESS.

MALAGA IS ISSUED FROM FOUR VINESTOCKS. THE "PEDRO-XIMENEZ" IS THE PROMINENT GRAPE WITH 60%. IT IS BLENDED WITH 20% OF "LAIREN", 15% OF MOSCATEL AND 5% FROM THE OTHER SPECIES OF THE AREA.

ALL THESE COMBINED WILL PRODUCE A STRONG, RICH AND DARK WINE. BEFORE THE GRAPES ARE PRESSED, THEY ARE LAID IN THE SUN ON STRAW MATS IN ORDER TO GET OVERRIPE AND SUGARY.

AFTER THE PRESSING THE NEW WINE IS POURED INTO OAK CASKS OR BUTTS AND REMAIN TO MATURE FOR TWO TO THREE YEARS.

DEPENDING ON THEIR OWN INDIVIDUAL CHARACTER OF SWEETNESS AND COLOR, THE WINE DEVELOPS IN DIFFERENT STYLES AS FOLLOW:

MALAGA "DULCE COLOR": VERY SWEET AND DARK

MALAGA "BLANCO DULCE": SWEET AND GOLDEN YELLOW

MALAGA "SEMI DULCE": SWEET YELLOW AND RED

MALAGA "BLANCO SECO": SEMI-DRY WITH A PALE GOLD COLOR

MALAGA "PEDRO-XIMENEZ": LUSCIOUS SWEET, DARK WITH REDDISH GLINT

MALAGA "TINTLLO": RED COLOR WITH LESSER ALCOHOL CONTENT

THE MAIN PRODUCERS AND EXPORTERS FROM MALAGA ARE:
HIJOS DE A. BARCELO, LUIS BARCELO, FLORES HERNANOS

FELIX GARCIA GOMEZ, JOSE GARIJO RUIZ, HIJOS DE JOSE SUAREZ VILLALBA.

CHAPTER TEN

Conclusion

The themes of vineyards and wine have flattered nature by the beauty and illustrations which were found in France, also, in the greatness of its historic resonance.

The most illustrious example is the history of champagne. During the fourteenth century, the country of wine in the minds of the bourgeois of Reims was precisely opposed to that poor dry champagne area. That is what they reported to King Charles V in a royal ordinance dated from 1578 about the vineyards of the Sevres and Saint-Cloud townships close to Paris which were among the most delicate growths of the kingdom. These testimonies had been printed and are available in the great libraries of France. One wonders why they are ignored by such a large public in a country where wine enjoys the greatest prestige.

It would be very pleasing to see the virtues of these French vineyards, the effects of a natural privilege of a particular grace given to the soil of France as it has been more honor for this country to receive from Heaven instead of men's pains.

The outstanding fertile soil where the French ancestors had found a subject of collective pride even before the feeling of French patriotism had been awakened in them.

Enjoy the wine you have chosen, but, please, sip it in moderation and responsibly.

The average consumer does not realize the fragility of wine, the effort, the vigilance, and to say it all, the love required to create and deliver these lofty beverages.

In ignoring all these matters, the buyer buys wine like he might buy beer or other industrial beverages without a thought to the nuances of the wines or the changes that the passage of time can produce. There are not enough words to say that the wine behaves like a living thing.

Excerpts of a wine-lover in his memoirs: By Ray Neuman

I can truthfully say since I reached the age of discretion, I have consistently, but with moderation, consumed more wine than most people would say was good for me, nor do I regret it.

Wine has been to me a firm friend and a wise counselor. Often wine has shown me matters in their true perspectives and has as though by the touch of a magic rod, reduced great disasters to small inconveniences.

Wine has lit up for me the pages of literature and revealed in life romance lurking in the commonplace.

Wine has made me bold but not foolish, has induced me to say stupid things but not to do them. Under its influence, words have often come too easily which had better not have been spoken, and letters have been written which had better not been sent, but if such small indiscretions were standing in the debit column of wine's account and were added up, they would amount to nothing in comparison with the vast accumulation on the credit side of the column.

Wine is the child of sun and Earth, but cannot come into existence without the help of work. Like all great achievements and great thoughts, it does not come from the wine-press ready to be swallowed immediately and without worries by a greedy stomach. It needs the collaboration of art and patience, of time and care. It needs along repose in the dark before arriving at the triumph of flavor which is a source of wonder to the brain as much as to the palate.

Wine is a true of the unnamed everyday drink which the laborer's honest thirst as of the product of those ancient vineyards whose heraldic bearings add lustre to the records of our loveliest provinces.

Wine has a triple mission. It is the medium of a triple communion.

First, communion with the soil into which it sinks its roots and from which it receive both soul and body.

Secondly, communion with ourselves. It is wine that gently warms and opens up our personalities, bringing our memories to life stimulating our imaginations, and, with the rosy fingers which Homer attributes to dawn, unveiling before us the most promising vision of the future. Wine instructs our taste, and by training us to turn our attention inwards, it frees the mind and illuminates the intelligence

And lastly, wine is the symbol and the means of social communion; round a table, all the guests are at the same level, and the cups goes round, it fills us with indulgence, understanding, and sympathy for our neighbors.

CHAPTER ELEVEN

Reference List

INDEX

1   THE BORDEAUX WINE CLASSIFICATION OF 1855:
        MÉDOC
        SAINT-EMILION
        POMEROL
        GRAVES AND SAUTERNES

2   VINTAGE CHART OF THE MÉDOC, OTHER PARTS OF BORDEAUX, BURGUNDY, ALSACE, THE GERMAN RHINE AND MOSELLE

3   SPECIMEN OF LABELS FROM THE MEDOC

4   SPECIMEN OF LABELS FROM THE COLLECTION OF CHÂTEAU MOUTON-ROTHSCHILD

5   LABELS OF CHÂTEAU PETRUS, LAFLEUR-GAZIN, (POMEROL) CHÂTEAU GLORIA AND CHÂTEAU CAMENSAC (MEDOC)

6   GLOSSARY OF WINE TERMS

BORDEAUX

A PERFECT VIEW OF A BORDEAUX MANSION, CALLED A CHÂTEAU
AND BUILT IN THE 19TH CENTURY

VIEW OF THE ESTATE OF CHATEAU LAFITE-ROTHSCHILD

THIS MANSION WAS ERECTED AT THE END OF THE 17TH CENTURY. THE ESTATE
OCCUPIES THE BEST EXPOSED CRESTS OF THE TERRITORY OF THE OUTSTANDING WINES
PRODUCED AT LAFITE GAVE THEM THE MERIT TO BE NAMED "PRINCE OF VINES"

THE WINE CLASSIFICATION OF 1855 FOR THE MÉDOC

FIRST GROWTHS - PREMIERS CRUS

CHÂTEAU LAFITE-ROTHSCHILD (Pauillac)

CHÂTEAU MARGAUX (Margaux)

CHÂTEAU LATOUR (Pauillac)

CHÂTEAU-MOUTON-ROTHSCHILD (Pauillac)

-0-

GRAVES

CHÂTEAU HAUT-BRION (Pessac, Graves)

OUTSTANDING GROWTH (CRU HORS CLASSE)

SAUTERNES

CHÂTEAU d'YQUEM

GRAND PREMIER CRU DE SAUTERNES

AREA OF SAINT-EMILION

SAINT-EMILION, PREMIER GRAND CRU CLASSÉ (A)

CHÂTEAU AUSONE

CHÂTEAU CHEVAL BLANC

SECOND GROWTHS - DEUXIÈMES CRUS
CHATEAU RAUSAN-SÉGLA (MARGAUX)
CHATEAU RAUZAN-GASSIES (MARGAUX)
CHATEAU LÉOVILLE LAS-CASES (Saint-Julien)
CHATEAU LÉOVILLE-POYFERRE (Saint-Julien)
CHATEAU LÉOVILLE-BARTON (Saint-Julien)
CHATEAU DURFORT-VIVENS (Margaux)
CHATEAU LASCOMBES (Margaux)
CHATEAU GRUAUD-LAROSE (Saint-Julein)
CHATEAU BRANE-CANTENAC (Cantenac-Margaux)
CHATEAU PICHON-LONGUEVILLE (Pauillac)
CHATEAU PICHON-LONGUEVILLE-LALANDE (Pauillac)
CHATEAU DUCRU-BEAUCAILLOU (Saint-Julien)
CHATEAU COS D'ESTOURNEL (Saint-Estephr)
CHATEAU MONTROSE (Saint-Stephen)

THIRD GROWTHS - TROISIÈMES CRUS
CHÂTEAU KIRWAN (Cantenac-Margaux)
CHÂTEAU D'ISSAN (Cantenac-Margaux)
CHÂTEAU LAGRANGE (Saint-Julien)
CHÂTEAU GISCOURS (Labored-Margaux)
CHÂTEAU LANGOA-BARTON (Saint-Julien)
CHÂTEAU MALESCOT-SAINT-EXUPERY (Margaux)
CHÂTEAU CANTENAC-BROWN (Cantenac-Margaux)
CHÂTEAU PALMER (Cantenac-Margaux)
CHÂTEAU LA LAGUNE (Loudon)
CHÂTEAU DESMIRAIL (Margaux)
CHÂTEAU CALON-SEGUR (Saint-Stephen)
CHÂTEAU FERRIERE (Margaux)
CHÂTEAU D'ALESME-BECKER (Margaux)
CHÂTEAU BOYD-CANTENAC (Cantenac-Margaux)

FOURTH GROWTHS - QUATRIÈMES CRUS

CHÂTEAU SAINT-PIERRE (Saint-Julien)

CHÂTEAU BRANAIRE-DUCRU (Saint-Julien)

CHÂTEAU TALBOT (Saint-Julien)

CHÂTEAU DUHART-MILON (Pauillac)

CHÂTEAU POUGET (Cantenac-Margaux)

CHÂTEAU LA TOUR-CARNET (Saint-Laurent)

CHÂTEAU LAFONT-ROCHET (Saint-Stephen)

CHÂTEAU BEYCHEVELLE (Saint-Julien)

CHÂTEAU PRIEURE-LICHINE (Cantenac-Margaux)

CHÂTEAU MARQUIS DE TERME (Margaux)

FIFTH GROWTHS - CINQUIÈMES CRUS

CHÂTEAU PONTET-CANET (Pauillac)

CHÂTEAU BATAILLEY (Pauillac)

CHÂTEAU HAUT-BATAILLET (Pauillac)

CHÂTEAU GRAND-PUY-LACOSTE (Pauillac)

CHÂTEAU GRAND-PUY-DUCASSE (Pauillac)

CHÂTEAU DAUZAC (Labored)

CHÂTEAU MOUTON BARON-PHILIPPE (Pauillac)

CHÂTEAU DU TERTRE (Arsis)

CHÂTEAU HAUT-BAGES-LIBERAL (Pauillac)

CHÂTEAU PEDESCLAUX (Pauillac)

CHÂTEAU BELGRAVE (Saint-Laurent)

CHÂTEAU CLERC-MILON-MONDON (Pauillac)

CHÂTEAU CROIZET-BAGES (Pauillac)

CHÂTEAU COS LABORY (Saint-Stephen)

CHÂTEAU CANTEMERLE (Macao)

LISTING OF THE COMMON OUTSTANDING GROWTHS OF THE MÉDOC - OR CRUS BOURGEOIS

CHATEAU ANGLUDET
CHATEAU BEAU-SITE
CHATEAU BEL-AIR MARQUIS D'ALEGRE
CHATEAU CAPBERN
CHATEAU CHASSE-SPLEEN
CHATEAU DUTRUCH GRAND-PUJEAUX
CHATEAU FOURCAS-DUPRE
CHATEAU FOURCAS-HOSTEIN
CHATEAU GLANA
CHATEAU GLORIA
CHATEAU GREYSAC
CHATEAU HAUT-MARBUZET
CHATEAU LABEGORCE
CHATEAU LANESSAN
CHATEAU LA TOUR-DE-MONS
CHATEAU LIVERSAN
CHATEAU LOUDENNE
CHATEAU MAUCAILLOU
CHATEAU MEYNET
CHATEAU LES ORMES DE PEZ
CHATEAU PAVEIL DE LUZE
CHATEAU PHELAN-SEGUR
CHATEAU POUJEAUX-THEIL
CHATEAU SIRAN
CHATEAU DU TAILLAN
CHATEAU TRONQUOY-LALANDE
CHATEAU VERDIGNAN

CLASSIFICATION OF THE DISTRICT OF SAINT-EMILION OFFICIAL RATING OF 1955

FIRST GREAT GROWTHS - PREMIERS GRANDS CRUS

CHÂTEAU AUSONE
CHÂTEAU CHEVAL BLANC
CHÂTEAU BEAUSEJOUR-DUFFAU-LAGAROSSE
CHÂTEAU FIGEAC
CHÂTEAU LA GAFFELIERE
CHÂTEAU MAGDELAINE
CHÂTEAU BEAUSEJOUR-FAGOUET
CHÂTEAU BELAIR
CHÂTEAU CANON
CHÂTEAU FOURTET
CHÂTEAU PAVIE
CHÂTEAU TROTTEVIEILLE

GREAT CLASSIFIED GROWTHS - GRANDS CRUS CLASSES

CHÂTEAU L'ANGELUS
CHÂTEAU BALESTARD-LA-TONNELLE
CHÂTEAU CANON-LA-GAFFELIERE
CHÂTEAU CORBIN
CHÂTEAU CURE-BON
CHÂTEAU DASSAULT
CHÂTEAU FONROQUE
CHÂTEAU GRAND CORBIN
CLOS DES JACOBINS
CHÂTEAU LA CLOTTE
CHÂTEAU LA GRACE-DIEU
CHÂTEAU SIMARD
CHÂTEAU LA DOMINIQUE
CHÂTEAU LARCIS-DUCASSE
CHÂTEAU LA TOUR-DU-PIN-FIGEAC
CHÂTEAU PAVIE-MAACQUIN
CHÂTEAU RIPEAU
CHÂTEAU SOUTARD
CHÂTEAU TERTRE-DAUGAY
CHÂTEAU TRIMOULET
CHÂTEAU TROPLONG-MONDOT
CHÂTEAU VILLEMAURINE
CHÂTEAU LAPELLETRIE

CLASSIFICATION OF THE DISTRICT OF GRAVES
OFFICIAL RATING OF 1955

<u>RED WINES</u>
CHATEAU HAUT-BRION, RATED FIRST GROWTH IN 1855 WITH THE MEDOC

CLASSIFIED GROWTHS - CRU CLASSES
CHATEAU BOUSCAUT

CHATEAUX CARBONNIEUX

DOMAINE DE CHEVALIER

CHATEAU HAUT-BAILLY

CHATEAU DE FIEUZAL

CHATEAU LA MISSION-HAUT-BRION

CHATEAU LARRIVET HAUT-BRION

CHATEAU LA TOUR HAUT-BRION

CHATEAU KRESSMAN LA TOUR

CHATEAU MALARTIC-LAGRAVIERE

CHATEAU PAPE CLEMENT

CHATEAU OLIVIER

CHATEAU SMITH-HAUT-LAFITE

<u>WHITE WINES</u>
CHATEAU BOUSCAUT

CHATEAU CARBONNIEUX

DOMAINE DE CHEVALIER

CHATEAU BARET

CHATEAU KRESSMAN LA TOUR

CHATEAU LAVILLE-HAUT-BRION

CHATEAU MALARTIC-LAGRAVIERE

CHATEAU LA LOUVIERE

RATING OF THE DISTRICT OF POMEROL

Pomerol vineyards have no official classification yet. However the best of them is CHÂTEAU PÉTRUS, one of the ten best Bordeaux. It is considered as an outstanding great growth.

CHÂTEAU BEAUREGARD

CHÂTEAU CERTAN-DE-MAY

CHÂTEAU CERTAN-GIRAUD

CHÂTEAU CLINET

CHÂTEAU GAZIN

CHÂTEAU LA CONSEILLANTE

CHÂTEAU LAFLEUR

CHÂTEAU LAFLEUR -PETRUS

CHÂTEAU LAGRANGE

CHÂTEAU LA POINTE

CHÂTEAU DE SALES

CLOS RENE

CHÂTEAU LATOUR-POMEROL

CLOS L'ÉGLISE

DOMAINE DE L'ÉGLISE

CHÂTEAU L'ÉGLISE-CLINET

CHÂTEAU L'EVANGILE

CHÂTEAU NENIN

CHÂTEAU PETIT-VILLAGE

CHÂTEAU ROUGET

CHÂTEAU TROTANOY

VIEUS-CHÂTEAU CERTAN

CHÂTEAU TAILLEFER

CLASSIFICATION OF THE DISTRICT OF SAUTERNES
RATING OF 1855

GRAND PREMIER CRU - FIRST GREAT GROWTH

CHÂTEAU D'YQUEM - CRU HORS LIGNE

FIRST GROWTH - PREMIER CRUS

CHÂTEAU LA TOUR BLANCHE
CLOS HAUT-PEYRAGUEY
CHÂTEAU COUTET
CHÂTEAU LAFAURIE-PERAGUEY
CHÂTEAU DE RAYNE-VIGNEAU
CHATEAU DE SUDUIRAUT
CHÂTEAU CLIMENS
CHÂTEAU GUIRAUD
CHÂTEAU RIESSEC
CHÂTEAU RABAUD-PROMIS
CHÂTEAU SIGALA-RABAUD

SECOND GROWTH - DEUXIEMES CRUS

CHÂTEAU MYRAT
CHÂTEAU DOISY-DAENE
CHÂTEAU DOISY-VEDRINES
CHÂTEAU NAIRAC
CHÂTEAU CAILLOU
CHÂTEAU SUAU
CHÂTEAU D'ARCHE
CHÂTEAU FILHOT
CHÂTEAU BROUSTET
CHÂTEAU DE MALLE
CHÂTEAU ROMER
CHÂTEAU LAMOTHE

VINTAGE YEARS GUIDE

IN ORDER TO PRODUCE A GOOD VINTAGE, YEAR AFTER YEARS, TWO FACTORS ARE ESSENTIAL LIKE ANY PRODUCTS GROWING FROM THE EARTH:

THE GENTLE MAGNETIC ACTION OF THE WEATHER AND THE INGENIOSITY OF MAN.

TODAY MAN CAN EXERCISE HIS SCIENCE MUCH BETTER AS YEARS AGO, FOR EXAMPLE: CONTROL OF THE HARVEST, THE VINIFICATION, THE BLENDING, THE ALCOHOL CONTENT, THE COLOR OF THE WINE AND THE RELATIVE DEGREE OF FRUITINESS THROUGH ARTIFICIAL MEANS.

ONE THING HE HAS NO CONTROL OVER IS THE PERFECT MATURATION OF THE GRAPE.

TO BE FRANK, A VINTAGE CHART IS TODAY A VALUABLE TOOL FOR WINE-BROKERS AND MERCHANTS, BUT ONLY FOR WINES PRODUCED ABOVE THE 43' PARALLELE IN EUROPE. A COUNTRY WITH FOUR SEASONS IS THE MOST ACCEPTABLE AREA TO GROW THE VINE.

IN THAT PERPECTIVE, FRANCE AND GERMANY ARE THE BEST TEMPERED REGION TO PRODUCE WINES, WELL BALANCED AND DELICATE.

THE CHART BELOW IS FROM 1990 TO 2005.

INDICATES EXCELLENT VINTAGE YEARS

GRADING: 20 EXCELLENT, 5 BELOW TO AVERAGE

10 TO 13 PASSABLE

13 TO 15 AVERAGE TO GOOD

15 TO 16 GOOD TO VERY GOOD 17 TO 20 EXCELLENT

	MEDOC	OTHER PART OF BORDEAUX		BURGUNDY	ALSACE	RHINE AND MOSELLE
1990	17*	17*	17*	N/A	N/A	N/A
1991	10	9	12	13	13	13
1992	12	12	12	12	13	13
1993	12	12	11	12	14	12
1994	13	13	12	16	14	16
1995	16	15	14	14	17	15
1996	15	14	16	13	15	15
1997	13	12	15	12	15	14
1998	15	15	15	12	16	15
1999	14	14	15	13	17*	14
2000	17*	16	16	14	14	14
2001	14	14	16	14	14	14
2002	15	13	16	13	13	14
2003	14	14	15	14	14	15
2004	15	16	14	14	14	15
2005	18*	18*	17*	15	16	17*

CHATEAU GLORIA

ST. JULIEN, DISTRICT OF THE MEDOC
CRU BOURGEOIS SUPERIEUR
HENRI MARTIN, PROPRIETOR

This Estate of 115 acres of vineyards is made-up solely with the great growths from St. Julien and Pauillac.

The Domain of Mr. Henri Martin, has acquired quickly a very great fame. His wines are appreciated not only because they are harvested from a soil composition of high quality, but as well as for the modern technique applied which does not neglect the teachings derived since the last three centuries from the vineyard of the proprietor's family.

It is above all under the label Château Gloria that the wines are sold, but in certain countries particularly in the Benelux (Belgiun-The Nederlands and Luxembourg) the brand name is known as Château Haut-Beychevelle-Gloria.

Henri Martin, also was a long time Mayor of the parish of Saint-Julien.

CHATEAU BALESTARD LA TONNELLE
Saint-EMILION "Grand Cru Classé"

HISTORY

THIS ANCIENT ESTATE IN THE DISTRICT OF SAINT-EMILION IS RENOWNED FOR ITS WINE AFFINITIES GOING BACK AS FAR AS THE 15TH CENTURY.

IT WAS ALSO PORTRAYED BY FRANCOIS VILLON (1421-1485, A FAMOUS POET OF THAT TIME AND A WINE CONNOISSEUR. HE WROTE A POEM WHICH HAS BEEN KEPT AT THE CHATEAU. IT WAS LATER PRINTED ON THE BOTTLE'S LABEL.

"VIERGE MARIE, GRANDE DÉESSE GARDE= MOI PLACE EN PARADIS OU QUE N'AURAI JOIE NI LIESSE ICI BAS, PUISQU'IL N'EST PERMIS DE BOIRE CE DIVIN NECTAR QUI PORTE LE NOM DE BALESTARD

"QU'A GENS FORTUNÉS EN CE MONDE, OR SUIS MISÉREUX ET PAUVRE SI DONC CE VIN ABONDE VIENS, DOUCE MORT, POINT NE M'EFFRAYE PORTE-MOI PARMI LES ELUS QUI LA-HAUT, SAVOURENT CE CRU"

BY FRANCOIS VILLON

(EXTRAIT DE ST. EMILION SON HISTOIRE, SES MANUSCRITS SES GRANDS VINS}.

PAR LE DR. PIERRE BERTON-ROULLEAU

"VIRGIN MARY, GENTLE GODDESS KEEP MY PLACE IN PARADISE WHEN I WILL HAVE NO MORE FUN OR HAPPINESS AS IN THIS WORLD, TO DRINK THIS NECTAR ONLY RICH PEOPLE CAN AFFORD BUT I AM IN MISERY AND VERY POOR, SO IF THERE IS ABUNDANCE OF THIS WINE IN YOUR KINGDOM COME SWEET DEATH, YOU DON'T SCARE ME TAKE ME WITH YOUR ELECTED FEW WHO UPSTAIRS ENJOY THIS VINTAGE"

THE WINE DISTRICT OF POMEROL

Label of the illustrious wine of Château Pétrus

SPECIMENS OF LABELS FROM THE COLLECTION OF THE CHÂTEAU MOUTON-ROTHSCHILD FROM 1961-1972

VINTAGE 1961

THE VINEYARD OF MOUTON-ROTHSCHILD CONSISTS OF 60 HECTARES
AND IS MOSTLY PLANTED WITH CABERNET SAUVIGNON.

THE WINE OF MOUTON IS POWERFULL, WITH A LOT OF CHARACTER AND FINENESS.
IT IS A WINE OF GREAT BREED. IN GOOD VINTAGE YEAR IT HAS A PRINCELY ELEGANCE.

THE LABEL OF 1961 WAS DESIGNED BY MATHIEU.

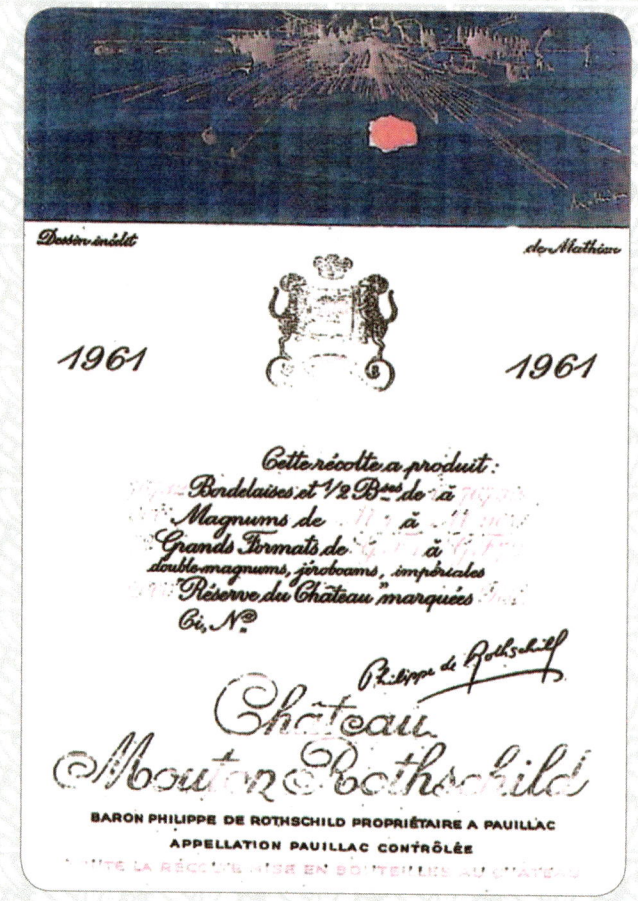

THE WINES FROM BORDEAUX

DRAWINGS OF LABEL COLLECTIONS, FROM 1962 TO 1972

THE MOUTON-ROTHSCHILD LABEL COLLECTION
THE DE MATTA PAINTING 1962
THE MOTTO IS" TON TENDRE VELOUTE SEDUIT LES PLUS REBELLES"
MEANING: YOUR TENDER VELVETINESS SEDUCES THE MOST REBELLIOUS.

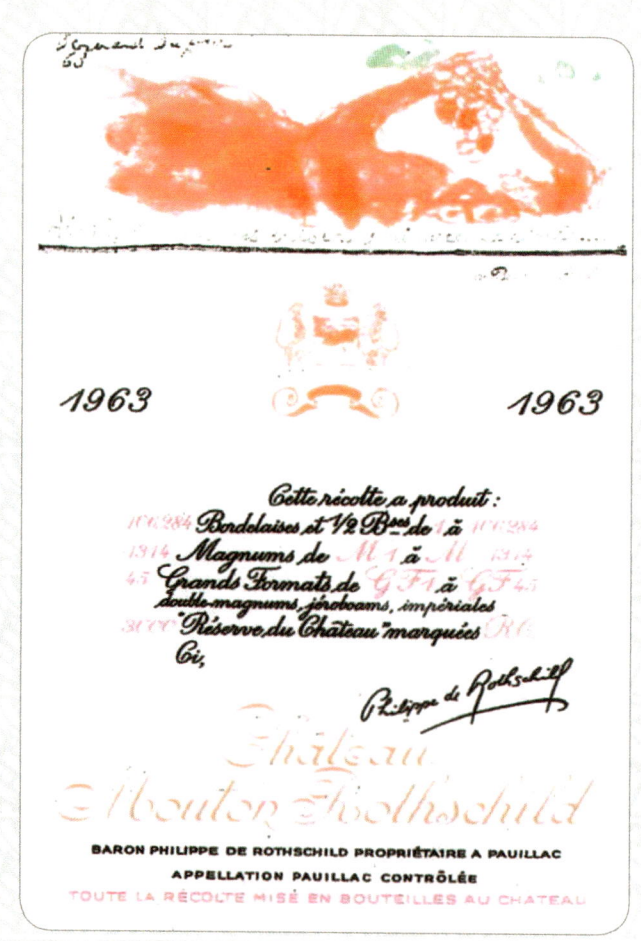

BERNARD DUFOUR'S MOTTO IS:
"AINSI, QUAND DES RAISINS, J'AI SUCÉ LA CLARTÉ"
TRANSLATED AS: "SO TO SPEAK, AS FOR THE GRAPES, I HAVE IMBIBED ITS BRIGHTNESS"

CHATEAU MOUTON-ROTHSCHILD
1964 AND 1966

PAINTING BY HENRY MOORE   PAINTING BY ALECHINSKY

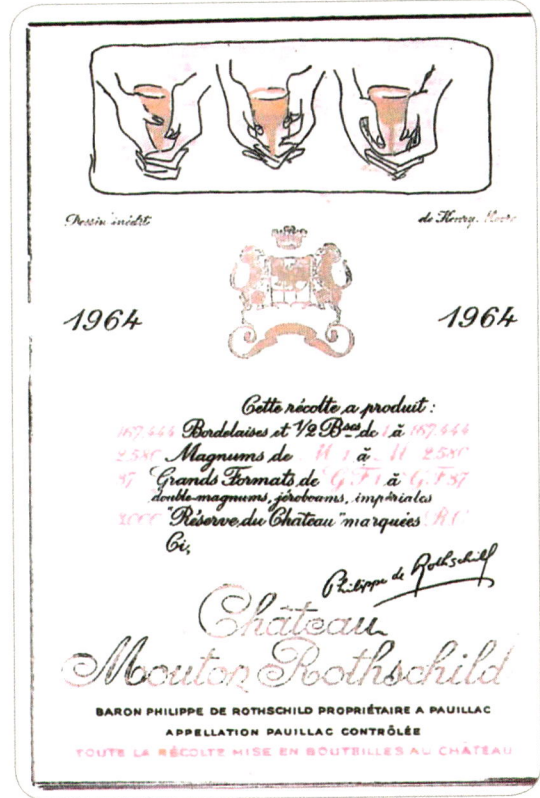

CHATEAU MOUTON-ROTHSCHILD
1965

PAINTING OF DOROTHEA TANNING

CHATEAU MOUTON-ROTHSCHILD
1967 AND 1968

PAINTING BY CESAR   PAINTING BY BONA

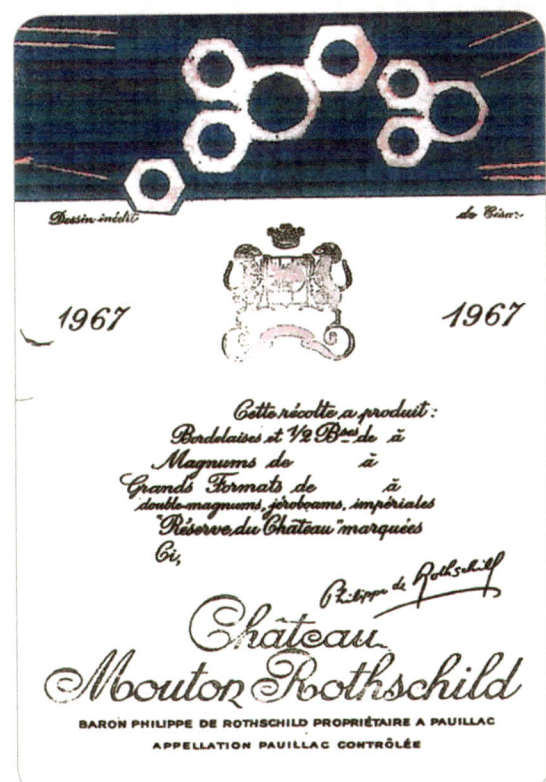

CHATEAU MOUTON-ROTHSCHILD
1970 AND 1971

PAINTING REALISED BY MARC CHAGALL
FOR THE MOUTON-ROTHSHILD 1970

UNPUBLISHED PAINTING 1971
BY KANDINSKY

CHATEAU MOUTON-ROTHSHILD
1969 AND 1972

UNPUBLISHED PAINTING
BY JOAN MIRÓ 1969

UNPUBLISHED PAINTING
BY SERGE POLIAKOFF 1972

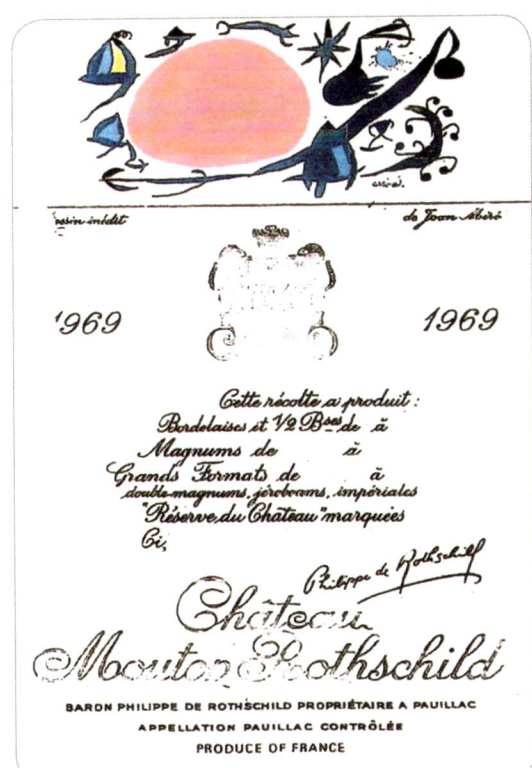

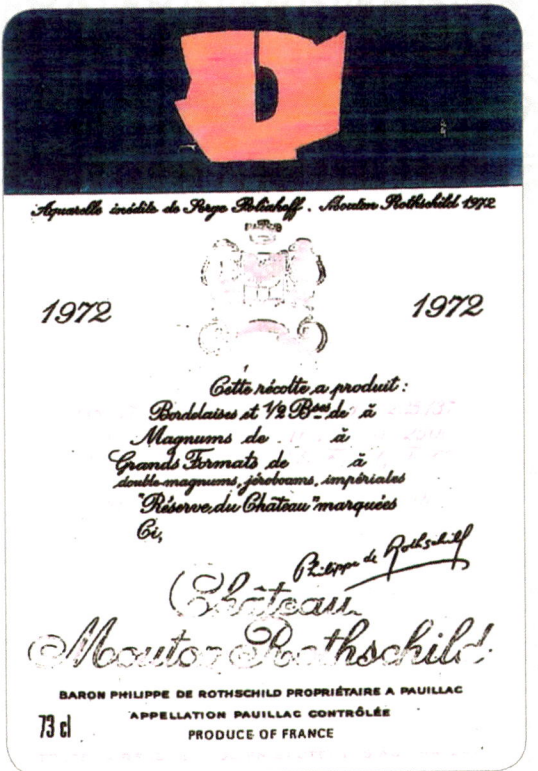

WINE TERMS' GLOSSARY

A

ACIDITY
A natural bitterness found in the grape and later in the wine.

ALCOHOL LEVEL
After the fermentation, the wine contains a percentage of alcohol represented by volume or proof.

ALIGOTÉ
A variety of grapevine which produces mostly acid wines due to the lack of sugar in the grape. In France, allowed for planting only in the Burgundy region. Not authorized anymore for blending with quality grapes.

APOTHECA
Greek word for amphora which is a container in clay, large and of a conic shape and used to store the wine.

ARTIFICIAL COLORATION
Dyes substances mixed in the wine to improve or darken the wine. Certain countries in Europe do not allow this practice.

AROMA
A general term meaning the vegetal smell of the wine.

AOC (appellation d'origine controlée)
French term for Appellation for wines grown in control areas specifically named. In other words, wines produced in a verified piece of land.

ASTRINGENT
Detection of an acid wine when tasted young and not freed of tanin and acid coming from the pips and stems.

ADULTERATION
That does not conform to authorized standard of processing.

B

BALANCE
A well-balanced wine when ready to taste and to consume when the gustative examination is met in a state of equilibrium.

BARREL
Wooden cylindrical container made of white or dark oak. The capacity is 32 US gallons. It can be easily transported.

BARRIQUE BORDELAISE contains 225 Liters or 59 US gallons.

BLEND
Used for a wine where some different varieties of grapes are mixed together.

BODEGA
Term used in Spain only meaning a wine cellar

BODY
Constitution of a wine described for its qualities (rich, fleshy powerful,) against its flaws like lean, thin, common, unrefined.

BOTTLED AGED
Last stage of a wine or a Champagne wine layed to rest and to mature. Red Bordeaux wines usually are ready to drink after seven years.

BOUQUET
A fruity floral scent which shows a certain steadiness and through the sense of taste can characterize the wine-growth.

C

CASK
contains 264 US gallons and is not easily removable.

CHÂTEAU
Mostly term used in Bordeaux describing an elaborated mansion built in the 19th century in the English style or a plain large house connected with wine-storages or cellars and delimited by a large vine-field.

CASSE
A disease of wine, the symptoms of which are cloudiness and a disagreeable taste.

CEPAGE
Means a variety of grape. CEP means an individual vine-stock.

CRISP
The characteristic of a slightly acid wine which is very dry.

D

DOMAINE
This term is mostly used in Burgundy, France meaning a wine estate

DRY
The opposite of sweet. A bone-dry wine means a wine with no flaws and without any fruit or floral scent.

E

EARTHY
Usually a note of a harsh wine
An earthy taste translated in French is "gout du terroir".

EDELZWICKER
Alsatian term meaning a wine made from quality grapes varieties. This name is issued from the German word "Edel", which means noble.

F

FERMENTATION
Natural transformation of the grape juice through the interaction of the yeasts and sugars.

FLAVOR
General term for a quality of a substance combining taste and smell.

FRUITY
The aroma suggesting the taste or smell of a fruit.

G

GENEROUS
When used as a wine term signifies a full-flavored and strong wine.

H

HOCK
Word used in England for the term of the Rhine wine.

HYBRID
In the viticultural language, it means the crossbreed of two grape species. Most hybrids are an attempt to combine the best qualities of the two

I

IMPERIALE
A large, usually a Bordeaux bottle, holding eight regular bottles of 24 oz.

L

LEES
Sediments also called dregs formed during the natural process of the wine fermentation.

M

MACERATION
One of the process, of fermentation when skin grapes and dregs which are allowed to soften and break down the component parts of the grape juice.

MINERAL
An inorganic substance found in the soil.

O

OIDIUM
A fungus of American origin which attacks the leaves, the shoots and tendrils of the vine. It did cause heavy damages in European vineyards when it first appeared in the mid 19th century. It can now be controlled.

P

PHYLLOXERA
A sickness caused by insects that attack the leaves and roots of the grapevines.

R

RESIDUAL SUGAR
Remaining sugar or left over at the end of the fermentation process

ROUND
A general term used in the wine language for the structure of a finished wine which after tasting and smell shows a balanced process between alcohol, sweetness and acids.

S

STEM
The stalk or part of the vine supporting the leaves, flowers and fruit

T

TANNIN
A natural phenolic compound absorbed from the grape skins and seeds. An important ingredient for the formation and longevity of the wine.

TASTING
The primaries impressions when you taste wine

TERROIR
A word used in French vineyards, describing the taste or flavor of a wine which has a taste of the earth caused by different influences.

TONNEAU: a wood container holding four barriques Bordelaise= 900 Liters.

THIN
A wine is called thin for lack of alcohol, tannin and flavors.

V

VARIETAL
Is the characteristics of a wine grape species.

VEGETAL
When tasting, you may observe a taste of greenery or green herbs.

VIN DE PAYS
This is an appellation of country wines which holds a lower status than legally controlled wines.

VINIFICATION
The process of making wine to a finish product.

VINTAGE
The grape harvest and making of a wine from a specific year

VITICULTURE
The unity of the activities concerning the planting and growing and in general the culture of the vine.

Y

YEAST
Micro-organic cell directed to launch and direct an alcoholic fermentation.